Parallel Logic Programming in PARLOG

The Language and its Implementation

International Series in Logic Programming

Series Editor
Keith Clark, Imperial College of Science and Technology

Associate Editors
Bob Kowalski, Imperial College of Science and Technology
Jean-Louis Lassez, IBM, Yorktown Heights, USA

Editorial Board
K Furukawa (ICOT, Japan)
H Gallaire (ECRC, Munich, FRG)
J W Lloyd (University of Melbourne, Australia)
J Minker (Maryland, USA)
J A Robinson (Syracuse University, NY, USA)
S-A Tärnlund (Uppsala University, Sweden)
M H van Emden (University of Waterloo, Canada)
D H D Warren (Manchester University, England)

Parallel Logic Programming in PARLOG

The Language and its Implementation

STEVE GREGORY

Imperial College of Science and Technology, London

ADDISON-WESLEY PUBLISHING COMPANY

Wokingham, England · Reading, Massachusetts · Menlo Park, California
Don Mills, Ontario · Amsterdam · Bonn · Sydney · Singapore
Tokyo · Madrid · Bogota · Santiago · San Juan

The programs presented in this book have been included for their instructional value.
They have been tested with care but are not guaranteed for any particular purpose.
The publisher does not offer any warranties or representations, nor does it accept
any liabilities with respect to the programs.

Cover design by Marshall Henrichs.
Typeset by Quorum Technical Services Ltd, Cheltenham.
Printed in Great Britain by R.J. Acford, Chichester.

ISBN 0-201-19241-1

Contents

Preface

Declarative (relational and functional) programming languages have become very widely used in recent years, largely because of their high-level nature: declarative programs can be understood without reference to the behaviour of any particular machine. An increasingly important argument in favour of such languages is that, owing to their lack of side-effects, they are well suited to parallel evaluation. Among declarative programming languages, those based on logic are claimed to be particularly human-oriented. However, the most common logic programming language, Prolog, embodies a control strategy which is designed for sequential evaluation.

In principle, two types of parallelism are possible in logic program evaluation: AND parallelism and OR parallelism. Many combinations of these are possible, but not all can be efficiently implemented. To investigate this is the subject of the research described in this book – a revised and updated version of my PhD thesis. The main result of the work is the design of a new parallel logic programming language: PARLOG.

PARLOG incorporates into logic programming the idea of committed choice non-determinism from Dijkstra's guarded commands and Hoare's CSP language. This feature, combined with 'mode' declarations, makes possible the AND parallel evaluation of relation calls as processes, with stream communication through shared logical variables. This 'stream AND parallelism' is the logic programming analogue of Kahn and MacQueen's model of parallel evaluation for functional programs. It constitutes a powerful programming paradigm, and one which can be implemented with reasonable efficiency on parallel computers.

I hope that this book will be of some use to anyone with an interest in Fifth Generation computing and logic programming. The first part is fairly tutorial in nature, outlining the principles of parallel logic programming and the design of PARLOG by means of examples. The final chapters discuss various issues concerning implementation of the language on a range of parallel architectures.

Acknowledgements

Above all, I am indebted to my friend, colleague and advisor Keith Clark, without whom this work would not have been possible.

I am grateful to Bob Kowalski for several reasons. The strength of the logic programming activity at Imperial College owes much to his efforts, as does the discipline itself. It was Bob who introduced me to logic programming several years ago, since when he has provided continued help and encouragement.

The support of Bruce Sayers, Head of the Department of Computing since September 1984, is much appreciated.

During the writing of my PhD thesis, I was very fortunate in working with Ian Foster, Graem Ringwood and Ken Satoh in the newly formed PARLOG Group. Their excellent work, especially in implementing PARLOG, made it possible for me to divert my attentions from productive research for the considerable time needed. I would also like to thank the more recent members of the PARLOG Group: Alastair Burt, Jim Crammond, Andrew Davison, David Gilbert, Matthew Huntbach, Tony Kusalik and Melissa Lam. More generally, I should thank of my colleagues at Imperial College, especially Krysia Broda, Frank McCabe and Mike Reeve.

The thesis benefited substantially from the comments of Ian Foster, Melissa Lam and Ken Satoh. Special thanks in this respect are due to Tony Field and Graem Ringwood, who took the trouble to wade through even the more tedious parts and provided numerous detailed and perceptive comments. In revising the thesis for publication, I have been helped by the comments, criticism and encouragement of numerous people. I am especially grateful to Mike Clarke, Michael Codish, Tom Conlon and Ronan Sleep for detailed comments.

Visits to other institutions have proved very beneficial to this research, and I would like to thank all who invited me and made these visits possible. I am particularly grateful to Alan Robinson of Syracuse University and to

Kazuhiro Fuchi, Koichi Furukawa and Yumiko Okada of ICOT, for their hospitality during my stays in 1980 and 1983, respectively.

My research has been supported by the Science and Engineering Research Council, currently by a SERC Advanced Fellowship. Other recent and current work of the PARLOG Group at Imperial College has been funded by the SERC, International Computers Limited, Fujitsu Laboratories Limited and Ericsson Telecom.

1
Introduction

1.1 Background

Programming languages play a pivotal role in computer science: they act as the interface between the problems to be solved (the applications) and the hardware (the implementation). An ideal programming language should be efficiently implementable on available technology but should also be 'human-oriented', providing ease of expression of problems and their solutions.

1.1.1 Declarative programming

The earliest programming languages were oriented much more towards the machine than the human programmer. These languages were simply abstractions of the 'von Neumann' organization of the machines on which they were implemented. Subsequent developments, such as Pascal and Ada, have raised the level of programming but these languages still inherit many of the characteristics of the von Neumann type of architecture, notably the concept of destructive assignment. Programs written in such **imperative** languages have only an operational semantics: they can be understood only by reference to their effect on the state of some (real or abstract) machine.

A quite different style of programming emerged with the appearance of LISP (McCarthy *et al.*, 1965). **Declarative** programming languages are distinguished by being based on an abstract formalism; in the case of LISP, the mathematical theory of functions known as the lambda calculus (Church, 1941). LISP was the first, and is still the most widely used, **functional** programming language.

A declarative programming language is one whose statements have a declarative interpretation; they contain no features which only make sense in machine-level terms, such as side-effects. Hence, a declarative program can be read as a formal description of a problem without recourse to the behaviour of any machine. This means that a program often acts as its own specification. Because of their formal basis and lack of side-effects, declarative programs can be developed and tested in a piecemeal fashion; such programs are also very amenable to systematic synthesis or transformation (Burstall and Darlington, 1977; Hogger, 1978; Clark and Darlington, 1980). Some of the benefits of declarative languages are discussed by Backus (1978).

Logic programming – another variety of declarative programming – is most broadly defined as the use of a programming language whose statements are sentences of first-order predicate logic. In practice, the term usually refers to programming in Horn clauses, the form of logical sentence to which Kowalski's (1974) pioneering work gave a procedural interpretation. The first, and still the most widely used, logic programming language was Prolog, which was designed and implemented by Colmerauer and others at Marseille in 1972 (Roussel, 1975).

Logic programming languages are claimed to be particularly human-oriented, being based on a formalism which was originally devised for the purpose of clarifying human thought. Moreover, logic is a formalism already familiar in computing, e.g. as a specification language and in relational databases. General aspects of computational logic are covered in Kowalski (1979a) and Robinson (1979), while for an introduction to logic programming, the reader is referred to Hogger (1984). The books by Clocksin and Mellish (1981) and Clark and McCabe (1984) are recommended as tutorials on Prolog programming.

Although the origins of declarative programming languages date back to the early days of computing, it is only in recent years that they have gained widespread acceptance. This may be attributed both to the extent of investment in existing languages and to the 'semantic gap' between declarative languages and conventional computers. Recent improvements in implementation technology (such as compiling techniques and microprogramming) have narrowed this gap considerably while, at the same time, there has been increasing realization of the benefits of declarative programming.

There is another, increasingly important, influence in favour of declarative languages. This is the advent of VLSI technology which has made possible the development of new, parallel, computer architectures.

Parallelism has long been a feature of computer architectures in the form of 'pipelining', i.e. parallel execution of different phases of each instruction. Multiprocessor computers have been developed (e.g. Denelcor, 1982; Sequent, 1985) comprising several (von Neumann-type) processors which usually share a common memory. Also, vector and array processors have been developed for specific applications of a regular, repetitive nature.

It is widely believed that the best long-term prospect for increased computational performance is the development of extensible, highly parallel architectures. Unlike 'conventional' parallel architectures, these will differ radically from the von Neumann model. Architectural research has further focussed attention on declarative languages which, because of their lack of side-effects, are eminently suited to parallel evaluation (at least in principle). New computational models have been developed over recent years, notably dataflow and reduction architectures (Treleaven, 1982).

It is worth noting that the main objective of the Japanese Fifth Generation Computer Systems project begun in 1982 (Kawanobe, 1984) is the development of highly parallel architectures for very fast execution of logic programs.

1.1.2 Control strategy

The difference between a declarative formalism (such as Horn clause logic or the lambda calculus) and a declarative *programming* language is that the latter includes some **control strategy**. To generalize Kowalski's (1979b) dictum 'Algorithm = Logic + Control':

Declarative programming language = declarative formalism
                                    + control strategy

It is the control strategy that enables a program to be executed on a computer. The nature of the control strategy determines the operational semantics of a program, while the declarative semantics is obtained by reading the program as a logical or functional formula.

Furthermore, the control strategy can often be viewed as comprising two parts:

Control strategy = evaluator
                    + control language

The **evaluator** is the mechanism that executes a program expressed in the declarative formalism. In some systems this operates autonomously. Other systems allow the programmer to influence the behaviour of the evaluator by means of some **control language** superimposed on the declarative part of a program.

The evaluators used in functional programming are usually based on reduction (described in Chapter 2). Roughly, functional expressions are reduced by applying the equations which constitute the declarative part of the program. Traditional evaluators (such as that of LISP) perform the reduction sequentially, in 'left-most inner-most' order. As will be explained in Chapter 2, evaluators which perform the reduction 'lazily' or concurrently have important advantages.

A separate control language is not usually considered necessary in functional programming (but see Schwarz, 1977). For example, in the sequential, 'eager' evaluation of a functional program, the only ordering that is important is that arguments of an expression should be evaluated before the expression itself; but the arguments are distinguished by the structure of the declarative program, not by a separate control language. In contrast, the essential ordering of calls and clauses in a sequential Horn clause (i.e. Prolog) program *is* expressed by a control language: namely, the textual order of calls and clauses in a program. This is regarded as a control language because the textual order does not affect the declarative reading of a program.

Another aspect of Prolog's control language is its 'cut' primitive, introduced as a means of restraining the non-determinism of the logic. For certain common types of program, the use of the cut (or a similar primitive) is essential. The effect of the cut depends upon the evaluation order of clauses and so makes this ordering even more crucial.

As a sequential logic programming language, Prolog embodies an evaluator (or **proof procedure**) which *sequentially* solves calls in a conjunction and clauses in a procedure, with a backtracking facility to handle non-determinism. This form of control has two important advantages. First, it can be implemented very efficiently on a conventional, sequential computer. Second, it provides a useful programming paradigm, enabling the elegant use of Prolog in certain application areas, e.g. parsing, database interrogation, plan formation, expert systems, etc.; these applications are well documented in the logic programming literature.

1.1.3 Parallel logic programming

Having accepted that logic programming (as well as functional programming) has attractions for both the programmer and the computer architect, how can parallel logic programming be realized in practice?

As explained in Chapter 2, the parallel evaluation of *functional* programs (Kahn and MacQueen, 1977) is relatively straightforward. Essentially, two kinds of parallelism can be identified, and exploited by suitable evaluators:

1. **Restricted parallelism**. The concurrent evaluation of several arguments of a functional expression. This is quite straightforward to implement since the arguments are independent.

2. **Stream parallelism**. The evaluation of a functional expression concurrently with one of its arguments. The value of the argument can be communicated incrementally to the expression.

The special significance of stream parallelism is that it provides a useful programming paradigm: that of parallel, communicating processes.

At first sight, logic programming would seem to offer even more scope for parallel evaluation: not only can calls in a conjunction be evaluated concurrently (**AND parallelism**), but also clauses in a procedure (**OR**

parallelism). However, there are technical difficulties which will be explained.

It should be clear that Prolog is not a suitable language for parallel evaluation. As noted above, Prolog programs are written under the assumption of sequential evaluation. Small-scale parallelism is certainly possible: Tick and Warren (1984) present a design for a pipelined Prolog processor. However, this is an application of conventional techniques and does not exploit the declarative nature of logic programming. Another proposal (Tamura and Kaneda, 1984), described in Chapter 2, can extract some parallelism from a Prolog program by exploiting its non-determinism while retaining the specified sequencing; however, the scope for parallelism in this scheme is rather limited.

There have been many proposals for parallel control strategies for (Horn clause) logic programs, some of which are described in Chapter 2. Some of these include a control language component to guide the parallel evaluation while others rely upon a sophisticated proof procedure to solve *pure* Horn clause programs concurrently. These proposals differ in the forms of parallelism that they implement.

The two forms of parallelism noted above for functional languages can be applied also to logic programming:

1. **Restricted AND parallelism**. The concurrent evaluation of several calls in a conjunction which are independent, i.e. do not share variables.

2. **Stream AND parallelism**. The concurrent evaluation of two calls which share a variable, with the value of the shared variable communicated incrementally between the calls.

In addition, the non-determinism of logic programs admits two further forms of parallelism (explained fully in Chapter 2):

3. **OR parallelism**. The concurrent application of several clauses in a procedure while solving a call.

4. **All-solutions AND parallelism**. The concurrent evaluation of several calls in a conjunction, each working on a *different* solution.

Of these four possibilities, 3 and 4 are perhaps the easiest to implement because each of the parallel processes is working on a different solution and so they are independent. There are therefore many proposals that incorporate these forms of parallelism.

Options 1 and 2 differ from the corresponding functional concepts in that the opportunities for AND parallel evaluation are not obvious from the structure of a Horn clause program. Some control language or a sophisticated proof procedure may be necessary to determine both the independence of calls and the direction of stream communication through shared variables. Moreover, stream AND parallelism is very difficult to implement in the presence of non-determinism, as explained in subsequent chapters. In order to implement stream AND parallelism efficiently, some means of constraining the non-determinism is necessary. For this reason, most proposals prior to the present work specifically excluded stream AND parallelism.

1.2   The research

1.2.1   Objectives of the research

The basic objective of the research reported herein is the design of a parallel Horn clause logic programming language.

The research has been guided by a principle most succinctly stated by Warren (1977):

Logic programming *is* programming.

That is, the logic programmer *has to* keep in mind the operational semantics (control strategy) of the language when writing a program. (It would require a proof procedure far more sophisticated than any yet devised to evaluate *any* correct Horn clause specification as a reasonable program; consider, for example, a sort program that merely specifies that a sorted version of list x is an ordered permutation of x.)

As noted above, the control strategy may comprise both a proof procedure and some form of control language. Some proposals (e.g. Pollard, 1981; Conery, 1983) advocate 'transparent control', i.e. that the proof procedure should be sufficiently sophisticated to avoid the need for a control language. This approach may well be suitable for applications such as deductive logic databases, where the user should be concerned only with the logic, but is arguably out of place in a general-purpose logic *programming* language. It is preferable to keep the proof procedure simple so that the programmer can predict its behaviour and, if necessary, guide it by means of a control language.

Indeed, the success of Prolog can be largely attributed to its provision of a simple proof procedure which can be exploited by the programmer to write useful programs *and* which can be efficiently implemented on sequential machines. A parallel logic programming language should therefore include a proof procedure which is efficiently implementable on parallel architectures and which provides suitable idioms for parallel programming.

Of the forms of parallelism identified in Section 1.1.3, it is stream AND parallelism that is by far the most useful from a programming viewpoint since it allows the expression of problems involving parallel systems of communicating processes.

The criteria to be satisfied by the language can be summarized as follows:

1. The proof procedure should provide stream AND parallelism. As will be explained, the fulfilment of this objective entails certain compromises in the language design.
2. Other forms of parallel evaluation should be provided, in order to achieve maximum exploitation of parallelism.
3. It should be possible to implement the language with reasonable efficiency on a range of parallel (or even sequential) computers. This should not require any special-purpose architectural features.
4. The language should include a control language component sufficient to give the programmer complete control over the evaluation. This is the philosophy taken in Prolog, except that there is an added dimension: the degree of parallelism.
5. The language should be reasonably simple: there should be as few primitive concepts as possible.

1.2.2 Contributions

The result of the research is a language named PARLOG (a PARallel LOGic programming language). The main original contributions are the following:

1. To incorporate into a logic programming framework the idea of committed choice non-determinism (as in Dijkstra's guarded commands).
2. To combine this with other language features to efficiently realize 'stream AND parallelism' in logic programming.
3. To develop a complete, practical parallel logic programming language, including an interface with the conventional 'don't-know' form of non-determinism.
4. To investigate new application areas for logic programming made possible by the implementation of stream AND parallelism.
5. To show how programs in the language can be largely compiled into efficient machine-oriented instructions.
6. To show how the language may be implemented on various types of parallel machine with no special architectural features.

The work has given rise to the development of other, closely related, parallel logic programming languages, notably Concurrent Prolog (Shapiro, 1983) and Guarded Horn Clauses (Ueda, 1985a). The relationship between PARLOG and these languages will be discussed in subsequent chapters, particularly Chapter 8.

1.3   Preview of contents

This book can be viewed as comprising two main parts.

Part 1 (Chapters 2 to 4) covers the motivation, design and application of the PARLOG language.

Chapter 2 begins with an overview of established concepts of logic and functional programming, and describes the issue of control in declarative programs. This is followed by a survey of the forms of parallel control that are possible in logic programming.

Chapter 3 follows on from the discussion of Chapter 2 by considering in more detail how stream AND parallelism might be realized in a logic programming language. The chapter proceeds by presenting the complete design of the PARLOG language.

Chapter 4 further illustrates the use of PARLOG by means of more substantial example programs than those appearing in Chapter 3. These programs are chosen to demonstrate several useful PARLOG programming techniques, notably a method of obtaining 'lazy' evaluation.

Part 2 (Chapters 5 to 7) will be of interest mainly to the reader interested in implementation. In these chapters, priority has been given to rigour rather than ease of presentation where a choice has had to be made, in an attempt to provide sufficient detail for a potential implementor of the language.

Chapter 5 presents in detail the algorithms needed in a PARLOG compiler to check that a PARLOG program satisfies certain properties described in Part 1. The chapter continues with an explanation of the general principles involved in compiling a PARLOG program; these are applied to two specific implementation models in Chapters 6 and 7.

Chapter 6 describes one possible computational model for the evaluation of PARLOG programs: the AND/OR tree model.

Chapter 7 describes another computational model: the AND tree model of PARLOG evaluation.

The work is concluded by Chapter 8 which summarizes the past and present research on PARLOG, and future plans, together with a survey of some of the related research.

2
Parallel logic programming

This chapter is primarily an overview of established concepts of logic programming. However, it is not intended to constitute an introduction to the subject; there are many such introductions available, including a recent book by Hogger (1984) to which the interested reader is referred.

The chapter begins by summarizing the syntax and semantics of (pure) Horn clause programs. This provides the opportunity to define certain terminology and concepts that will be used and developed in subsequent chapters, and also sets the scene for the rest of this chapter. After a short diversion into functional programming, there follows a discussion of the control component of logic programs including the control strategy employed in Prolog.

The final section surveys some of the ways in which parallel evaluation of logic programs can be realized. This is an attempt to place into a coherent framework some of the many schemes for parallel logic programming that have been proposed.

2.1 Syntax of Horn clause programs

A **program** is a set of clauses. A **clause** is a sentence of the form:

$$H <- B_1, B_2, ..., B_n.$$

H is termed the **clause head** and is an atomic formula. $B_1,...,B_n$ $(n \geqslant 0)$ is the **clause body**. Each of $B_1,...,B_n$ is a literal. If n is 0, the clause is written without the '$<-$' symbol, and is an **assertion**. Otherwise, the clause is an **implication**.

An **atomic formula** takes the form:

$$R(t_1,...,t_k)$$

9

where R is the **relation name** and the **arguments** $t_1,\ldots,t_k$ ($k \geqslant 0$) are terms. R is said to be a k-ary relation, or to have **arity** k. In the uncommon case where k is 0, the parentheses can be omitted.

A **literal** is either a positive literal or a negative literal. A positive literal is simply an atomic formula, while a negative literal is written:

$\sim R(t_1,\ldots,t_k)$

A **term** is either a variable, a constant or a structured term.

A **variable** is an unquoted alphanumeric identifier (possibly including the '−' character) beginning with a lower-case letter. For example, x, y12 and next-B are all variables.

A **structured term** acts as a data structure in logic programs. It takes the form:

$F(t_1,\ldots,t_j)$

where F is the **function name** and the **arguments** $t_1,\ldots,t_j$ ($j \geqslant 1$) are terms. The j-ary function F is a constructor function, not one that will be evaluated. An example of a structured term is T(E,2,E) which might represent a labelled tree whose root node has label 2 and which has empty left and right subtrees, each represented by the constant E.

A **constant** is either a number or a structured term with no arguments; the parentheses are omitted. A constant name must be syntactically distinct from a variable name, so it must either be an identifier beginning with an upper-case letter, or any character string enclosed in quotes. Examples of constants are 213, X, 'merge' and 'No more solutions'.

For convenience, a special syntax is used for lists, a common type of structured term. A list with head h and tail t is written as the structured term $[h|t]$ while the empty list is denoted by the constant '[]'. The nested list term:

$[h_1|[h_2|[\ldots[h_i|t]\ldots]]]$

can be written as:

$[h_1,h_2,\ldots,h_i|t]$

In the special case where the tail t is the empty list '[]', this can be further shortened to:

$[h_1,h_2,\ldots,h_i]$

As a final piece of syntactic sugar, infix notation will occasionally be used for binary atomic formulas and structured terms. For example, the atomic formula:

<(1,y)

for the arithmetic relation 'less than' will often be written as:

1 < y

As an example, Program 2.1 defines the Sibling relation. Sibling(x,y) is true when x and y have a common parent and they are different individuals. The program comprises three implications and seven assertions.

Sibling(x,y) <− Parent(z,x), Parent(z,y), Dif(x,y).

Parent(Alice,Caspar).   Dif(x,y) <− Dif1(x,y).
Parent(Caspar,Eric).   Dif(x,y) <− Dif1(y,x).
Parent(Alice,Brian).
Parent(Alice,Dexter).   Dif1(Brian,Caspar).
                                         Dif1(Brian,Dexter).
                                         Dif1(Caspar,Dexter).

Program 2.1   The Sibling relation.

A program is invoked by a **query** which has the syntax:

: $B_1, B_2, ..., B_n.$

where $B_1,...,B_n$ are literals, like a clause body. This query invokes the evaluation of the conjunction $B_1,...,B_n$, which might instantiate some of the variables in the conjunction.

It is convenient at this point to define two further terms inspired by the procedural interpretation of logic programs. A **procedure** for relation R is the set of all clauses whose heads have the relation name R. Program 2.1 contains four procedures: for Sibling, Parent, Dif and Dif1. A **relation call** is any atomic formula appearing in a clause body or query, i.e., one that is not a clause head.

A variable in a logic program is initially an **unbound variable**. In the evaluation of a logic program, an unbound variable may be **instantiated** by being **bound** to a term t. Once instantiated, a variable cannot be bound to a different term; that is, there is no destructive assignment. Any term which is not a variable is a **non-variable term**. A term which contains no unbound variables is known as a **ground term**.

2.2   Semantics of Horn clause programs

2.2.1   Declarative semantics

As sets of logical sentences, Horn clause programs have a straightforward declarative reading. Each procedure is read as the conjunction of its clauses. A clause:

$R(t_1,...,t_k) <- B_1, B_2, ..., B_n.$

is read as:

'$R(t_1,...,t_k)$ if B_1 and B_2 and ... and B_n'

Any variables in the clause are implicitly universally quantified. For example, the clause for Sibling in Program 2.1 can be understood as:

'For all x,y,z: Sibling(x,y) if
Parent(z,x) and Parent(z,y) and Dif(x,y)'

The logical interpretation of a query, such as:

: Sibling(x,y).

is taken to be a denial:

'For no x,y: Sibling(x,y)'

Resolution inference systems (see Section 2.2.3) solve a query by proving that the denial is logically inconsistent with the set of clauses comprising the program.

The semantics of logic programs were investigated by van Emden and Kowalski (1976). They considered operational semantics and two kinds of declarative semantics: model-theoretic and fixpoint. The model-theoretic semantics is based on the classical theory of predicate logic, and deals with concepts such as truth and logical implication. van Emden and Kowalski proved the equivalence of model-theoretic semantics with the fixpoint semantics applicable to programming languages in general.

In the model-theoretic semantics, the meaning or denotation of a k-ary relation R in a program A is defined as the set of k-tuples of terms $(t_1,...,t_k)$ such that $R(t_1,...,t_k)$ is **logically implied** by the clauses in A.

In Program 2.1, the denotation of the Sibling relation is clearly the set {(Caspar,Brian),(Caspar,Dexter),(Brian,Dexter)}.

2.2.2 Operational semantics

In the operational semantics, the denotation of a k-ary relation R in a program A is the set of k-tuples $(t_1,...,t_k)$ such that there exists a derivation of $R(t_1,...,t_k)$ from the clauses in A. This denotation depends upon the nature of the inference system used.

2.2.3 Resolution

Most logic programming systems are based on top-down (or **goal-oriented**) resolution. Resolution is a constructive proof procedure that solves a query:

   : $B_1, B_2, ..., B_n$.

and, at the same time, generates bindings for variables in the query. This means that if $(t_1,...,t_k)$ is a solution of relation R according to the declarative semantics, the solution can be found by a resolution proof of the query:

   : $R(x_1,...,x_k)$.

which will construct a **substitution** (a set of variable=term bindings), namely $\{x_1=t_1,...,x_k=t_k\}$.

If e is a term and s is a substitution, $e.s$ (read 's applied to e') is a **substitution instance** of e. If s is the set $\{x_1=t_1,...,x_k=t_k\}$, $e.s$ is the term obtained by replacing $x_1,...,x_k$ in e by $t_1,...,t_k$, respectively.

A resolution proof reduces a given query to an empty query by a series of resolution steps.

2.2.3.1 *Resolution step*

Each resolution step, applied to a query Q, consists of the following actions:

1. Select any relation call P from the query Q. Let the relation name of this call be R.
2. Select any clause C from the procedure for R, and ensure that all variables in C are new, i.e. not used elsewhere in Q.
3. Unify the call P with the head of clause C, with most general unifier s (see Section 2.2.3.2).
4. Replace P in Q by the body of clause C, to obtain a new query NQ.
5. Apply the unifying substitution s to NQ, to obtain a new query QQ.

The resolution step is repeated with QQ as the query until an empty query results. If any of actions 2 to 5 are impossible, the resolution step **fails**. Depending upon the particular inference system, failure of a resolution step need not be fatal. It often causes backtracking to try a different choice of clause in a previous resolution step.

2.2.3.2 *Unification*

Two atomic formulas P and H can be **unified** if there exists a substitution s such that $P.s$ and $H.s$ are syntactically identical. The unifying substitution s should be the **most general unifier** (Robinson, 1965) of P and H, i.e. a unifying substitution that is not an instance of any other (more general) unifying substitution.

In unifying a relation call P with a clause head H, the unifying substitution is often classified into two parts. The **input substitution** is the set of bindings to variables in H, and the **output substitution** contains the bindings to variables in P. For example:

relation call:	R(T(x,2,y),z,M)
clause head:	R(T(E,u,E),K,w)
input substitution:	{u=2,w=M}
output substitution:	{x=E,y=E,z=K}

2.2.4 Non-determinism

Among declarative programming languages, a distinguishing feature of logic programming is its non-determinism. Two sources of non-determinism are apparent in the above definition of a resolution step. In 1, any relation call can be selected from the query while, in 2, any clauses for the appropriate relation can be selected. It is the latter that causes non-determinism in the solutions computed; the former affects only the behaviour.

2.2.5 The logical variable

Another extremely important feature of logic programming is the 'logical variable'. This is the ability of a relation call to construct a partially instantiated data structure (i.e. containing unbound variables) in such a way that the variables in it can be instantiated by another call. Such a data structure can be successively modified by instantiating the variables *in place*, without the need to copy the structure. The logical variable is a consequence of the bidirectional nature of unification, as discussed in Section 2.4.1.3.

The logical variable endows logic programming with much of the power of imperative languages but in a declarative style, and is heavily exploited in Prolog programs. Warren (1980) demonstrates the advantages of logic programming for compiler writing. His compiler features a dictionary which is a partially instantiated data structure, containing variables in place of addresses which have been referenced but are not yet known. As these addresses are defined, they are inserted in the dictionary simply by instantiating the variables.

2.2.6 Correctness and completeness

Any resolution inference system is **correct** (Kowalski, 1979a). That is, the set of solutions representing the denotation under the operational semantics is a subset of that under the model-theoretic semantics. The two denotations are equivalent only if the inference system is also **complete**; an incomplete system may not compute all of the solutions that a program logically defines.

Although there exist complete inference systems for predicate logic, that of Prolog is incomplete, and the same is true of the PARLOG language to be described in subsequent chapters. The reasons for the incompleteness of these languages will be explained in detail below. It is likely that any practical logic programming language must sacrifice completeness in the interests of efficiency.

2.3 AND/OR trees

The 'AND/OR tree' (Kowalski, 1979a) is a graphical representation of problem solving. It will be used here to illustrate the solution of a query using a given (Horn clause) logic program. This representation has the weakness (or advantage) that it reveals nothing about the control, i.e. how the problem is solved. The examples shown here use the form of AND/OR tree given by Pollard (1981).

OR nodes are labelled by a 'problem', comprising a single relation call in the form of a query, such as :Parent(z,x). Each subtree of an OR node is an **OR branch**, representing an alternative solution to the problem. The offspring of an OR node are AND nodes, one for each clause that unifies with the given relation call. The arcs joining an OR node to its offspring AND nodes are shown as double lines. If the unification involves an output substitution, this is shown on the connecting arc. Input substitutions are not shown but are applied directly to the offspring.

An **AND node** is labelled by a clause head, after application of the input substitution generated in unifying with the parent's problem. The subtrees of an AND node are **AND branches**. There is one offspring OR node for each relation call in the body of the corresponding clause. The arcs joining an AND node to its offspring OR nodes are shown as single lines.

For descriptive purposes, OR nodes are named *O1*, *O2*, etc. and AND nodes are named *A1*, *A2*, etc.

The AND/OR tree in Fig. 2.1 depicts the solution of the query:

: Sibling(Brian,Caspar).

with Program 2.1. For brevity, the constants in Program 2.1 will henceforth be abbreviated to A, B, C, D and E. In Fig. 2.1, the query :Sibling(B,C) labels *O1*, the root node of the AND/OR tree. Node *A1* is labelled by the (instantiated) head of the Sibling clause, while *O2*, *O3* and *O4* correspond to the calls in the body of this clause. Nodes *O2* and *O3* are each labelled by a call which is solved by an assertion; both of these have an output substitution z=A. These assertions label nodes *A2* and *A3*, respectively. The tree shows that, for this example query, there is one solution, which binds the (internal) variable z to A.

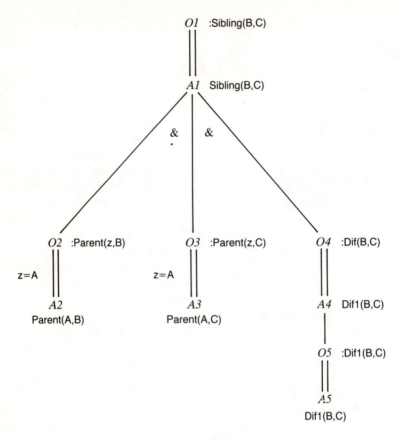

Fig 2.1   AND/OR tree.

Fig. 2.2 shows a more interesting AND/OR tree, for the query:

: Sibling(x,Caspar).

This time, node *O2* is labelled by the problem :Parent(z,x) which has four unifying clauses, each giving a different output substitution for z and x. Node *O3* has one offspring as before, while node *O4* is labelled by :Dif(x,C) which has two solutions.

The solutions to the query at the root of an AND/OR tree are obtained by finding compatible sets of branches; that is, those labelled by compatible substitutions. One compatible set of branches in Fig. 2.2, identified by the set of their leaf nodes, is {*A4,A6,A9*} and the other is {*A5,A6,A10*}. These yield substitutions {z=A,x=B} and {z=A,x=D}, which in turn give the two solutions of x to the original query.

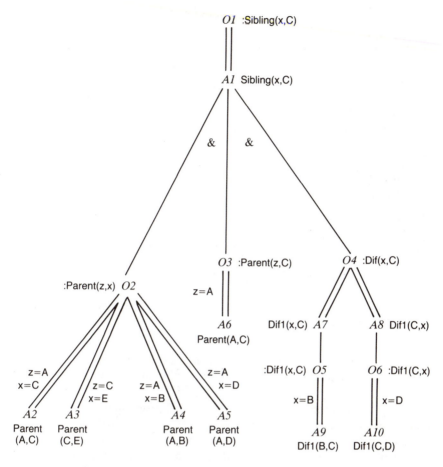

Fig 2.2   AND/OR tree.

2.4   Functional programming

Although this book is primarily concerned with logic programming, this section is devoted to a brief discussion of functional programming languages. This is worthwhile since many of the control issues in logic programming, discussed below in this chapter, can be described in a functional programming framework. Moreover, functional languages enjoy some properties which are advantageous in a parallel environment, so it is instructive to consider these carefully in any investigation of parallel logic programming.

Whereas logic programming is derived from predicate logic, functional programming is based on the lambda calculus (Church, 1941). Nevertheless, the two kinds of programming language have much in common. For a general introduction to functional programming, the reader is referred to Henderson (1980), while comparisons of logic and functional languages appear in Kowalski (1983) and in two recent papers (Darlington *et al.*, 1985; Reddy, 1985b).

Functional programs deal with expressions built from two types of function: rewritable functions and constructor functions. Rewritable functions are analogous to relations in logic programs, and are defined by a set of equations. An example of a functional program is the following, which defines the Flatten function; this maps a labelled tree structure to a list of its leaf nodes, by an inorder traversal:

Flatten(T(T(xx,xu,xy),u,y)) = Flatten(T(xx,xu,T(xy,u,y))).
Flatten(T(E,u,y)) = [u|Flatten(y)].
Flatten(E) = [].

The corresponding Horn clause program appears in Program 2.2. It will be apparent that the two programs are very similar. Each equation in the functional program corresponds to a clause in the logic program. Each *n*-ary rewritable function F is replaced by an $(n+1)$-ary relation R such that:

$$F(x_1,...,x_n) = y \leftrightarrow R(x_1,...,x_n,y)$$

Kowalski (1983) gives a simple proof that, using such a translation, any computable function can be translated to an equivalent Horn clause program; the converse is not true.

Points often quoted in favour of functional programming are that the notation is more 'user friendly' than relational notation, and that it is more amenable to higher-order programming. The former is largely a matter of taste, while the latter advantage is offset somewhat by the absence of the 'logical variable' described above. (This is not to suggest that the logical variable endows logic programming with expressive power *equivalent* to that provided by higher-order facilities.)

The reasons why functional programming lacks the two distinguishing features of logic programming, namely non-determinism and the logical variable, can be clarified by considering its operational semantics. This is normally based on reduction (but see Section 2.4.2). A reduction evaluation **reduces** an expression containing rewritable functions to one which contains only constructor functions. An expression involving only constructors is analogous to a ground term in logic programming parlance.

2.4.1 Reduction

2.4.1.1 *Reduction step*

Each step of a reduction evaluation of an expression X consists of the following actions:

1. Select any subexpression SX (for some rewritable function F) from the expression X.

2. Match the expression SX with the left-hand side (LHS) of an equation E for F, possibly producing input bindings for the variables in the LHS.

3. Replace SX in X by the right-hand side (RHS) of equation E, with *all* variables replaced by their bindings from the LHS, to obtain a new expression NX.

This is repeated with NX as the expression until an expression is obtained which contains only constructors. If any actions are impossible, a run-time error occurs.

The only non-determinism here is in the order in which subexpressions are reduced: in 1, any subexpression can be selected. This choice does not affect the solution computed. Only one solution can ever be computed because, in 2, only one equation can be used to rewrite any selected subexpression. The reason for this determinism is a desire to adhere to the theory of functions underlying functional programming. Note that there is no syntactic restriction that prevents the writing of a 'non-deterministic function' in which more than one equation can be selected.

2.4.1.2 Matching

A notable feature of reduction is that, in 2, **term matching** is used instead of unification. The matching of a subexpression with the LHS of an equation conveys data only 'into' the equation. The variables of the equation are used only to carry values from the LHS expression to the RHS, *all* variables in an equation being bound by the matching. Any 'output' from the equation is a consequence of the rewriting of the selected subexpression to the RHS expression of the equation.

2.4.1.3 Directional logic programs

In the logic program equivalent of a functional program, discussed above, each n-ary function F is replaced by an $(n+1)$-ary relation R. Let the first n arguments of R be termed **input arguments** and the $(n+1)$th argument an **output argument**. Because of the nature of the functional program F, the equivalent logic program R exhibits two interesting properties.

First, in each resolution step, when a call to R is unified with the head of a clause for R, the unifier for each of the input arguments is always an input substitution while that for the output argument is an output substitution.

Second, in each clause in the procedure for R, the variables in the input arguments in the clause head occur in the clause body only in input arguments of calls, and other variables occur no more than once as output arguments of calls.

The first property is a consequence of the unidirectional nature of term matching while the second is guaranteed by the syntax of functional programs. A logic program equivalent of a functional program is an example of what might be termed a **directional** logic program. In general, this term will be applied to any logic program satisfying the above two properties; a relation might have more than one output argument in the general case.

The pragmatic effect of directionality in logic programs is that the arguments are **strong**, or 'definite' (Reddy, 1985b). That is, for each argument of a relation call, the argument is either completely constructed by that call (if an output argument) or by another call (if an input argument). There can never be an output substitution for any variable in an input argument, nor an input substitution for any variable in an output argument. Note that this does not preclude the construction of a data structure containing unbound variables; it does mean that any such variables cannot be instantiated by any other call. Therefore, the logical variable (Section 2.2.5) is not possible in directional programs. To allow the logical variable, weak arguments must be allowed; this is discussed further in Chapters 3 and 5.

2.4.2   Narrowing

It should be noted that an alternative operational semantics for functional programming has been proposed: **narrowing** (Reddy, 1985a). This differs from reduction in allowing output substitutions through arguments in order to implement the logical variable. That is, narrowing uses unification whereas reduction uses matching. Functional languages based on narrowing include Eqlog (Goguen and Meseguer, 1984) and the current version of Qute (Sato and Sakurai, 1984) (not to be confused with the earlier version of the language (Sato and Sakurai, 1983)).

The reason for adopting narrowing as an operational semantics is to provide more of the power of logic programming in an equational framework. Indeed, if narrowing is combined with non-determinism – an extension considered by Reddy (1985b) – the only difference from logic programming appears to be the equational syntax.

While narrowing adds to the power of functional programming, it loses some of the simplicity that is an argument in favour of the functional approach. Narrowing will therefore not be considered in detail in this book: all references to 'functional programming' should be taken to mean the conventional, reduction-based semantics.

2.4.3   Control in functional programs

In declarative programming languages, the declarative semantics of a program determines the solution(s) that *can* be computed. In addition, there is a control strategy which determines exactly *which* solution(s) are computed and *how*. In functional programming, the control strategy specifies the choices that can be made within the constraints of the reduction algorithm described in Section 2.4.1.

The only choice here concerns the order in which subexpressions are selected for rewriting; this is the 'computation rule'. This choice affects the behaviour of the evaluation. It may determine whether or not the evaluation terminates, i.e. whether the solution to the function is actually computed. This issue is analogous to completeness in logic programs.

Several computation rules are analysed from a theoretical standpoint in Manna (1974). The choice of computation rule also has important pragmatic implications, which are considered here.

2.4.3.1 *Call-by-value*

LISP (McCarthy *et al.*, 1965), the most widely used functional language, traditionally uses the 'call-by-value' rule. This is a sequential computation rule whereby the arguments of a functional expression are completely evaluated, sequentially, before the expression itself is reduced. If the arguments are evaluated in left–right order, as is usual, the rule is known as 'left-most inner-most'.

2.4.3.2 *Lazy evaluation*

An alternative computation rule, 'call-by-need' (Vuillemin, 1973; Wadsworth, 1971), was proposed for LISP independently by Henderson and Morris (1976) and Friedman and Wise (1976). This has become known as **lazy** evaluation. In the lazy evaluation scheme, a functional expression may be reduced before its arguments are completely evaluated, the arguments being reduced only on demand. Lazy evaluation has been implemented not only for LISP (Henderson *et al.*, 1983), where the list constructor is the only constructor function, but also in other, more modern, functional languages. HOPE (Burstall *et al.*, 1980) features an optional lazy list constructor. Turner's languages SASL and KRC (Turner, 1981) feature lazy evaluation for all functions.

As pointed out by its originators, lazy evaluation subsumes the concepts of streams (Landin, 1965) and coroutines (Conway, 1963). A unary function and its argument act as a pair of coroutined processes. The value of the argument is transmitted to the outer function by **incremental communication**, a series of partial approximations to the final value.

A classic example illustrating streams and coroutines is the Sameleaves function, which evaluates to True if its two argument trees have the same labels in the same order:

Sameleaves(x,y) = Eqlist(Flatten(x),Flatten(y))

where Eqlist is a function that compares two lists and returns True or False. Using lazy evaluation, Sameleaves will Flatten the trees on demand and yield a False result as soon as a different pair of nodes is encountered. In the call-by-value scheme, the two trees would be Flattened completely, even if they differed at an early stage.

Lazy evaluation also makes possible programming with infinite data structures. Because arguments of a function are evaluated only on demand, there is no problem if they evaluate to infinite data structures. In PARLOG, lazy evaluation can be achieved by a programming technique which is discussed in Chapter 4.

2.4.3.3 Parallel evaluation

Both the call-by-value and the lazy evaluation schemes were, at least originally, intended for implementation on sequential computers. Kahn and MacQueen (1977) presented a functional language which generalized the idea of lazy evaluation to include parallelism.

In Kahn and MacQueen's language, each function call in an expression is viewed as a process in a network. As with lazy evaluation, the processes communicate by incremental communication. A function which requires input on one of its arguments is modelled by a (consumer) process performing a *GET* operation on the channel connected to the producer process evaluating its argument. When the producer eventually generates output, it performs a *PUT* operation on the channel connected to its consumer process.

In the lazy or coroutine mode of execution, a *GET* operation by a consumer causes transfer of control to the producer in the event that no data is available. A *PUT* operation by the producer switches control to the consumer if the consumer requires data.

The eager or parallel mode of execution is obtained by allowing consumer and producer processes to run in parallel. Now, a *GET* operation by a consumer merely causes that process to suspend, i.e. it is 'blocking'; there is no transfer of control. A *PUT* operation is 'non-blocking'; it does not cause the producer to suspend, but it might reactivate a suspended consumer.

Eager parallel evaluation can give advantages over and above those obtainable by lazy evaluation, by exploiting multiprocessing. For example, the function:

Sumtree(t) = Sum(Flatten(t))

evaluates to the sum of all nodes on its tree argument by Flattening the tree to a list and summing the list. This will potentially run faster if the Flatten and Sum functions are evaluated concurrently as independent processes. The two processes communicate by incremental generation of the frontier list.

The drawback of eager evaluation is that there is no restraint upon the evaluation of a producer. The producer could 'run ahead' of the consumer process to an arbitrary extent, perhaps doing unnecessary computation, even evaluating an infinite function. Kahn and MacQueen propose the use of an 'anticipation coefficient' to restrain eager evaluation: if the coefficient is n, the producer may run ahead by no more than n items. A coefficient of

0 results in lazy evaluation, while the eager parallel form of control results from a coefficient of infinity.

Keller and Lindstrom (1981) observe that eager evaluation can be obtained in a lazy environment by adding strict operators, i.e. those that 'demand' their arguments. They define an anticipate function which is the identity function, but which has the operational effect of demanding each part of its argument data structure, so that it is evaluated eagerly. They then refine this idea to implement the anticipation coefficient of Kahn and MacQueen. This is done by a buffer function which begins by generating demand 'tokens' for as many values as there are spaces in the buffer. Each time a value is supplied by the producer, the buffer generates a further demand token.

2.5   Control in logic programs

The resolution algorithm in Section 2.2.3 shows that the control strategy for logic programs must determine both the order in which relation calls are selected (the **computation rule**), and the order in which clauses are chosen from among those whose heads unify with the call (the **search rule**). Alternative control strategies can be obtained by varying the computation rule and search rule.

2.5.1   Prolog's sequential control

The control strategy of Prolog, which requires no detailed description here, is a sequential one. At each resolution step, the computation rule selects one relation call from the query and evaluates it. As with functional languages, the computation rule is usually fixed throughout the evaluation. Also, the choice of a relation call is never retracted: there is no backtracking to select a different relation call from the query. This is usually acceptable since the computation rule affects only the behaviour of the evaluation, not the results computed.

In Prolog, the computation rule traditionally selects the left-most call but variations have been suggested. For example, Warren (1981) proposes the selection of the call having the fewest solutions; this is more efficient, especially for database relations having many solutions. IC-PROLOG (Clark and McCabe, 1979; Clark *et al.*, 1982) provides annotations by means of which the programmer may specify the selection of relation calls in an order dependent upon the mode of use. PRISM (Kasif *et al.*, 1983) provides a similar control language. Conery (1983) uses a run-time algorithm to arrange 'dependent' calls in the most efficient order, in his AND/OR process model, described in Section 2.6.4.

The search rule of Prolog selects the left-most clause from the procedure for the selected relation. Because the choice of clause determines which solution is computed, Prolog features a backtracking mechanism. If a resolution step fails, the system backtracks to the last choice of a clause, selects the next clause in the procedure, and proceeds with this new choice.

2.5.1.1 AND/OR tree interpretation

In terms of the AND/OR tree representation, Prolog's control strategy performs a left–right depth-first traversal. In the example of Fig. 2.2, the AND/OR tree is traversed in the following order, showing the variable bindings and nodes traversed:

> *O1 A1 O2* (z=A,x=C) *A2 O3* (z=A)   *A6 O4 A7 O5* (x=B)

Because this traversal results in incompatible bindings to x, the system backtracks repeatedly until compatible bindings are obtained:

> *O1 A1 O2* (z=A,x=C) *A2 O3* (z=A)   *A6 O4 A8 O6* (x=D)
> *O1 A1 O2* (z=C,x=E) *A3 O3* (z=A)   *A6 O4 A7 O5* (x=B)
> *O1 A1 O2* (z=C,x=E) *A3 O3* (z=A)   *A6 O4 A8 O6* (x=D)
> *O1 A1 O2* (z=A,x=B) *A4 O3* (z=A)   *A6 O4 A7 O5* (x=B) *A9*

The last traversal represents a solution to the query. If more solutions are required, the system again backtracks:

> *O1 A1 O2* (z=A,x=B) *A4 O3* (z=A)   *A6 O4 A8 O6* (x=D)
> *O1 A1 O2* (z=A,x=D) *A5 O3* (z=A)   *A6 O4 A7 O5* (x=B)
> *O1 A1 O2* (z=A,x=D) *A5 O3* (z=A)   *A6 O4 A8 O6* (x=D) *A10*

This is the second solution. Any further backtracking will immediately fail the evaluation.

2.5.1.2 Incompleteness of Prolog

As noted in Section 2.2.6, Prolog is an incomplete inference system. That is, a Prolog evaluation of a logic program may not compute all of its solutions (defined according to the declarative semantics). The solutions that will not be found are those involving a branch to the right of an infinite branch in the corresponding AND/OR tree. This incompleteness is a consequence of the left–right depth-first control strategy of Prolog.

For example, Program 2.1 can be changed to one which has the same declarative semantics but very different operational semantics, when evaluated by Prolog. Suppose the definition of the Dif relation of Program 2.1 is replaced by the following procedure:

```
Dif(Brian,Caspar).
Dif(x,y) <- Dif(y,x).
Dif(Brian,Dexter).
Dif(Caspar,Dexter).
```

Then, the AND/OR tree of Fig. 2.2 is changed: the subtree rooted at node
O4 is replaced by that illustrated in Fig. 2.3.

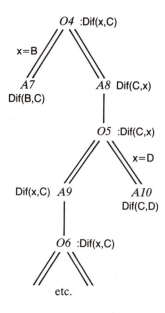

Fig 2.3   Infinite branch in AND/OR tree.

The first solution is found by a left–right depth-first traversal ending in:

O1 A1 O2 (z=A,x=B)   *A4 O3* (z=A)   *A6 O4* (x=B)   *A7*

but any backtracking will immediately cause the system to explore the
infinite branch:

O4 A8 O5 A9 O6 ...

so that the second solution will never be computed.

2.5.2   'Don't-know' and 'don't-care' non-determinism

The backtracking ability of Prolog is one method of implementing what is
known as 'don't-know' non-determinism (Kowalski, 1979a). Loosely, this
term means that the system 'doesn't know' how to obtain a solution to a
problem, and so may need to search through many alternative evaluation
paths.
    The opposite is 'don't-care' non-determinism, in which the system
'doesn't care' how a solution is obtained, so does not need to search.

Don't-care non-determinism is the basis of Dijkstra's language of guarded commands (Dijkstra, 1976). Kowalski (1979a) points out that don't-care non-determinism is a form of intelligent backtracking, since it eliminates unnecessary searching. In Prolog, a 'cut' primitive is often used to realize don't-care non-determinism. However, the undisciplined use of the cut can result in obscure programs, so the cut is the subject of some controversy.

2.5.3   AND parallelism and OR parallelism

The term 'AND parallelism' refers to a computation rule in which relation calls are evaluated concurrently. 'OR parallelism' is parallelism in the search rule, such that several clauses are acted upon concurrently.

Within these categories, many variations and combinations are possible, not all of which can be implemented efficiently. For example, it is not straightforward to implement AND parallelism as is found in functional programming, with incremental communication of solutions between concurrent relation calls. This is because of the non-determinism of logic programs. For this reason, most proposals for parallel logic programming restrict communication between calls to complete, rather than incrementally constructed, solutions. Even with this restriction, a form of AND parallelism is still possible, as is OR parallelism.

A detailed discussion of parallelism is deferred to Section 2.6.

2.5.4   A functional logic program interpreter

Before considering in detail the potential for parallel evaluation of logic programs, it is useful to outline the definition of a logic program interpreter as a functional program. This will allow several of the possible control strategies for logic programming to be related to concepts of functional programming.

The heart of such an interpreter is a Solns function, which evaluates to the set of *all* solutions to a given relation call. It has two arguments: a relation call, and an initial substitution for the variables in the call. These two arguments together determine a partially instantiated relation call, i.e. a call that might contain unbound variables. The result of the function is a bag (a set with members possibly duplicated) of substitutions which are the solutions to the relation call. The bag of solutions is represented as a list; the order of list members depends upon the definition of Solns. Each substitution is itself a bag (represented as a list) of variable = term bindings.

For example, given the definition of the Parent relation in Program 2.1:

Solns(Parent(z,x),[])

evaluates to:

[[z=A,x=C],[z=C,x=E],[z¬A,x⊑B],[z=A,x=D]]

in some order: the four solutions to Parent(z,x) in the case where z and x are unbound variables. For the call Parent(z,C), however, there is only one solution:

Solns(Parent(z,x),[x=C])

evaluates to:

[[z=A]]

2.5.4.1 *Disjunction*

For a relation defined by more than one clause, the solutions obtained from each of the clauses are combined in some way. For example, given the following procedure for relation P:

P(x) <− P1(x).
P(x) <− P2(x).

the solutions to P are defined by the equation:

Solns(P(x),sub) =
    Combine(Solns(P1(x),sub),Solns(P2(x),sub)).   (D)

In other words, to find the solutions of P(x) when x is instantiated according to some substitution sub, obtain the solutions of P1(x) and P2(x) starting with the same solution sub, and Combine the two bags. Here, Combine is a function which evaluates to the union of two bags represented as lists.

    In D, the two arguments of Combine are independent, so they could easily be evaluated concurrently, thus realizing OR parallelism.

2.5.4.2 *Conjunction*

There are two different methods that might be used to obtain the solutions of a conjunction. Suppose that Q is defined by the conjunction:

Q(x) <− Q1(x), Q2(x).

    One possibility is the 'join method', whereby solutions are obtained from each call independently and intersected:

Solns(Q(x),sub) =
    Join(Solns(Q1(x),sub),Solns(Q2(x),sub)).   (CJ)

The solutions to Q1(x) and Q2(x) are computed independently, starting with the same initial substitution sub. The two bags of solutions are 'joined', producing a bag of solutions upon which both calls agree. For example, the solutions of the query:

: Sibling(x,Caspar).

are found by the following evaluation:

Solns(Sibling(x,y),[y=C])

$\Rightarrow$ Join(Solns(Parent(z,x),[y=C]),
            Join(Solns(Parent(z,y),[y=C]), Solns(Dif(x,y),[y=C])))

$\Rightarrow$ Join([[y=C,z=A,x=C],[y=C,z=C,x=E],[y=C,z=A,x=B],[y=C,z=A,x=D]],
            Join([[y=C,z=A]], [[y=C,x=B],[y=C,x=D]]))

$\Rightarrow$ [[y=C,z=A,x=B],[y=C,z=A,x=D]]

An alternative to CJ is the 'nested loops method', as used by Prolog, whereby each solution obtained from the left-most call in a conjunction is 'passed on' to the rest of the conjunction:

Solns(Q(x),sub) =
        Combineall(Solns(Q1(x),sub),Q2(x)).   (CN1)

Combineall([],body) = [].   (CN2)
Combineall([sub|subs],body) =
        Combine(Solns(body,sub),Combineall(subs,body)).   (CN3)

Here, the solutions to Q1(x), starting with the initial substitution sub, are obtained by the expression Solns(Q1(x),sub) in equation CN1. For each of these solutions to Q1, the bag of solutions to Q2 is computed, and all of these bags are Combined.

In the nested loops method, it is advantageous to order the calls so that the call with the smallest set of solutions is solved first, thus reducing the number of invocations of subsequent calls. In the example of Program 2.1, the Sibling clause should be reordered to:

Sibling(x,y) <− Parent(z,y), Dif(x,y), Parent(z,x).

for use with the query:

: Sibling(x,Caspar).

The first call, Parent(z,y) where y is bound to Caspar, has only one solution. The nested loops method solves the query as follows:

Solns(Sibling(x,y),[y=C])

⇒ Combineall(Solns(Parent(z,y),[y=C]),(Dif(x,y),Parent(z,x)))

⇒ Combineall([[y=C,z=A]],(Dif(x,y),Parent(z,x)))

⇒ Solns((Dif(x,y),Parent(z,x)),[y=C,z=A])

⇒ Combineall([[y=C,z=A,x=B],[y=C,z=A,x=D]],Parent(z,x))

⇒ Combine(Solns(Parent(z,x),[y=C,z=A,x=B]),
    Solns(Parent(z,x),[y=C,z=A,x=D]))

⇒ Combine([[y=C,z=A,x=B]],[[y=C,z=A,x=D]])

⇒ [[y=C,z=A,x=B],[y=C,z=A,x=D]]

Of the two methods outlined, the nested loops method is probably the most practical. First, unlike the join method, the amount of computational effort can be minimized by suitable ordering of calls (Warren, 1981). Second, the join method may incur a large space overhead for the storage of intermediate solutions.

On the other hand, the join method offers more scope for parallelism, since all calls are independent. This can be seen by the form of equation CJ.

2.5.4.3 *Applications*

Various computation rules can be applied to the functional program comprising equations in the form of D with either CJ or CN1–3. The call-by-value rule (Section 2.4.3.1) results in a scheme in which whole relation extensions are manipulated. Such a scheme is similar to the Relational Programming system of MacLennan (1981) except that his language is not limited to Horn clauses. The evaluation of a query produces all solutions to the query. If a relation is defined by a conjunction, all solutions will be found to each call in the conjunction, in turn, and they will be combined using either CJ or CN1–3. Similarly, D will combine all solutions found by the application of each clause.

An interesting, if not original, observation is that the interpreter comprising D and CN, using lazy evaluation (Section 2.4.3.2), yields the Prolog control strategy. The lazy evaluation ensures that the clauses defining a relation are applied, one at a time, in a left–right order. Here, Combine could be implemented as a function that concatenates two lists. Successive solutions to a query are found by fully lazy evaluation of the Solns, Combine and Combineall functions. Demanding the nth member of the list produced by Solns is analogous to backtracking to find the nth solution to a Prolog query.

To summarize, the two sequential computation rules for functional programs – call-by-value and lazy evaluation – can be applied to the simple logic program interpreter above, each resulting in a different sequential logic programming control strategy. One of these happens to be that of Prolog, while the other is an even simpler scheme, perhaps more suitable for database-style applications than for general programming.

In Section 2.6, parallel computation rules are considered and are shown to reveal ways of incorporating parallelism into logic program evaluation.

2.6   Forms of parallelism in logic programs

Section 2.5.3 introduced the concepts of AND and OR parallelism. This section considers how such parallelism can be realized in logic programming systems.

2.6.1   All-solutions AND parallelism 1

There is a form of AND parallelism which can be implemented quite easily. This involves the concurrent evaluation of relation calls in a conjunction, in such a way that the calls are working concurrently on *different* solutions. This might be termed **all-solutions AND parallelism** to distinguish it from forms of AND parallelism in which many calls can be active on the same solution concurrently. Note that all-solutions AND parallelism is therefore effective in exploiting parallelism only for programs with some don't-know non-determinism (Section 2.5.2).

The first variant of all-solutions AND parallelism, described in this section, is an extension of the Prolog control strategy. To understand this scheme, consider the conjunctive query:

   : Q1(x), Q2(x).

In Prolog, the solutions to Q1(x) are found sequentially. As each solution is computed, it is 'passed on' to the remainder of the conjunction, Q2(x), which is evaluated in the context of that solution. Subsequent solutions to Q1(x) are computed only when required by Q2(x).

To introduce parallelism, successive solutions to call Q1(x) can be sought immediately, even before they are required by Q2(x). The second and subsequent solutions to Q1(x) are being produced while Q2(x) is working on Q1's first solution, resulting in a form of AND parallelism analogous to pipelining.

Within this scheme, there are at least two further alternatives. In the first, the solutions to Q1(x) found by the 'pre-search' are buffered until required by Q2(x). In the second, as soon as each solution to Q1(x) is found, a new invocation of Q2(x) is created and evaluated. The second alternative clearly yields greater parallelism. Both of these are considered by Conery and Kibler (1981) in the framework of their AND/OR process model, described more fully in Conery (1983).

These two schemes can be described in terms of the simple logic program interpreter of Section 2.5.4. They are modifications of the nested loops method and can be obtained by the use of equations CN1–3 with different computation rules. The first scheme, in which the solutions found by the pre-search are buffered, results from applying a parallel (eager) computation rule to equation CN1. The first argument (Solns) of the Combineall function (underlined) is evaluated in parallel with the outer function:

Solns(Q(x),sub) =
    Combineall(Solns(Q1(x),sub),Q2(x)).

This means that solutions to the first call, Q1(x), are computed eagerly.

The second scheme is obtained by *additionally* applying a parallel computation rule to equation CN3. The second argument of the Combine function is evaluated in parallel with the outer function:

Combineall([sub|subs],body) =
    Combine(Solns(body,sub),Combineall(subs,body)).

Now, not only are the solutions to the first call computed eagerly – they are also eagerly consumed by the Combineall function.

Tamura and Kaneda (1984) describe a multiprocessor implementation based on the first of these schemes, which they call **pipelining parallelism**. Theirs is an implementation of an AND/OR process model similar to Conery and Kibler's. As a refinement of the above scheme, processes are provided with bounded message buffers. This limits the extent of the 'pre-search' for solutions, thus restraining the parallelism. In terms of equation CN1, this bounded buffer is analogous to the use of an anticipation coefficient, described in Section 2.4.3.3.

As Tamura and Kaneda note, the use of a buffer of size zero (corresponding to lazy evaluation of equation CN1) results in a Prolog-style evaluation. They also point out that, provided the search for solutions is sequential, i.e. no OR parallelism, the cut primitive may still be used to control backtracking, as in Prolog.

Another proposal (Lindstrom and Panangaden, 1984) combines all-solutions AND parallelism with OR parallelism in an implementation of logic programming on a hybrid reduction/dataflow architecture. This form of parallelism is also a feature of the PRISM system (Kasif *et al.*, 1983).

The use of all-solutions AND parallelism results in a potential speed gain for non-deterministic programs. However, it is more likely than Prolog to enter a non-terminating evaluation, since many branches of the

AND/OR tree are traversed concurrently, possibly including an infinite branch. Moreover, in the absence of OR parallelism (see Section 2.6.3), an evaluation will still, like Prolog, fail to compute solutions corresponding to branches to the right of an infinite branch in the AND/OR tree.

2.6.2 All-solutions AND parallelism 2

Section 2.6.1 presented a control strategy based on the nested loops method with a parallel computation rule. Another variant of all-solutions AND parallelism uses the join method. To solve the conjunctive query:

   : Q1(x), Q2(x).

the two relation calls can be evaluated concurrently, each computing a set of solutions. The two sets of solutions are joined by a further concurrent process.

   This scheme corresponds to the use of equation CJ, with an eager parallel computation rule:

Solns(Q(x),sub) =
   Join(Solns(Q1(x),sub),Solns(Q2(x),sub)).   (CJ)

Here, the two arguments of Join, and the Join function itself, are all evaluated concurrently.

   This scheme has greater potential for parallelism, because the solutions to the individual relation calls are computed independently, but the join method has disadvantages, noted in Section 2.5.4.2. It appears that this scheme is to be used in a dataflow implementation of the OR parallel subset of ICOT's KL1 (Kernel Language version 1) (Ito *et al.*, 1985).

2.6.3 OR parallelism

OR parallelism refers to concurrency in the search for solutions to a single relation call. It can be combined with any of the schemes involving AND parallelism, as in Sections 2.6.1 and 2.6.2, or with an 'AND sequential' strategy as in Prolog. In a procedure such as:

   P(x) <− P1(x).
   P(x) <− P2(x).

all clauses are invoked concurrently and the solutions obtained by each clause are combined.

   OR parallelism can be explained quite simply in terms of equation D of Section 2.5.4.1:

Solns(P(x),sub) =
    Combine(Solns(P1(x),sub),Solns(P2(x),sub)).

An eager parallel computation rule applied to this equation results in OR parallelism. That is, the two arguments of Combine, and the Combine function itself, are all evaluated concurrently.

The nature of the Combine function now becomes important. There are two obvious choices. If Combine is the Append function, that concatenates two lists, the solutions will be produced in an order determined by the order of clauses in the procedure. That is, even if P2(x) computes a set of solutions very quickly, these will not be produced as solutions to P(x) until all solutions to P1(x) have been computed. If, however, Combine acts as a Merge function, interleaving two lists in time-dependent order, solutions to P(x) will be produced in the order in which they are found. (In the latter case, Combine is not a function on lists; it *is*, however, a function on bags.)

Regardless of the way in which solutions are combined, OR parallel evaluation renders the cut primitive meaningless. The cut as used in Prolog assumes an 'OR sequential' search.

OR parallelism is related to breadth-first search and tends to be 'more complete' than Prolog. Because OR branches of the AND/OR tree are traversed concurrently, even solutions to the right of an infinite branch can be computed. For example, in Program 2.1 as modified in Section 2.5.1.2, both solutions to the example query will be computed.

There have been many proposals for OR parallel logic programming architectures. Conery's AND/OR process model (Conery, 1983) provides both sequential and parallel OR processes. (Other references include Pollard, 1981; Kasif *et al.*, 1983; Ciepielewski, 1984; Lindstrom and Panangaden, 1984; Moto-oka *et al.*, 1984.)

2.6.4 Restricted AND parallelism

The above techniques of all-solutions AND parallelism, as well as OR parallelism, rely upon the non-determinism of logic programs for their effectiveness. If a program is highly non-deterministic, in the 'don't-know' sense of having a large number of (final or intermediate) solutions, there is greater scope for exploiting parallelism. For largely deterministic programs, however, little parallelism will be exhibited.

To extract AND parallelism from deterministic programs, many relation calls must work concurrently on each individual solution. This contrasts with all-solutions AND parallel schemes in which calls are evaluated sequentially for each solution.

If several relation calls have no shared variables, so that they are independent, there is no difficulty in evaluating them in parallel. The concurrent evaluation of such independent calls is sometimes known as **independent** or **restricted AND parallelism** (DeGroot, 1984). The parallelism is 'restricted' in that mutually dependent calls are still evaluated sequentially, in some order.

The point is illustrated by the example of Program 2.1. In the AND/OR tree shown in Fig. 2.1, nodes *O2* and *O3* are mutually dependent, owing to their shared variable z, but they are both independent of node *O4*. Whenever the Sibling procedure is called *with both arguments given*, the Dif call in its clause body can be evaluated in parallel with the sequential evaluation of the two Parent calls. This could be written:

Sibling(x,y) <− (Parent(z,x) & Parent(z,y)), Dif(x,y).

using ',' to indicate parallel evaluation and '&' for sequential, left to right, evaluation.

In the AND/OR tree of Fig. 2.2, node *O2* has a variable in common with both nodes *O3* and *O4*, but the last two are mutually independent. This means that for any call to Sibling with just the second argument given, the second and third calls could be evaluated concurrently, but they must be evaluated either before or after the first call. One way to write this control is:

Sibling(x,y) <− Parent(z,x) & (Parent(z,y), Dif(x,y)).

(This clause is not at all efficient, because of the non-determinism of the first Parent call.)

PRISM (Kasif *et al.*, 1983), a parallel logic programming system, features a control language that enables a programmer to guide the evaluation of a pure Horn clause program. This includes the ability to specify, as above, either sequential or parallel evaluation of calls within a clause. IC-PROLOG (Clark and McCabe, 1979; Clark *et al.*, 1982) provides a similar control language and, additionally, allows different control to be specified for each pattern of call, as in the two uses of Sibling above.

The control languages of IC-PROLOG and PRISM allow the programmer to specify, statically, whether parallel or sequential evaluation should be used and, in the case of sequential evaluation, the order of evaluation of calls. The same decisions are made dynamically, at run time, in Conery's AND/OR process model (Conery, 1983). Conery's system includes algorithms to detect dependencies between calls, as well as heuristics to select the optimal ordering for the sequential evaluation of dependent calls.

Conery's run-time detection of dependent calls is generally more effective in exploiting potential parallelism than the use of a static control language, because variables shared between calls in the source program may actually be instantiated by the time the clause is invoked, rendering the calls independent. However, the complex algorithms involved can constitute a substantial computational overhead. DeGroot (1984) proposes a method using simpler run-time algorithms which is claimed to be computationally cheaper than Conery's, though perhaps less thorough in detecting the independence of calls.

2.6.5   Stream AND parallelism

None of the AND parallel schemes considered above allow the concurrent evaluation of calls that share a variable, while working on a single solution. **Stream AND parallelism** does just this. It is a form of AND parallelism in which calls can be evaluated concurrently, communicating incrementally through bindings to a shared variable. This incremental communication is analogous to that found in both the lazy and eager parallel evaluation of functional programs, considered in Section 2.4.3.

There is no difficulty in implementing stream AND parallelism for deterministic logic programs. Since functional programs can always be rewritten as (deterministic) logic programs, Kahn and MacQueen's model of parallel evaluation (Section 2.4.3.3) carries over naturally. This was investigated by van Emden and de Lucena (1982).

An example of a deterministic logic program is the relational equivalent of the Sameleaves function of Section 2.4.3.2:

Sameleaves(x,y) $<-$ Flatten(x,z), Flatten(y,z).

By evaluating the Flatten calls in parallel, the value of the shared variable z can, in principle, be constructed cooperatively by the two calls. The effect of this is similar to that of the corresponding functional program, using unification in place of an Eqlist function.

Program 2.2 defines the Sumtree relation. This is the logic program corresponding to the Sumtree function of Section 2.4.3.3. Sumtree(t,n) has the logical reading: n is the sum of all labels on tree t. Flatten(t,z) is the relation: z is the list of nodes on tree t. Sum(z,n) is read: n is the sum of items on list z. The calls to Flatten and Sum can be evaluated in parallel and communicate by incremental generation, by Flatten, of the frontier list z.

Fig. 2.4 shows the AND/OR tree for a query:

: Sumtree(T(T(E,2,E),3,E),n).

Because the program is deterministic, the AND/OR tree has no more than one OR branch. This kind of AND/OR tree is known as a **proof tree**.

Sumtree(t,n) $<-$ Flatten(t,z), Sum(z,n).

Flatten(T(T(xx,xu,xy),u,y),z) $<-$ Flatten(T(xx,xu,T(xy,u,y)),z).
Flatten(T(E,u,y),[u|z]) $<-$ Flatten(y,z).
Flatten(E,[]).

Sum(z,n) <– Sigma(z,0,n).

Sigma([u|z],m,n) <– Plus(u,m,um), Sigma(z,um,n).
Sigma([],n,n).

Program 2.2 Program to sum a tree.

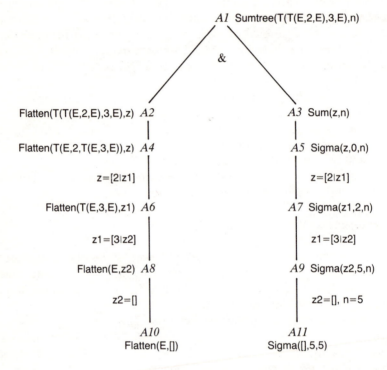

A1 Sumtree(T(T(E,2,E),3,E),n)

&

Flatten(T(T(E,2,E),3,E),z) *A2*

Flatten(T(E,2,T(E,3,E)),z) *A4*

z=[2|z1]

Flatten(T(E,3,E),z1) *A6*

z1=[3|z2]

Flatten(E,z2) *A8*

z2=[]

A10
Flatten(E,[])

A3 Sum(z,n)

A5 Sigma(z,0,n)

z=[2|z1]

A7 Sigma(z1,2,n)

z1=[3|z2]

A9 Sigma(z2,5,n)

z2=[], n=5

A11
Sigma([],5,5)

Fig 2.4 Proof tree.

The implementation of stream AND parallelism requires that each relation call computes no more than one solution. Deterministic logic programs, like Sumtree, have this property. It is also a property of systems based on don't-care non-determinism, such as PARLOG, described in Chapter 3. The single solution can be generated incrementally by a series of approximations. If this is done in such a way that each partial solution is not subsequently retracted, they can be conveyed immediately to other calls, i.e. shared variables have the **single-assignment** property. It is this property that makes stream AND parallelism easy to implement.

Stream AND parallelism contrasts with the schemes for parallelism outlined in Sections 2.6.1–2.6.4 in two respects. It has the advantage that solutions are communicated incrementally, but the disadvantage that only one solution can be computed. However, stream AND parallelism is, in a sense, a more primitive form of parallelism in terms of which other schemes can be implemented. If many solutions are required to a call to a relation *R*, these solutions can be computed as members of a list, which is the single solution to another relation *R'*. By the incremental construction of the solution list, the solutions can be made available one at a time.

2.6.6 The reconciliation approach

There is a class of logic programs that can make use of what might be termed **non-deterministic incremental communication**. These are programs of the 'generate and test' type, where candidate solutions to be tested can usefully be made available incrementally; one such program is a coroutined solution to the 'eight queens' problem (Clark, 1979). This type of program is typified by the 'naive sort' program of Program 2.3, which appeared in this context in Kowalski's original paper (Kowalski, 1974).

The relations defined in Program 2.3 have the following logical reading. Sort(x,y): y is the sorted version of list x. Perm(x,z): z is some permutation of list x. Delete(u,x,y): y is list x with item u removed. Ord(x): x is a list partially ordered by the '=<' relation.

Sort(x,z) <− Perm(x,z), Ord(z).

Perm([],[]).
Perm(x,[v|z]) <− Delete(v,x,y), Perm(y,z).

Delete(v,[v|x],x).
Delete(v,[u|x],[u|y]) <− Delete(v,x,y).

Ord([]).
Ord([u]).
Ord([u,v|z]) <− u =< v, Ord([v|z]).

Program 2.3 Naive sort program.

A list is sorted by a query of the form:

: Sort([3,4,1],z).

which immediately reduces to the conjunctive query:

: Perm([3,4,1],z), Ord(z).

The intention is that the Perm call should *generate* successive permutations of the given list [3,4,1] as values of z, each of which is *tested* by the Ord call to check whether it is ordered.

As Kowalski (1974) noted, if the Perm and Ord calls communicate incrementally, each candidate permutation can be tested by the Ord call before it is completely constructed; if the Ord call fails at an early stage, there is no need to construct the remainder of the permutation. This algorithm relies upon non-deterministic incremental communication: not only is a data structure constructed incrementally, but at each step there are several alternative partial solutions:

```
z=[3|z1]   z1=[4|z2]   z2=[1|z3]
   ...     z1=[1|z2]
z=[4|z1]   z1=[3|z2]
   ...     z1=[1|z2]
z=[1|z1]   z1=[3|z2]   z2=[4|z3]   z3=[]
```

Non-deterministic incremental communication is feasible in a system with centralized control, such as IC-PROLOG (Clark and McCabe, 1979; Clark *et al.*, 1982) and MU-PROLOG (Naish, 1982). IC-PROLOG achieved it by a coroutining evaluation, with incremental communication between calls. In the event of the failure of a 'test' call, the *entire* evaluation was backtracked to try the next solution to the 'generate' call.

In a parallel implementation with distributed control, non-deterministic incremental communication is not easy to implement. If the 'generate' and 'test' calls are running on separate processors, the failure of the 'test' call for a particular partial solution must be communicated to the 'generate' call. This process must in turn undo all of the effects of producing the rejected solution, probably notifying several other processes that have received the rejected solution, and so on. This has been called 'distributed backtracking'.

The first proposal to incorporate non-deterministic incremental communication in a parallel context was Pollard's AND/OR proof procedure (Pollard, 1981). This scheme can achieve the maximum possible (AND and OR) parallelism from any pure Horn clause program. Kasif and Minker (1984) have recently proposed a scheme for AND/OR parallelism which seems to have much in common with Pollard's approach.

Pollard's AND/OR scheme performs a completely unrestrained parallel traversal of the AND/OR tree in the search for compatible sets of branches. In parallel with the traversal of the tree, there are administrative processes responsible for **reconciliation** and **pruning**. Unifying substitutions on different branches of the AND/OR tree are reconciled, to produce **filters** that identify sets of mutually incompatible branches. By a process of **promoting** filters, the proof procedure detects branches that cannot contribute to any solution; such branches are dynamically pruned.

Because all activities are performed concurrently, there is incremental communication of solutions between AND branches, even if each branch forks into several OR branches. OR branches contributing unsatisfactory partial solutions will be pruned.

Clearly, Pollard's scheme incurs a great deal of computational overhead and is not possible to implement efficiently on any present-day architecture. Additionally, there is the risk of an explosion in parallel activity. Remedies to some of these problems are put forward by Pollard.

3
PARLOG: a parallel logic programming language

This chapter presents the design of the parallel logic programming language PARLOG.

As noted in Chapter 1, the main objective in the language design is the provision of stream AND parallelism. The chapter begins by considering how this can be achieved in a practical programming language. The outcome of this discussion is a decision to use 'committed choice' non-determinism as the basis of the language semantics; various aspects of this are discussed in Section 3.2, where 'guarded clauses' are introduced.

There follows a comparison of parallel and sequential evaluation of programs, and how this relates to the 'granularity' of a parallel implementation. Section 3.5 defines the operational semantics of PARLOG more precisely by introducing a lower-level 'standard form' of the language.

The 'logical variable' is an important feature of logic programming and can be exploited very effectively in PARLOG. This is demonstrated in Section 3.6, followed by a discussion of various aspects of unification. Section 3.8 considers the imposition of priorities among alternatives, which is sometimes required in non-deterministic programs.

Metalevel programming in PARLOG is considered in Section 3.9. Because of the parallelism and the committed choice non-determinism of the language, a more general metacall primitive than that of Prolog is required. Section 3.10 presents the logical justification and implementation of negation as failure in PARLOG. The final section introduces the 'set constructor' primitives, by which the language may be interfaced to a 'don't-know' non-deterministic language of pure Horn clauses.

3.1 Stream AND parallelism in PARLOG

Program 2.2 defined the Sumtree relation. This program computes the sum of the nodes on a tree by Flattening the tree to a list and Summing the elements of the list:

Sumtree(t,n) <− Flatten(t,z), Sum(z,n).

It was pointed out in Section 2.6.5 that parallelism can be exploited by evaluating the two calls concurrently, with incremental communication via the shared variable z. This program was compared with the functional program for Sumtree:

Sumtree(t) = Sum(Flatten(t)).

in Kahn and MacQueen's (1977) model of parallel evaluation.

This analogy is qualified by the fact that, unlike functional programs, Horn clauses have a 'flat' structure. That is, no direction of communication between calls is expressed in a Horn clause program. This is often quoted as an advantage of Prolog over, say, LISP: a relation such as Append(x,y,z) can be used either to concatenate two given lists x and y *or* to split a given list z into two sublists x and y. In practice this feature is little more than a curiosity in Prolog because, if a clause body contains more than one call, the order of these calls (which are always sequentially evaluated) will normally be efficient only for one 'mode' of use.

The flat nature of Horn clause programs gives rise to a problem when stream AND parallelism is introduced. If the Sumtree logic program is run in the intended mode of use, with its first argument (a tree) given, a query:

: Sumtree(t,n).

immediately reduces to the query:

: Flatten(t,z), Sum(z,n).

where t is a given tree and the two calls are to be evaluated concurrently. The intended behaviour is that the Flatten call should incrementally generate a list binding for z, the shared variable, for which there is only one solution. But, because of the bidirectional nature of unification, there is no restraint on the Sum call 'guessing' the value of z, by binding z non-deterministically to either [u|z1] or '[]' (the first head argument term of each of the two clauses for Sigma, to which the Sum call reduces). This binding may have to be retracted when Flatten produces the correct binding for z.

To implement stream AND parallelism efficiently, it is essential that shared variables have the single-assignment property noted in Section 2.6.5. That is, bindings made to shared variables should never be retracted.

3.1.1 Constraining the communication

The above problem does not arise in the functional program for Sumtree. Here, the syntax of the program specifies that the Flatten function produces, incrementally or otherwise, a value of which the Sum function is the consumer. The process evaluating Sum would suspend if its input, produced by the Flatten process, is not available. Exactly the same effect can be obtained in the equivalent logic program by declaring a **mode** for each relation, stating whether each argument is input or output. This is the method employed in PARLOG.

In a PARLOG program, every relation definition (procedure) is accompanied by a **mode declaration** of the form:

mode $R(m_1,...,m_k)$.

Each m_i is either '?' or '↑'. A '?' specifies that the argument in that position is **input**, while a '↑' indicates that the argument is **output**.

In the Sumtree program, the relations Sumtree, Flatten and Sum should all have mode (?,↑); the auxiliary relation Sigma has mode (?,?,↑). In general, in a PARLOG equivalent of a functional program, each relation has several input arguments and one output argument. The output argument of a call is always an unbound variable and is given a value which is functionally determined by the input arguments.

The complete PARLOG program is shown in Program 3.1. It is identical to Program 2.2 except for the addition of the mode declarations. To emphasize that it is a PARLOG program, lower-case identifiers are used for the relation names. Henceforth, all PARLOG programs will be written with this convention, while Prolog programs and other Horn clause programs will have relation names beginning with an upper-case letter. Each example program will include mode declarations for all relations defined and used therein, even if some relations have been defined or used elsewhere. In a real PARLOG program, just one mode declaration is required for each relation.

```
mode sumtree(?,↑), flatten(?,↑), sum(?,↑), sigma(?,?,↑).

sumtree(t,n) <− flatten(t,z), sum(z,n).

flatten(T(T(xx,xu,xy),u,y),z) <− flatten(T(xx,xu,T(xy,u,y)),z).
flatten(T(E,u,y),[u|z]) <− flatten(y,z).
flatten(E,[]).

sum(z,n) <− sigma(z,0,n).

sigma([u|z],m,n) <− plus(u,m,um), sigma(z,um,n).
sigma([],n,n).
```

Program 3.1 PARLOG program to sum a tree.

In a PARLOG program, the ',' is used as the parallel conjunction operator. So, in the sumtree clause and in the first clause for sigma, the calls in the body are evaluated concurrently.

Primitive relations, such as plus as used in this program, have an implicit mode declaration as well as the usual implicit procedure. plus is implicitly defined with the following mode declaration and procedure, comprising a very large number of assertions:

mode plus(?,?, ↑).

plus(0,0,0).   plus(0,1,1).   plus(0,2,2). ...
plus(1,0,1).   plus(1,1,2).   plus(1,2,3). ...
...

The mode declaration for a relation constrains the unification of a call with a clause head for that relation: the unifier for each input argument must comprise only an input substitution. This is termed the **input constraint**.

A clause may be used to solve a call only if the input arguments of the call unify with the corresponding arguments of the clause head, *satisfying the input constraint*. The unification of the input arguments will often be termed **input matching**, in recognition of the input constraint. If a call argument c and the corresponding head argument h do not unify, the attempt to use the clause **fails**. If c and h would unify with a substitution that binds variables in c (violating the input constraint), the attempt to use the clause **suspends** *unless* there are other arguments that fail to unify, in which case it fails.

An effect of the mode declarations is to force the evaluation of a relation call to suspend if its input arguments are not available. This happens if all clauses either suspend or fail, and there is at least one suspended clause. In the query:

: flatten(t,z), sum(z,n).

where t is instantiated to a tree structure, both flatten and sum calls can be evaluated. If the sum call is evaluated, it is first unified with the head of the sum clause, satisfying the input constraint. The query becomes:

: flatten(t,z), sigma(z,0,n).   (1)

Now, in attempting to unify the sigma call with the head of each clause for sigma, the input constraint is not satisfied because z (the first argument of the call) is not a substitution instance of either [u|z1] or '[]' (the first head argument of each sigma clause). The attempt to use each clause suspends, so the call to sigma suspends. It remains suspended until the input matching can proceed, i.e. until z is bound to a suitable term (a list pattern or an empty list) by the evaluation of the flatten call.

Because of the use of modes, many PARLOG programs have a graphical interpretation identical to Kahn and MacQueen's model for functional programs (Kahn and MacQueen, 1977). A query which is a parallel conjunction can be viewed as a network of communicating processes. Variables shared between calls act as communication channels between processes. The declared modes determine the direction of communication along channels. A shared variable appears as an output argument of exactly one call in the query, the **producer**, while there may be any number of **consumers** for the variable.

As an example, Fig. 3.1 shows the graphical representation of query 1. Supposing that the call flatten(t,z) reduces to flatten(t1,z1) with an output binding z=[u|z1], the call sigma(z,0,n) can also be reduced using the first sigma clause, giving the query:

: flatten(t1,z1), plus(u,0,um), sigma(z1,um,n).   (2)

The network corresponding to query 2 is shown in Fig. 3.2.

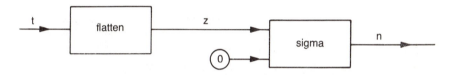

Fig 3.1   Graphical representation of query.

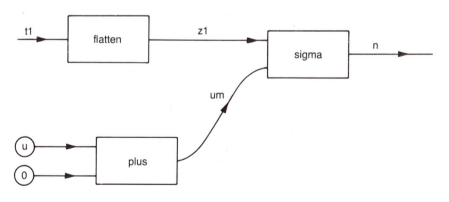

Fig 3.2   Reconfigured graph.

The mode declarations of PARLOG were inspired by analogy with functional languages. They do, however, bear a superficial resemblance to the *optional* mode declarations of DEC-10 Prolog (Bowen *et al.*, 1982). In

DEC-10 Prolog, however, there is no concept of suspension: an error *always* occurs if a mode constraint is not satisfied. In PARLOG, the main purpose of modes is their effect on a program's behaviour. In both DEC-10 Prolog and PARLOG, mode declarations allow the compilation of efficient code for unification. The compilation of unification in PARLOG is discussed in Section 3.5 and in Chapter 5.

3.2   Non-determinism and time-dependent programs

As noted above, the relations defined in Program 3.1 are deterministic in their declared modes. This is not necessarily true of PARLOG programs; non-deterministic evaluation is both desirable and easy to implement.

Many concurrent systems are inherently non-deterministic. That is, the overall behaviour of a system often depends upon the relative speeds of the component processes. For example, if several 'client' processes are sharing some resource, requests from the clients are typically granted in the order in which they are generated. Non-determinism is essential for such time-dependent evaluation.

Kahn and MacQueen's model of parallel evaluation deliberately excludes non-deterministic, time-dependent behaviour. This is because of a desire to adhere to the semantics of functions on which the model is based. However, many practical parallel functional languages introduce non-determinism, usually via some special primitive; the nature of this primitive varies. Friedman and Wise (1980) propose a special list constructor frons, while Henderson (1982) and Jones (1984) use a non-deterministic merge 'function' in their operating systems programs. A merge primitive is also proposed for dataflow languages by Dennis (1974) and Arvind and Brock (1982).

3.2.1   Committed choice non-determinism

As a logic programming language, PARLOG is naturally non-deterministic. Although the output arguments of many PARLOG relations are functionally determined by their input arguments, this need not be the case. As an example, Program 3.2 shows a PARLOG procedure for the merge *relation*. The logical reading of merge(x,y,z) is: if x and y are lists, z is *some* interleaving of x and y. Note that the output argument of merge is not a function of its inputs. For example, in the call merge([A,B],[C,D],z), z will be one of {[A,B,C,D], [A,C,B,D], [A,C,D,B], [C,A,B,D], [C,A,D,B], [C,D,A,B]}.

---

mode merge(?,?, ↑).

```
merge([u|x],y,[u|z]) <- merge(x,y,z).
merge(x,[v|y],[v|z]) <- merge(x,y,z).
merge([],y,y).
merge(x,[],x).
```

Program 3.2   Merge.

Consider the query:

  : flatten(t1,x), flatten(t2,y), merge(x,y,z), writelist(z).

where t1 and t2 are two given trees. writelist has the mode (?), and has the effect of displaying its argument list incrementally, as its members become available. The list printed will be some interleaving of the two frontier lists x and y, determined by the rate at which the flatten processes run.

The operational semantics of PARLOG incorporates 'don't-care' or **committed choice** non-determinism (Section 2.5.2). The evaluation of a relation call for R proceeds by performing a *parallel* search for a candidate clause (see below) from among the procedure for R. When candidate clauses are found (there may be more than one), *one* of them is arbitrarily chosen and the call reduces to the body of the selected clause. There is no backtracking on the choice of clause; the evaluation **commits** to this choice.

In the absence of guards (see Section 3.2.2), the search for a candidate clause is controlled by the **input matching** (i.e. the unification of the input arguments). In solving a call, a clause is a **candidate** if the input matching for every argument of the call with the clause head arguments succeeds, rather than failing or suspending. After a clause is selected, the **output unification** is performed for the clause (i.e. the unification of the output arguments). Since the evaluation commits to the use of the clause, it is also committed to the effects of the corresponding output unification. There is no backtracking on the choice of clause, so the bindings made to variables in output arguments are never retracted. The operational semantics of PARLOG will be made more precise after guards are introduced, in Section 3.2.2.

The evaluation of the call merge(x,y,z) in the above query begins with a concurrent attempt to apply each merge clause. All clauses are suspended, because of the input constraint, until either x or y is bound to a non-variable term by another call. Supposing that the first flatten call binds x to a list term [A|x1], the input constraint of the first merge clause is satisfied, so that clause is a candidate and z is bound to [A|z1]. If, instead, the second flatten call binds y to [C|y1], the second merge clause is a candidate and z is bound to [C|z1]. If both x *and* y are bound thus, both the first and second merge are candidates, so either of them can be selected; the choice of which candidate clause is selected is not specified by the operational semantics, so either A or C may be output on z in this case.

The net effect of this operational semantics is that a relation call computes no more than one solution for each of its output arguments.

Moreover, bindings to variables are never retracted, so shared variables have the single-assignment property (Section 2.6.5). Committed choice non-determinism is the result of combining non-determinism with the single-assignment property required for efficient parallel implementation. The committed choice non-determinism of PARLOG is similar to that of Dijkstra's (1976) guarded commands and Hoare's CSP (Hoare, 1978, 1983), which strongly influenced the original design of PARLOG.

3.2.2 Guarded clauses

It was stated above that a clause is a candidate if its input matching succeeds. The input matching allows a pattern match on the input arguments to determine whether a clause is a candidate, but this is not always sufficient: sometimes a more general test on the input arguments is required. By analogy with Dijkstra's guarded commands and Hoare's CSP, this is done in PARLOG by **guarded clauses**.

The **guard** is an optional conjunction that may precede the body of a clause; it is separated from the body conjunction by a ':', termed the **commit operator**. The syntax of a general PARLOG clause is therefore:

$$R(t_1,...,t_k) <- G_1, ..., G_m : B_1, ..., B_n.$$

$G_1,...,G_m$ ($m \geqslant 0$) is the clause guard. If m is 0, as in the merge procedure of Program 3.2, the ':' is omitted.

The ':' has the declarative reading of conjunction, so the above clause is read as:

'$R(t_1,...,t_k)$ if G_1 and ... and G_m and
B_1 and ... and B_n.'

Operationally, the guard is a test that must be evaluated successfully, in addition to the input matching, before the clause is selected. The ':' is similar to Prolog's cut primitive, except that its use is symmetric due to the parallel search among the clauses, just as a guarded command set (Dijkstra, 1976) is a symmetric version of the conditional *if...then...else*. In Prolog the cut is optional, but every PARLOG clause has a commit operator (even though the ':' symbol can be omitted when the guard is empty).

Program 3.3 shows a procedure employing guards. It defines on-ord-tree(key,value,tree) which has the logical reading: tree is an ordered tree containing a node labelled with the pair P(key,value). Operationally, it is a procedure to search for a given key in a given tree and return the associated value. The first clause handles the case where the root node of tree contains a pair with the given key. The second and third clauses handle, respectively, the cases where key is less than and greater than the key of the root node of tree. The guards are necessary in the second and third clauses to determine whether to search for the key in the left or right subtree. '<' is a primitive relation with mode (?,?), and x < y has the logical reading: x is less than y (according to some arithmetic or lexical ordering relation).

```
mode on-ord-tree(?, ↑ ,?).

on-ord-tree(key,value,T(x,P(key,value),y)).
on-ord-tree(key,value,T(x,P(rkey,rvalue),y)) <- key < rkey :
    on-ord-tree(key,value,x).
on-ord-tree(key,value,T(x,P(rkey,rvalue),y)) <- rkey < key :
    on-ord-tree(key,value,y).
```

Program 3.3   Ordered tree search program.

With the introduction of guards, the operational semantics of PARLOG must be refined, as follows. Initially, the evaluation of each relation call is suspended. The evaluation then invokes a concurrent attempt to apply each clause of the appropriate procedure. For each clause, the input matching is performed and the guard (if any) is evaluated. The guard evaluation is begun in parallel with the input matching, so a guard may fail even if the input matching suspends (i.e. if the input constraint is not satisfied), thus causing the clause to be a non-candidate.

- A **candidate clause** is one in which both the input matching *and* the guard evaluation succeed.
- A **non-candidate clause** is one in which either the input matching *or* the guard evaluation (or both) fail.
- A **suspended clause** is one in which either the input matching *or* the guard evaluation are suspended, and neither of them fail.

If at least one clause is a candidate, such a clause can be selected. The call is then reduced to the body of the chosen clause and the output unification for that clause is performed. If all clauses are non-candidates, the call fails. If there are no candidate clauses but there *are* suspended clauses, the call remains suspended. Each clause begins in a suspended state and eventually becomes either a candidate or a non-candidate clause. Therefore, a suspended call will eventually fail or be reduced to a clause body.

A conjunction succeeds if *all* calls in it succeed. A conjunction fails if *any* of the calls in it fails. A conjunction is suspended if none of its calls fails but at least one of them is suspended.

Note that, if one call in a parallel conjunction fails, the evaluation of the other calls in the conjunction must be terminated. Similarly, when the evaluation commits to the use of a candidate clause, the evaluation of the guards of the other clauses in the procedure must be aborted.

The evaluation of a PARLOG program is a variant of resolution, as defined in Section 2.2.3. The selection of relation calls from the query proceeds in parallel. The selection of a clause with which to solve a call is a committed choice. The unification between call and clause head is restricted, in that matching is used for input arguments.

3.2.3 Committed OR parallelism

The parallel search for a candidate clause, together with the committed choice, provides PARLOG with a limited form of OR parallelism; this will be termed **committed OR parallelism**. The guards of alternative clauses are evaluated concurrently until one of them successfully terminates, when the evaluation commits to that clause. When the evaluation commits to the clause, the evaluation of sibling guards (guards of other clauses in the procedure) is aborted. Committed OR parallelism is an OR parallel search for a single solution, in contrast to full OR parallelism, where *all* solutions are computed concurrently.

An example of this committed OR parallelism is shown by the on-tree procedure of Program 3.4. It defines the relation on-tree(key,value,tree) which has the logical reading: tree is a tree (not necessarily ordered) containing a node labelled with the pair P(key,value). It has the same mode of use as the on-ord-tree procedure of Program 3.3. Because the tree is not necessarily ordered, both left and right subtrees must be exhaustively searched for the given key. A call to on-tree performs this tree search in parallel. The process forks into two (OR parallel) on-tree processes, one for each subtree, and a process to check the root node. When the search of one branch succeeds, the search of the other branch is terminated.

```
mode on-tree(?, ↑ ,?).

on-tree(key,value,T(x,P(key,value),y)).
on-tree(key,value,T(x,P(rkey,rvalue),y)) <−
    on-tree(key,value,x) :.
on-tree(key,value,T(x,P(rkey,rvalue),y)) <−
    on-tree(key,value,y) :.
```

Program 3.4 Tree search program.

3.2.4 Safe guards

A property that PARLOG has in common with the languages Concurrent Prolog (Shapiro, 1983) and Guarded Horn Clauses (Ueda, 1985a) is that, during the search for a candidate clause with which to solve a call, a guard evaluation must not be allowed to bind any variables in the call. If this were allowed, a guard might bind a variable in the call even if the guard subsequently fails; such bindings must only be made after commitment. The three languages differ in the method used to ensure this property.

The operational semantics of PARLOG specifies that output unification is performed *after* commitment to a candidate clause. At this point, the output arguments in the head of the selected clause are unified with the corresponding arguments of the call. Variables in the head argument terms may have been instantiated by the input matching or by the guard evaluation but these bindings will not affect the output arguments of the call until the output unification is performed.

In addition, it must be ensured that variables in *input* arguments of a call are not bound by a guard evaluation. For this purpose, PARLOG imposes an additional requirement: every guard must be **safe**. A safe guard is one that only *tests* values of variables obtained by input matching; it is not allowed to *bind* any variable in an input argument in the head of the clause. A guard may only bind variables appearing in the guard, body and in the output arguments of the clause head.

The fact that guards must be safe in PARLOG avoids the need for a complex implementation, like that needed for Concurrent Prolog. Concurrent Prolog does not impose any constraint on the form of guards but requires an elaborate and expensive run-time mechanism to ensure that bindings made by a guard remain in a local environment until the time of commitment, when they are 'exported'. (It should be noted that simpler subsets of Concurrent Prolog have been developed to overcome this problem; see Chapter 8.) Guarded Horn Clauses uses a simpler mechanism, but one which still involves some run-time overhead: a guard suspends if it attempts to bind a variable in a call.

The safety of guards could be verified at run time. However, by checking the safety at compile time, the implementation of PARLOG is simplified still further; there is then no special mechanism required to support OR parallel evaluation. This means that an OR parallel search can always be transformed to an AND parallel evaluation, an example of which appears in Chapter 4. Compile-time and run-time safety checks are discussed in Chapter 5, where the use of safe guards is compared with other approaches from an implementation viewpoint.

3.2.5 Correctness and completeness

Because the PARLOG inference system is based on resolution, it is correct. That is, any solution that a program computes is a solution according to the declarative semantics. The main deviation from pure resolution (Section 2.2.3) is that specialized unification is used, i.e. input matching. But if the input matching of a pair of terms t_1 and t_2 succeeds, the unification of t_1 and t_2 would also succeed. Therefore, the correctness is preserved.

However, due to the committed choice non-determinism, PARLOG is incomplete. That is, at most one of the solutions specified by the declarative semantics can be computed by any particular PARLOG evaluation. This means that an evaluation may result in failure or indefinite suspension, even if solutions exist according to the declarative semantics.

3.2.6   PARLOG programming style

3.2.6.1   Sufficient guards

The incompleteness of PARLOG demands a certain style of programming. In particular, care should be taken to choose the guard appropriately. In solving a relation call, the input matching and the guard of each clause should be sufficient to ensure that, if the clause is a candidate, either:

1. a solution to the call can be computed using that clause, or

2. no solution can be found using any other clause.

This will be termed the **sufficient guards property**. Informally, it guarantees that if solutions to a call exist, the call will not fail. Although it is not enforced by PARLOG, this criterion is desirable in general and essential to ensure correct implementation of negation as failure; negation is discussed in Section 3.10.

The sufficient guards property *could* be satisfied by placing the entire right-hand-side conjunction of each clause in its guard, as in Program 3.4. However, this has several disadvantages. First, the amount of computation required to select a candidate clause may be increased because it will potentially require all guards to be evaluated; on the other hand, the evaluation of the guards can exploit OR parallelism. Second, the output unification is performed after commitment to a clause. If the guard is larger than necessary, the output unification is delayed and this will delay any other process that is waiting for the output bindings. Third, there is a strong likelihood of the resulting guard being unsafe. Ideally, to minimize wasted computation and to maximize the degree of parallelism, the guard of a clause should be chosen to contain the smallest conjunction that satisfies the sufficient guards property.

This special programming style is different from that of Prolog, where a failure at any point in a clause can invoke backtracking to try an alternative clause. However, even in Prolog, care must be taken not to backtrack into a non-terminating evaluation. Moreover, the backtracking ability of Prolog is tempered in practice by the often essential use of the cut primitive. It is probably true that the PARLOG programming style is no more difficult than that of Prolog, although the two styles are rather different.

3.2.6.2 *Data dependency*

The sufficient guards property guarantees that the evaluation of a call will not fail if any solutions exist. It is still possible, however, for a call to be suspended perpetually, so that no solution is computed. An example of such a call is merge(x,y,z), where x and y are variables with no producers. This is **deadlock**, and is the extreme case of a less serious situation: when, because of a data dependency, *some* solutions (according to the declarative semantics) cannot be computed by any PARLOG evaluation. This is analogous to what Keller has called the 'merge anomaly' (quoted by Brock and Ackerman, 1981).

A (somewhat contrived) example similar to that in Brock and Ackerman (1981) can be rendered in PARLOG as follows:

```
mode merge(?,?, ↑ ), one(?, ↑ ).

one([u|x],[1]).

: merge([0],y,z), one(z,y).
```

The relation one(x,y) has the logical reading: x is a non-empty list and y is the singleton list comprising 1. The value of z, according to the logical reading of the above query, is an interleaving of the lists [0] and [1], i.e. either [0,1] or [1,0]. Operationally, only the first of these solutions can be computed, because the 0 must be output on z, the third argument of merge, before its second argument, y, can be instantiated.

Brock and Ackerman use a similar example to argue that 'history relations' are insufficient for characterizing the behaviour of a program. They propose a theory of 'scenarios' to explain the behaviour.

In PARLOG, the problem is just a consequence of incompleteness; it is certainly possible to write a program whose logical reading is a relation arbitrarily larger than the set of solutions that can actually be computed. The problem can often be avoided in PARLOG by reformulating the program so that the two sets coincide. Then, the behaviour is adequately characterized by the logical reading of the program.

3.3   Sequencing

The language introduced above has employed both AND parallel and (committed) OR parallel evaluation exclusively. This is theoretically adequate but, for reasons that will be explained, PARLOG provides the option of sequential conjunction and clause search.

3.3.1   Sequential conjunction

The sequential conjunction operator is '&', which may be mixed with the parallel conjunction operator ','. No syntactic precedence is assumed, so parentheses must be used if the operators are mixed. All conjunctions, in queries, clause guards and bodies, may be constructed using the ',' and '&' operators. Both of them have the declarative reading 'and'.

$$C_1 , C_2$$

indicates that C_1 and C_2 are to be evaluated concurrently, while:

$$C_1 \ \& \ C_2$$

specifies that the evaluation of C_1 must terminate successfully before the evaluation of C_2 is begun.

The sequential operator '&' is useful in PARLOG for two main purposes: programming with side-effects and controlling the degree of parallelism of algorithms.

3.3.1.1 Side-effects

As a systems programming language, PARLOG, like Prolog, provides primitive relations that have side-effects. It is not intended that these should be used indiscriminately, scattered throughout a declarative program, as is traditional in Prolog programming. Instead, they are provided so that stream handling procedures can be written in PARLOG. These procedures may use side-effect primitives but the remainder of the program can then be free from side-effects. (In a production PARLOG system, it may be desirable to enforce the separation of procedures that use side-effects from the declarative part of the program.)

The sequential conjunction operator enables the side-effects to be performed in some specified order. For example, Program 3.5 shows a procedure for the writelist relation used above. In the declarative reading, writelist(x) is the relation: x is a list, but the procedure has the side-effect of printing a stream of items, provided they are ground terms. As each item is received on the input argument, it is printed on a new line. The write and NL primitives are as used in Prolog (Bowen *et al.*, 1982): they are executed immediately, with no suspension for input matching. The use of the '&' operator ensures that the items on the list are printed in the correct order.

```
mode writelist(?).

writelist([message|list]) <-
    write(message) &
    NL &
    writelist(list).
writelist([]).
```

Program 3.5   Program to write a list of ground terms.

Incidentally, it is worth noting that, provided parallel clause search is used, the order of clauses is insignificant. In some Prolog systems, the base clause(s) must be written before the recursive clause to allow tail recursion optimization. Committed choice non-determinism makes tail recursion optimization easy to implement in PARLOG and the order of clauses is immaterial.

3.3.1.2   Controlling parallelism in algorithms

The other principal use of sequential conjunction is to constrain the concurrency in an evaluation. Different degrees of parallelism result in different algorithms. Program 3.6 is an alternative procedure for on-tree which avoids a search of the left and right subtrees in the event that the root node contains the given key. This is achieved by placing an extra (inequality) test ~ key == rkey at the beginning of each guard, which must succeed before the recursive on-tree call is evaluated. Note that the use of the '&' in the guards is essential to obtain this behaviour. The '==' primitive has mode (?,?) and tests the syntactic identity of two terms; it will be described in detail in Section 3.5.1.2.

```
mode on-tree(?, ↑ ,?).

on-tree(key,value,T(x,P(key,value),y)).
on-tree(key,value,T(x,P(rkey,rvalue),y)) <−
    ~ key == rkey & on-tree(key,value,x) :.
on-tree(key,value,T(x,P(rkey,rvalue),y)) <−
    ~ key == rkey & on-tree(key,value,y) :.
```

Program 3.6   Modified tree search program.

3.3.2   Sequential clause search

A PARLOG procedure should be considered as a whole, not as a set of individual clauses. According to this view, the '.' following each clause is not treated as a clause terminator as it is in Prolog. Instead, it is regarded as a binary operator, with the exception of the '.' following the final clause of a procedure, which acts as the procedure terminator. For example, the procedure:

Clause$_1$.
Clause$_2$.
Clause$_3$.

is parsed as .(Clause$_1$,.(Clause$_2$,Clause$_3$)). The '.' symbol has the logical reading of conjunction.

The '.' is the parallel search operator of PARLOG. The clauses in a '.'-separated group are searched in parallel to find a candidate clause, as explained above. PARLOG also provides a sequential search operator ';'. A ';' in a procedure specifies that the clauses following the ';' should not be checked for candidacy until *all* of the clauses preceding the ';' have been found to be non-candidate clauses, i.e. their input matching and/or guard evaluation has failed. For example, consider the procedure:

> *Clause$_1$*;
> *Clause$_2$*.
> *Clause$_3$*;
> *Clause$_4$*.

As with the conjunction operators ',' and '&', the clause search operators '.' and ';' can be mixed, using parentheses if necessary. To enable parentheses to be omitted, '.' is assumed to be the more tightly binding operator. So the above procedure is parsed as ;(*Clause$_1$*,;(.(*Clause$_2$*,*Clause$_3$*),*Clause$_4$*)).

In evaluating a relation call for which the above is a procedure, only *Clause$_1$* is tried at first. If this clause is suspended, the call suspends. If *Clause$_1$* is a candidate, it is selected. *Only* if *Clause$_1$* is a non-candidate does the search proceed beyond the ';'. In this event, *Clause$_2$* and *Clause$_3$* are tried concurrently for candidacy. If these two clauses are both non-candidates, *Clause$_4$* is tried.

The use of sequential clause search *does* affect the logical reading of a procedure: ';' is *not* simply read as 'and'. A procedure of the form:

> $R(x_1,...,x_k) <- G_1 : B_1$;
> $R(x_1,...,x_k) <- G_2 : B_2$;
> $R(x_1,...,x_k) <- B_3$.   (S)

has the same logical reading as:

> $R(x_1,...,x_k) <- G_1 : B_1$.
> $R(x_1,...,x_k) <- \sim G_1 \& G_2 : B_2$.
> $R(x_1,...,x_k) <- \sim G_1 \& \sim G_2 : B_3$.   (P)

That is, to each guard must be added the negation of the guards of the clauses preceding the last ';' operator. The behaviours of procedures S and P are different in that, in S, the previous guards are not re-evaluated for each clause.

3.3.2.1   *Default handling*

As noted above, sequential clause search can avoid the redundant re-evaluation of a guard test. The on-tree procedure of Program 3.6 can be further modified (Program 3.7). Here, the use of ';' ensures that the second and third clauses are tried only if the first clause is a non-candidate, i.e. if the given key is not on the root node of the tree. There is therefore no need for an inequality test ~ key == rkey in the guards of these clauses.

```
mode on-tree(?, ↑ ,?).

on-tree(key,value,T(x,P(key,value),y));
on-tree(key,value,T(x,P(rkey,rvalue),y)) <−
    on-tree(key,value,x) :.
on-tree(key,value,T(x,P(rkey,rvalue),y)) <−
    on-tree(key,value,y) :.
```

Program 3.7 Modified tree search program.

3.3.2.2 Controlling parallelism in algorithms

Sequential clause search can be used to control the degree of OR parallelism in an algorithm. As an example, Program 3.8 shows another procedure for on-tree. This program performs a sequential, left–right depth-first, search of the tree, because of the ';' between the second and third clauses.

```
mode on-tree(?, ↑ ,?).

on-tree(key,value,T(x,P(key,value),y));
on-tree(key,value,T(x,P(rkey,rvalue),y)) <−
    on-tree(key,value,x) :;
on-tree(key,value,T(x,P(rkey,rvalue),y)) <−
    on-tree(key,value,y) :.
```

Program 3.8 Sequential tree search program.

3.3.3 The need for sequencing

It is worth considering at this stage whether sequential operators ought to be included in the language. As the examples in Sections 3.3.1 and 3.3.2 show, it is sometimes necessary to sequence events, but the sequential operators are not the only way to do this. Section 3.3.3.4 demonstrates how sequencing can be obtained by mode constraints, while Section 3.4 relates sequencing to the issue of granularity.

3.3.3.1 Guards and sequential conjunction

It should be emphasized that the commit operator ':' is not equivalent to '&' and should not be used to obtain sequencing of calls. The purpose of the ':' is to delimit the guard conjunction, and this should be the smallest conjunction that can determine that the clause is a candidate (Section

3.2.6). It follows that, if a procedure has only one clause, its guard should be empty; the same applies to the final clause in a sequence. In any case, no more than one ':' is allowed in a clause.

More importantly, the ':' cannot be used to delay the evaluation of a call without also withholding its output. This is because the guard G of a clause:

$$H <- G : B.$$

must not bind variables in the invoking call, for reasons explained in Section 3.2.4. Hence, any output from G will not be visible to the caller of H until G has successfully terminated. This is true not only of PARLOG, but also of the related languages Concurrent Prolog (Shapiro, 1983) and Guarded Horn Clauses (Ueda, 1985a). In the case of PARLOG, it is guaranteed by the guard safety property.

In contrast, in the clause:

$$H <- G \& B.$$

the only effect of the '&' is to delay the evaluation of B until G terminates; any output from G is available immediately and incrementally to the caller of H. An extensive discussion of this subject appears in Clark and Gregory (1984) and, independently, in Kusalik (1984b).

3.3.3.2   *Representing a state by side-effects*

Consider a database which is to be accessed by processes via a stream of request messages. A process is responsible for managing the database and receives the messages, which are of three types: to ADD an item, DELETE an item, and enquire whether an item is IN the database.

One way to represent the database is as a global data structure, modified destructively by a manager process executing primitives with side-effects, such as the assert and retract primitives of Prolog. This is quite acceptable in PARLOG since, as noted in Section 3.3.1.1, the side-effects are localized: the only access by the rest of the program to the database is via the request stream.

Program 3.9 defines such a database manager SE-dbase, having an argument which is the stream of request messages. The logical reading of SE-dbase(cmds) is: cmds is a valid list of request messages for an initially empty database. SE-dbase uses the SE-trans relation which performs a 'transaction' for a single message, possibly updating the database destructively. SE-initialize has the side-effect of initializing the database. SE-trans and SE-initialize do not have a declarative reading; they are used only to implement SE-dbase, and their details are not relevant here.

mode SE-dbase(?), SE-dbase1(?), SE-trans(?), SE-initialize.

SE-dbase(cmds) <− SE-initialize & SE-dbase1(cmds).

SE-dbase1([cmd|cmds]) <− SE-trans(cmd) & SE-dbase1(cmds).
SE-dbase1([]).

Program 3.9 Side-effect database manager.

Because Program 3.9, like Program 3.5, uses side-effects, the order of updates must be sequenced by the use of '&'. One message must be served completely before the next message is accepted. Since this message stream is the only interface to the database, its integrity is preserved.

3.3.3.3 *Representing a state by local variables*

As an alternative to Program 3.9, the database may be represented without the need for side-effects, as the arguments of a recursively defined relation. Program 3.10 shows a procedure for dbase, which has the same logical reading as SE-dbase of Program 3.9. The dbase relation is defined in terms of the relations initialize and trans, which have a valid declarative reading, as follows, initialize(initdb): initdb is an empty database. trans(cmd,db,newdb): if cmd is a valid database message, newdb is the database db after updating according to cmd. trans is defined in Program 3.12.

mode dbase(?), dbase1(?,?), trans(?,?, ↑), initialize(↑).

dbase(cmds) <−
    initialize(initdb), dbase1(cmds,initdb).

dbase1([cmd|cmds],db) <−
    trans(cmd,db,newdb), dbase1(cmds,newdb).
dbase1([],db).

Program 3.10 Declarative database manager.

Unlike Program 3.9, Program 3.10 can be read declaratively, as a set of relations on request messages and databases represented as terms. Operationally, for each message, a whole new term representing the database is built and used by subsequent messages. Old versions of the database can be removed by garbage collection when no longer referenced.

Here, a program which calls itself recursively with different arguments implements a 'perpetual process' (Warren, 1982) with an internal state which is modified without resorting to side-effects. This programming technique appears to be relatively new to logic programming, perhaps because (in Prolog) it relies upon the use of tail recursion optimization to be feasible. It was used in the supervisor program of the micro-PROLOG system in 1980. In Prolog, however, only one such process can exist at any time. In parallel logic programming languages such as PARLOG, the technique is more widely applicable since any number of processes can be active concurrently.

The first demonstration of 'perpetual processes' in parallel logic programming appeared in Gregory (1980), where a CSP program from Hoare (1978) was rendered as a concurrent logic program. The same technique has been exploited in functional programming, for example, in the work of Henderson (1982) and Jones (1984) who define operating systems as sets of communicating processes.

In Program 3.10, because of the representation of the database as a term, the sequential conjunction operator is not necessary; the request messages are served in sequence by virtue of the 'dataflow' through shared variables, constrained by the declared modes.

Fig. 3.3 depicts a possible state of the evaluation of dbase([CMD1,CMD2,CMD3]) before the initialize call has terminated. Assuming that the trans relation requires its second (input) argument, a database, to be (at least partially) instantiated before it can be updated according to a message, all trans processes are initially suspended. When the initialize process supplies the term representing the empty database (initdb), the first trans process can be evaluated, to serve message CMD1. The second trans process will be suspended until the first supplies a value for db1, and so on.

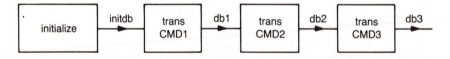

Fig 3.3   State of a dbase evaluation.

3.3.3.4   *Mode constraints for sequencing*

The simple example of Program 3.10 illustrates a very common situation in PARLOG programs: where mode constraints are sufficient to impose a suitable order of evaluation among calls that share a variable. If no such shared variable exists, one can be introduced as an extra argument of the calls, for no other purpose than synchronization. Kusalik has called this the 'control token' approach, in his survey of serialization techniques in Concurrent Prolog (Kusalik, 1984b).

Chapter 4 presents an example of a technique whereby a PARLOG program using a sequential '&' operator can be *transformed* to one with only parallel conjunction, using such a 'synchronization flag'. Utilizing this technique together with a special 'control call' primitive (Section 3.9), Chapter 5 demonstrates how a PARLOG program using '&' and ';' can be automatically *compiled* to another in which sequential conjunction and sequential clause search are obtained by mode constraints.

Sequential conjunction is omitted from most versions of Concurrent Prolog (Shapiro, 1983). However, a sequential clause search facility *is* included in that language (Shapiro and Takeuchi, 1983). This is the otherwise primitive, a restriction of PARLOG's ';' operator that specifies that a certain clause is to be tried only after all other clauses have become non-candidates.

Although sequential operators are not essential in PARLOG, programs that use them are often easier to write and to understand than those obtaining sequencing by mode constraints. In a programming experiment performed using PARLOG, Flat Concurrent Prolog (Mierowsky *et al.*, 1985) and Delta-Prolog (Pereira and Nasr, 1984), Butler *et al.* (1986) found the use of the sequential conjunction operator more convenient than synchronization via a control token (as required in Flat Concurrent Prolog).

Additionally, programs employing sequential operators are likely to run more efficiently on a coarse-grained architecture which can directly support sequential evaluation. This issue of **granularity** is discussed in the next section.

3.4 Granularity

In parallel processing, the 'grain' or degree of parallelism is a very important consideration. It is widely acknowledged that too much parallelism may be harmful, possibly overwhelming the system with communication overheads. On the other hand, if the parallelism is too coarse-grained, there may be little opportunity to exploit concurrency. See, for example, the discussion in Pollard (1981), page 61.

Parallel computer architectures can be viewed as a set of 'agents' of some kind, which do not necessarily coincide with physical processors. Different architectures vary widely in their granularity, i.e. the power of the individual agents and what kind of operations they can perform (MacQueen, 1979). These range from (fine-grained) dataflow architectures, (e.g. Gurd *et al.*, 1980, 1985; Arvind *et al.*, 1978), in which the agents (nodes) are capable only of simple 'stateless' operations such as arithmetic, to coarse-grained systems in which the agents are powerful, general-purpose machines capable of evaluating recursive programs.

In keeping with the philosophy of 'language first, architecture second' (Sleep, 1980), there exist several parallel architectures specially designed to execute a certain type of language. Architectures designed for functional languages include AMPS (Keller *et al.*, 1979), ZAPP (Sleep and Burton, 1981) and ALICE (Darlington and Reeve, 1981). All of these have a level of granularity corresponding to a programmer-defined function. In other words, an agent has the ability to evaluate an expression internally unless it includes a subexpression involving some programmer-defined function. In that case, the subexpression is evaluated by another agent and the result returned to the first agent. The computation performed by an agent is roughly a reduction step; see Section 2.4.1.1. These agents therefore have more power than a node in a dataflow graph: they can internally execute simple sequential programs, but not arbitrary recursive programs.

A similar approach is taken in the EPILOG system (Wise, 1982, 1984), an abstract parallel architecture for a variant of Prolog. The computation performed by an EPILOG agent is a resolution step; see Section 2.2.3.1.

In Concurrent Prolog (Shapiro, 1983), the natural level of granularity is also a resolution step, since all calls in a clause guard or body are evaluated concurrently and, in evaluating a relation call, the clauses are concurrently tested for candidacy.

3.4.1   The PARLOG approach

Despite the attractions of the 'language first' approach, PARLOG is not intended to be a language that will run efficiently only on a specially designed architecture. Instead, it should be possible to implement it on a range of parallel architectures, even the extreme case: a sequential machine. In a discussion of multiprocessing algorithms, Lusk and Overbeek (1984) write:

> A concerted attempt should be made to reduce the perception of machine peculiarities to simply recognizing that different machines will support different levels of granularity ... Thus, it seems to make sense to create multiple implementations ... differentiated by the granularity of the parallelism supported on different physical incarnations.

Although the above quotation concerns the implementation of algorithms, a similar argument could be applied to language implementations. To produce efficient implementations of PARLOG on different parallel machines, the implementation strategy should cater for different levels of granularity. This is described in detail in Chapters 5–7.

Since no assumptions are made concerning the granularity of the target architecture, there is no reason to enforce a particular level of granularity on the PARLOG programmer. That is, a program utilizing sequential operators ('&' and ';') may be more efficient on a coarse-grained architecture, while greater use of parallel operators (',' and '.') may be desirable for a fine-grained machine. This is a further justification for the inclusion of sequential operators in the language (Section 3.3.3).

As an example, consider the sigma procedure of Program 3.1:

```
sigma([u|z],m,n) <- plus(u,m,um), sigma(z,um,n).
sigma([],n,n).                                          (P)
```

Given this procedure, a sigma process 'forks' for each received member of the first argument list: one process is spawned to perform the input matching of each clause. When the first clause is selected, there are still two processes: one for each call (plus and sigma), although the plus process is short-lived.

This may well be a suitable program for a sufficiently fine-grained machine. On a more coarse-grained architecture, the parallelism may be excessive: the overhead in spawning processes may outweigh any speed gains from evaluating the plus and sigma calls concurrently. Because the calls are so simple, they would probably be evaluated using some form of pseudo-parallelism. This would be no faster than sequential execution and there would be some extra overhead in catering for the possible suspension of processes.

Since there is no need for AND and OR parallelism in the evaluation of sigma, the relation may equally well be defined by a completely sequential procedure:

```
sigma([u|z],m,n) <- plus(u,m,um) & sigma(z,um,n);
sigma([],n,n).                                              (S)
```

This program can be evaluated as a single process; there is no forking. It has different behaviour; e.g., if a plus call suspends, the whole sigma process will suspend.

On a coarse-grained architecture, procedure S is clearly more efficient than P, which involves unnecessarily spawning processes or implementing some form of multiprogramming. Moreover, the sequential procedure S can still be run on a fine-grained implementation. By techniques described in Chapter 5, it could be compiled to a program using only parallel operators, in which the sequencing is obtained by communication constraints (modes). The problem with this is that there would then be some overhead, compared with procedure P, in imposing unnecessary sequencing.

The different kinds of sequencing operators will prove particularly useful in the next section and in the chapters on implementation. For, even in a language with only parallel operators like Concurrent Prolog, there are semantic issues such as the order in which the unification of arguments and the guard evaluation are performed. In PARLOG, any sequencing can be expressed in the language itself. Section 3.5 shows how the order of unification can be made explicit by a translation of a PARLOG program to a lower-level form.

To summarize, the granularity of a program should, but need not, match that of the target architecture. A coarse-grained program (one using '&' and ';') can be implemented on a finer-grained architecture by compilation but with sequencing overhead. A fine-grained program can be run on a coarser-grained machine by multiprogramming but, again, at some expense.

Perhaps the best approach is to avoid overspecifying the granularity of the program. This can be done in PARLOG by using a 'neutral' conjunction operator 'and' and a neutral clause search operator '..'. These can be used whenever the programmer is not concerned about the sequencing. The 'and' operator will ultimately be replaced by either ',' or '&' while '..' is translated to either '.' or ';', depending upon the particular implementation. Both 'and' and '..' are read as conjunction. For example, the sigma program can be written:

```
sigma([u|z],m,n) <- plus(u,m,um) and sigma(z,um,n)..
sigma([],n,n).
```

This can be translated, by the PARLOG compiler, to either procedure P or S or some hybrid form. The neutral operators should not be regarded as primitives of PARLOG. Rather, they are 'macros' that enable a program to be efficiently ported to implementations of a different granularity.

In subsequent program examples, the neutral operators will be used wherever possible. As another example, Program 3.11 defines the relation partition(u,x,x1,x2): x is a list of items, x1 is the sublist of x comprising items less than u and x2 is the remainder of x. The relative order of items in x1 and x2 is the same as in x.

```
mode partition(?,?, ↑ , ↑ ).

partition(u,[v|x],[v|x1],x2) <- v < u :
    partition(u,x,x1,x2)..
partition(u,[v|x],x1,[v|x2]) <- u =< v :
    partition(u,x,x1,x2)..
partition(u,[],[],[]).
```

Program 3.11   List partition.

3.5   Standard form of PARLOG clauses

In a critique of Concurrent Prolog, Gelernter (1984) complains that the behaviour ('logical flow') of a Concurrent Prolog program does not coincide with its textual order. To understand the behaviour of a Concurrent Prolog procedure, one has to consider the inputs, then the guard evaluation, then the output of data performed upon commitment, and finally the new state that the process assumes. A similar criticism could be applied to PARLOG. However, the behaviour of a PARLOG program is clarified by considering a translation to a lower-level program in which, for each clause, the inputs, tests, outputs and new state are written in chronological order.

The language to which PARLOG programs are translated will be named **Kernel PARLOG**, as distinct from **source PARLOG**. A Kernel PARLOG program has no mode declarations; these are used purely to control the translation from source PARLOG. The structure of each PARLOG procedure is unchanged, but each clause is translated to **standard form**.

In the standard form of a PARLOG clause, all head arguments are distinct variables; the input matching and output unification are done by explicit calls to unification primitives which are added to the guard and body of the clause. The input matching calls appear in the guard and the output unification calls in the body.

Although it is possible, it is not suggested that one should necessarily program in standard form; the source PARLOG form of a program has a clearer declarative reading. Kernel PARLOG is preferable if one wishes to understand the behaviour. Moreover, the translation to Kernel PARLOG constitutes the first stage of the compilation of a PARLOG program, which is detailed in Chapter 5.

The ability to translate a source PARLOG program to Kernel PARLOG automatically is a result of the distinction between input and output arguments resulting from mode declarations. This distinction allows most of the unification (the input matching) to be compiled into simple efficient code. This is not possible in Concurrent Prolog because that language uses a variant of unification, constrained by read-only variables. The input/output use of a Concurrent Prolog procedure is determined by each call to it, not by the procedure itself.

3.5.1 Standard form of a general PARLOG clause

To transform a general PARLOG clause:

$$R(t_1,\ldots,t_k) <- G : B.$$

to standard form, the head arguments are replaced by distinct variables. Then a call to a primitive '$<=$' is added to the guard for each input argument, and a call to '$=$' is added to the body for each output argument. If a variable q occurs more than once in the input argument terms, new variables $q_1,\ldots,q_j$ are introduced in place of the repeated occurrences and calls to a '$==$' primitive $q == q_1,\ldots, q == q_j$ are added to the guard to *test* that every occurrence of the variable is given the same value.

Suppose that the mode declaration for R states that the first i arguments are input and the remaining arguments $(t_{i+1},\ldots,t_k)$ are output. Then the standard form of the clause is:

$$R(p_1,\ldots,p_i,p_{i+1},\ldots,p_k) <-$$
$$t'_1 <= p_1, \ldots, t'_i <= p_i,$$

    <test unifications for repeated variables of $t_1,...,t_i$>,
G :
    $p_{i+1} = t_{i+1}$ and ... and $p_k = t_k$ and
    B.   (SF)

in which $t'_1,...,t'_i$ are the input argument terms $t_1,...,t_i$ with all but the first occurrence of each variable q replaced by new variables $q_1,...,q_j$. The syntactic identity of q with each of $q_1,...,q_j$ is checked by the 'test unifications' (calls to '==') included in the guard of clause SF.

    Note that all primitive calls added to the guard are placed in parallel with each other and with the original (source PARLOG) guard. The ',' operator is used for this purpose. The '=' calls are added to the body using 'and'. That is, they may be evaluated concurrently, or sequentially in the specified order.

3.5.1.1   The '<=' primitive

'<=' is the **one-way unification** primitive of PARLOG. It will also be referred to as the **matching** primitive, since it implements term matching as described in Section 2.4.1.2. The mode of '<=' is (?,?); its left argument is 'weak', as explained in Section 3.6. The call:

    $t_1 <= t_2$

unifies t_1 and t_2 by binding variables in t_1 in order to make t_1 and t_2 syntactically identical. If it could proceed only by binding variables in t_2, the call suspends. Ultimately the call will succeed if and only if it is possible to unify t_1 and t_2; otherwise it will fail.

    In the case where t_1 is a variable, the call cannot suspend. Neither can it fail *unless* the occur check is implemented; see Section 3.7.2.

3.5.1.2   The '==' primitive

'==' is the **test unification** primitive; it has mode (?,?). A call to '==' unifies its two arguments, but without binding variables in either argument. The call suspends if it could proceed only by binding a variable in one of the terms. Ultimately the call will either succeed or fail, depending upon whether the terms are syntactically identical.

    Two terms t_1 and t_2 are syntactically identical if they are both the *same* variable, or the same constant, or are both structured terms with the same function name and syntactically identical arguments.

3.5.1.3   The '=' primitive

'=' is the **full unification** primitive. It has mode (?,?), and both arguments are weak. The call:

    $t_1 = t_2$

simply unifies t_1 and t_2; it can only succeed or fail, never suspend. In the case that t_1 and t_2 are both unbound variables, t_2 should be bound to a reference to t_1 (though t_1 could be bound to t_2).

In the standard form of a clause, each input argument of a call (i.e. $p_1,...,p_i$) appears on the right of a '<=' call whose left argument is an input argument term $(t_1,...,t_i)$ from the head of the clause. This states explicitly the requirement that t_1 can only be used for input matching with p_1, and so on. By the definition of the one-way and test unification primitives, no variables in the call arguments may be instantiated by the '<=' calls or the '==' calls in the guard. Moreover, because of the requirement that G is 'safe', G cannot bind any variables in $t_1,...,t_i$. This guarantees that the guard of the standard form clause SF cannot bind any variables in the call to R.

Each output argument of a call (i.e. $p_{i+1},...,p_k$) appears on the left of a '=' call *in the clause body*, reflecting the fact that the output unification is performed after commitment.

3.5.2 Examples of standard form

Applying the above rules, the standard form of Program 3.7 is as follows:

```
on-tree(p1,p2,p3) <−
      key <= p1, T(x,P(q1,value),y) <= p3, key == q1 :
      p2 = value;
on-tree(p1,p2,p3) <−
      key <= p1, T(x,P(rkey,rvalue),y) <= p3,
      on-tree(key,value,x) :
      p2 = value.
on-tree(p1,p2,p3) <−
      key <= p1, T(x,P(rkey,rvalue),y) <= p3,
      on-tree(key,value,y) :
      p2 = value.
```

In each clause, the head arguments have been replaced by distinct variables and a call to '<=' introduced for each input argument: the first and third. Note the introduction of a call to '==' in the first clause. Since the variable key occurs in both of the input arguments in this clause, the second occurrence has been replaced by a new variable q1 and key is compared with q1 by the test call key == q1. In all three clauses, a full unification call is added to the (previously empty) body, for the second (output) argument.

This example illustrates a simple optimization in the standard form of a clause: if a head argument in an input position is a variable, there is no need to add a '<=' call to the guard for that argument.

This optimization is justified as follows. The variables in the left argument of each introduced '<=' call are distinct, owing to the method of replacing repeated variables in input arguments so, for example, key (above) could not appear on the left of another introduced '<=' call. key *could* appear in the guard as an argument of an introduced '==' call (as in the first clause) but such a call cannot instantiate key. The only other possible location for key in the guard is in the guard of the source PARLOG program (as in the second and third clauses for on-tree). Because of the 'safe' guard requirement (Section 3.2.4), this guard is not allowed to instantiate key. Hence, when the call key <= p1 is evaluated, key is guaranteed to be an unbound variable, and the only effect of the call would be to assign to key the value of p1. Therefore, the call key <= p1 can be dropped from all of the above clauses and key replaced by p1 throughout each clause:

```
on-tree(p1,p2,p3) <-
    T(x,P(q1,value),y) <= p3, p1 == q1 :
    p2 = value;
on-tree(p1,p2,p3) <-
    T(x,P(rkey,rvalue),y) <= p3, on-tree(p1,value,x) :
    p2 = value.
on-tree(p1,p2,p3) <-
    T(x,P(rkey,rvalue),y) <= p3, on-tree(p1,value,y) :
    p2 = value.
```

The standard form of the on-tree clauses reveals explicitly the unification constraints that are implicit in the original (source PARLOG) program. To solve a call on-tree(p1,p2,p3), the first clause will be tried first (owing to the use of the ';' operator). This will invoke two guard calls:

```
T(x,P(q1,value),y) <= p3, p1 == q1
```

The first call will match p3 with the term T(x,P(q1,value),y), i.e. a tree structure with a pair as its label. This will suspend if p3 is an unbound variable, *or* if it is instantiated to T(x,z,y) but z is an unbound variable. The other call, p1 == q1, will be suspended until p1 and q1 are found to be identical terms, when it will succeed, or different terms, in which case it will fail. Notice that q1 will remain unbound until the matching call succeeds. If the entire guard succeeds, the evaluation will commit and the variable p2 will be bound to the value of value (obtained by the input match with p3).

If the guard of the first clause fails, those of the remaining clauses will be evaluated concurrently. Each of these guards comprises an input match and a call to a programmer-defined relation, e.g.:

```
T(x,P(rkey,rvalue),y) <= p3, on-tree(p1,value,x)
```

The matching call and the recursive on-tree call are evaluated in parallel. The latter will eventually perform a similar input match with x, which cannot proceed until the matching call has accessed the value of x.

The partition procedure of Program 3.11 can be translated to the following standard form:

```
partition(p1,p2,p3,p4) <- [v|x] <= p2, v < p1 :
    p3 = [v|x1] and p4 = x2 and partition(p1,x,x1,x2)..
partition(p1,p2,p3,p4) <- [v|x] <= p2, p1 =< v :
    p3 = x1 and p4 = [v|x2] and partition(p1,x,x1,x2)..
partition(p1,p2,p3,p4) <- [] <= p2 :
    p3 = [] and p4 = [].
```

Here, a single '<=' call has been added to the guard of each clause (for the second argument). By the above optimization, no '<=' call is necessary for the first argument, since it is a variable. In each clause, a '=' call has been added to the body to perform the output unification for the third and fourth arguments.

In fact, a further optimization is possible. In the first clause, the call p4 = x2 could be removed and x2 replaced by p4 throughout the clause. This is because x2 is a variable which is guaranteed to be unbound at the time of commitment, since it does not occur in the guard. Similarly, the call p3 = x1 is redundant in the second clause. In general, a full unification call need not be introduced for an output argument if the head argument term is a variable which does not appear in the input arguments or the guard of the source PARLOG clause. The resulting standard form of partition is:

```
partition(p1,p2,p3,p4) <- [v|x] <= p2, v < p1 :
    p3 = [v|x1] and partition(p1,x,x1,p4)..
partition(p1,p2,p3,p4) <- [v|x] <= p2, p1 =< v :
    p4 = [v|x2] and partition(p1,x,p3,x2)..
partition(p1,p2,p3,p4) <- [] <= p2 :
    p3 = [] and p4 = [].
```

3.5.3 Operational semantics

The translation of PARLOG programs to Kernel PARLOG simplifies the operational semantics because the unification is made explicit, as calls to primitives. The search for a candidate clause proceeds as described in Section 3.2.2, but the definition of each class of clause is simpler, as follows.

- A **candidate clause** is one in which the guard evaluation succeeds.

- A **non-candidate clause** is one in which the guard evaluation fails.

- A **suspended clause** is one in which the guard evaluation is suspended.

3.6   The logical variable in PARLOG

In Section 3.1.1, mode declarations were introduced as a communication constraint similar to that used in the parallel evaluation of functional programs: the arguments of a functional program correspond to the equivalent PARLOG program's input arguments, and the result of the function corresponds to the output arguments. As explained in Section 2.4.1.3, a functional program rewritten as a logic program is 'directional'. That is, its arguments are 'strong'.

The above examples of PARLOG programs have all been directional, so they do not feature the logical variable. However, PARLOG programs need not be directional. By allowing an input argument to be 'weak' (described below), a call may instantiate variables in an input argument term, thus enabling the use of the logical variable. This is perhaps the most significant difference between PARLOG and functional languages.

A **weak** input argument of a call to relation R is one in which variables might be instantiated by the evaluation of the call. For example, if R has mode (?) and is defined by the clause:

R(F(x,y)) <− S(x).

the evaluation of R will suspend until its input argument is instantiated to a term of the form F(x,y), owing to the input constraint imposed by modes (Section 3.1.1). But the value of x need not be supplied by another process running in parallel with the R call – it may instead be instantiated by the call S(x). This will occur if the mode of S is (↑), *or* if it is (?) but the argument of S is itself weak. In either of these cases, the argument of R is said to be weak. If, however, S has a *strong* input argument, the argument of R is also strong since it cannot be further instantiated by the call to R.

In directional programs, guards are necessarily safe (Section 3.2.4) because input variables (i.e. variables in input arguments) of a clause cannot be bound by any call in the guard (or even in the body). The introduction of weak input arguments means that a more complex check for guard safety is required. Essentially, if an input argument of a clause is weak 'because of' a call in the guard, the guard is unsafe. For example, if the argument of S is output *or* is a weak input argument, the clause:

R(F(x,y)) <− S(x) :.

is unsafe, because x may be bound by a guard call.

Directional programs, weak arguments and safe guards are fully discussed in Chapter 5.

3.6.1   Back communication

The logical variable is an even more powerful technique in parallel logic programming languages than in Prolog. In Prolog, a relation call may construct a structure containing variables to be instantiated by a subsequent call. In PARLOG, however, the call generating the structure may be running concurrently with one that consumes the structure and instantiates variables in it. When the consumer process binds a variable in the structure, an immediate 'back communication' occurs, from the consumer to the producer, which might affect the subsequent behaviour of the producer. This realizes two-way communication between concurrent calls, on a single shared variable (i.e. communication channel).

3.6.1.1 Back communication for resource allocation

Program 3.10 showed a procedure for a relation dbase, to be evaluated as a process to manage a database. The dbase process consumes a stream of messages of three types: to ADD or DELETE an item, and to enquire whether an item is IN the database. Suppose that the valid messages are of the form:

```
IN(key,reply)
ADD(key,value,reply)
DELETE(key,reply)
```

In each case, the last argument of the message, reply, will normally be (but need not be) an unbound variable when the message is received by the dbase process; the other arguments will be non-variable terms. (Messages containing unbound variables have been called **incomplete messages** (Shapiro and Takeuchi, 1983).) The intention is that the dbase process should receive each message in the stream, perform the requested action and then bind the reply variable to a response, which can then be read by the sender of the message.

The dbase process is a typical example of a resource allocator, controlling access to a resource (the database) by a number of 'clients'. By the use of messages containing variables, a 'resource' process (e.g. the database) may communicate with an arbitrary, possibly dynamically varying, number of client processes. The message streams from the clients are merged into a single stream to be served by the resource process. A reply to each message is effectively returned to the sending process without the need for a separate channel. The use of the dbase process is illustrated in Fig. 3.4. The solid lines represent the shared variables (communication channels) while the dotted lines show the direct 'back communication'. The figure illustrates the situation where the message sent by client2 reaches dbase before that sent by client1.

Arvind and Brock (1982) discuss the problem of resource sharing in a parallel functional language. Having introduced a non-deterministic merge 'function' to provide the essential time-dependency, they recognize the difficulty of connecting a resource process to an arbitrary and dynamically varying number of clients. This is a problem in functional languages due to

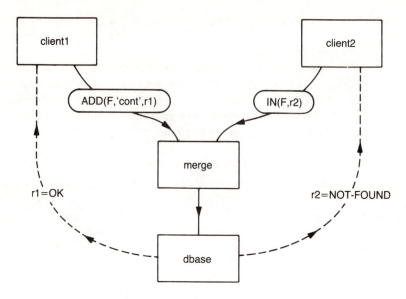

Fig 3.4   Communication with a resource allocator.

their directionality. For each client process, two channels are required: one for the messages and another for responses. To solve this deficiency, they extend the language by a special construct: a **manager**, similar in use to Hoare's **monitor** (Hoare, 1974). A manager handles, at the implementation level, the return addresses for responding to the client processes. In a parallel logic language, no additional construct is needed: the problem is solved by the logical variable; variables in messages act as return addresses.

In an earlier version of PARLOG – the Relational Language (Clark and Gregory, 1981) – only strong input arguments were allowed. It was soon discovered that the logical variable would greatly increase the expressiveness of the language, so the mode constraints were relaxed to their present form. Independently, another descendant of the Relational Language was developed: Concurrent Prolog (Shapiro, 1983). Concurrent Prolog featured a different communication constraint: read-only variables (see Section 3.7.5.4), which allowed the logical variable by default. The use of 'incomplete messages' for resource allocation was first exploited by Shapiro (1983).

The dbase procedure of Program 3.10 made use of a trans relation, which is defined here. trans(cmd,db,newdb) has the logical reading: newdb is the database db updated according to the cmd message. A procedure for trans is shown in Program 3.12. Here, the database is represented by an ordered tree term, so the on-ord-tree relation (Program 3.3) can be used to search for an item's value given the key. The program also uses two extra relations, insert-ord-tree and delete-ord-tree, whose definitions are not given here.

insert-ord-tree(P(key,value),tree,newtree) is the relation: there is no pair with the given key on the ordered tree tree, and the ordered tree newtree is the same as tree but augmented by the given P(key,value) pair.

delete-ord-tree(key,tree,newtree) has the meaning: tree is an ordered tree containing a pair with the given key, and newtree is tree with this pair removed.

```
mode trans(?,?, ↑ ), on-ord-tree(?, ↑ ,?),
    insert-ord-tree(?,?, ↑ ), delete-ord-tree(?,?, ↑ ).

trans(IN(key,reply),db,db) <−
    on-ord-tree(key,value,db) :
    reply = value..                                              (T1)
trans(ADD(key,newvalue,reply),db,newdb) <−
    insert-ord-tree(P(key,newvalue),db,newdb) :
    reply = OK..                                                 (T2)
trans(DELETE(key,reply),db,newdb) <−
    delete-ord-tree(key,db,newdb) :
    reply = OK;                                                  (T3)
trans(IN(key,reply),db,db) <−
    reply = NOT-FOUND..                                          (T4)
trans(ADD(key,newvalue,reply),db,db) <−
    reply = ALREADY-EXISTS..                                     (T5)
trans(DELETE(key,reply),db,db) <−
    reply = NOT-FOUND;                                           (T6)
trans(message,db,db).                                            (T7)
```

Program 3.12   Database transaction program.

The procedure for trans is in three parts, separated by ';'. Clauses T1 to T3 deal with the successful processing of each of the three types of message, the next three clauses handle the unsuccessful case, while clause T7 simply ignores an invalid message. For each valid message type, there are therefore two clauses. For a message IN(key,reply), reply will be unified with the value associated with the given key if it is in the database, otherwise reply is unified with NOT-FOUND. For a message ADD(key,newvalue,reply), the pair P(key,newvalue) will be added to the database if possible and reply unified with OK, otherwise the reply will be ALREADY-EXISTS. If the message is DELETE(key,reply), the item with the given key will be deleted if it is in the database and reply unified with OK, otherwise reply will be NOT-FOUND.

In the first three trans clauses, T1 to T3, the guard contains a substantial computation: updating or searching the database. If the sequential clause search operator ';' were not used following T3, the guards would need to be re-evaluated in clauses T4 to T6 to compute their negation. For the logical reading, the second group of three clauses, T4 to T6, should be read as though they included the negation of the guard of the corresponding clause in the first group. For example, clause T4 is read logically as:

```
trans(IN(key,reply),db,db) <-
    ~ on-ord-tree(key,value,db) :
    reply = NOT-FOUND.
```

The back communication is achieved in each clause by an explicit unification call which binds the reply variable in the message (assuming that reply is unbound). Because reply appears in a weak input argument position (an argument of a call to '=') in the body, the first argument of trans is weak, as defined above.

A more natural way to write clause T4 would be:

```
trans(IN(key,NOT-FOUND),db,db).                              (T4')
```

but this would result in incorrect behaviour. Because the first argument of trans is declared to be input, a call to trans would suspend, waiting for the argument to be a term of the form IN(key,reply) *and* waiting for reply to be instantiated to NOT-FOUND. This can be seen from the standard form of clause T4':

```
trans(p1,p2,p3) <- IN(key,NOT-FOUND) <= p1 :
    p3 = p2.
```

The translation to standard form introduces a '=' call into the body for output arguments (here, the third argument) but not for output components of input arguments (the term NOT-FOUND). Therefore, this output must be done by an explicit call to '=' in the source PARLOG program.

Similarly, clause T1 could more naturally be written:

```
trans(IN(key,reply),db,db) <-
    on-ord-tree(key,reply,db) :.                              (T1')
```

but this would make the guard unsafe (see Section 3.2.4) because the guard would bind reply, an input variable of the clause. The second (output) argument of the on-ord-tree call must be a new variable which is unified with reply after commitment. This is done by the explicit '=' call in the body of the original clause T1 in Program 3.12.

Ideally, the compiler would be able to translate clauses of the form T1' and T4' into clauses T1 and T4. However, this would require a method of indicating which are the output subterms of an input head argument. Such a facility was provided in an earlier version of PARLOG (Clark and Gregory, 1983): an annotation could be placed on output subterms of input arguments in clause heads. However, the annotation proved difficult to understand and use, so it was abandoned in favour of the present method: the explicit use of the '=' in the clause body in the source PARLOG program.

3.6.1.2 Back communication for input/output

Back communication provides a means of programming demand-driven input from an external device. A process requiring an input term from the device can send a message, containing an unbound variable, to the device handling process. When the data is available, the variable in the message is bound to it.

Consider the example of input/output to a conventional teletype-like terminal. The output streams from the various processes can be merged and displayed, interleaved, by the writelist procedure of Program 3.5. This program can be extended to handle input simply by adding an extra clause at the beginning of the procedure; see Program 3.13.

```
writelist([REPLY(prompt,reply)|list]) <−
    write(prompt) &
    read(reply) &
    writelist(list);
writelist([message|list]) <−
    write(message) &
    NL &
    writelist(list).
writelist([]).
```

Program 3.13   Program to read and write a list.

The new clause recognizes a message of the form REPLY(x,y) as a request to *read* an item; all other forms of message are displayed as usual by the second writelist clause. If a REPLY message is received, its first argument is displayed as a prompt, and an item is then read and unified with the second argument of the message (usually a variable). This transmits the read item directly to the sender of the message by a back communication. The read primitive is an imperative one, as used in Prolog; it has mode (↑). The back communication is apparent by the occurrence of an input argument variable, reply, in an output argument in the body of the clause.

The read primitive has the property that no output can be displayed at the terminal while a term is being input. This may delay the display of some output that is being sent to the writelist process. However, owing to the order-preserving nature of merge, all previous messages produced by a process sending a REPLY(x,y) message must have been displayed before this message prompts the user for input. By including a prompt as an argument of the message, the sending process can be identified to the user. This is very desirable if there are many processes accessing the same terminal for I/O.

This example suggests how back communication with variables in messages can provide the effect of lazy, or demand-driven, evaluation. Taking this idea to its extreme results in messages which *are* variables. By incrementally sending a stream of variables to a process, each variable may act as a *demand* for the next value computed by the process. This technique is illustrated in Chapter 4.

3.7   Unification

3.7.1   Implementation of the unification primitives

The unification primitives, '<=', '==' and '=', are introduced by the compilation from source PARLOG to Kernel PARLOG. They may also be used freely in source PARLOG programs; the introduced calls are simply added to any that already appear in the source program. For example, in Program 3.12, the '=' primitive was (necessarily) used explicitly to effect back communication.

Even though the unification in PARLOG is translated to calls to special primitives, it is not suggested that these calls should be implemented in the same way as calls to programmer-defined relations. They should be compiled wherever possible, whether used by the programmer or introduced by the compiler. (In addition, calls to other PARLOG primitives, including arithmetic relations, etc., can often be compiled to efficient code due to the fact that their mode is known.)

As explained in Chapter 5, calls to the term matching primitive '<=' that are introduced by the translation of a clause to standard form can always be compiled to efficient code, comprising simple, non-recursive instructions.

3.7.2   Correctness of the unification primitives

As explained in Section 2.2.6, any resolution inference system is correct. That is, any solutions to a program computed by a resolution-based system will conform to the declarative reading of the program. However, resolution is defined in terms of full unification, which is not always used in PARLOG. In PARLOG, the unification of a call $R(s_1,...,s_k)$ with the head of a clause $R(t_1,...,t_k)$ is achieved by breaking down the call arguments and the head arguments into subterms which are unified by a mixture of '<=',

'==' and '=' primitive calls. Clearly, if all of these primitives performed full unification, the result would be the same as unifying $R(s_1,...,s_k)$ with $R(t_1,...,t_k)$.

PARLOG is a correct inference system because '=' *is* full unification, while each of the other two unification primitives is a *restriction* thereof: if $t_1 <= s_1$ succeeds, then the unification of t_1 and s_1 would succeed; similarly for $t_1 == s_1$. The only difference is that these specialized unification calls might suspend instead of succeeding, thus preventing some or all of the solutions of a program being computed. However, this affects only the completeness, *not* the correctness. In a PARLOG program, the primitives '<=', '==' and '=' should all be read as the equality relation.

The correctness of resolution depends upon the 'occur check' in unification. The unification of a variable v and a term t should fail if v occurs in t. If the unification is allowed to succeed, binding v to t, incorrect solutions may be computed. However, almost all practical logic programming systems omit the occur check for reasons of efficiency.

In PARLOG, the occur check should also be implemented if it is desired to preserve correctness. However, the implementation overhead may be less than in Prolog. In a call to '==', no variables can be bound so the occur check is not necessary. A call to '<=' may require the occur check, though most uses of it do not: the '<=' calls introduced for input matching by the transformation to standard form *mostly* have the property that their left argument is a term containing new variables that cannot occur in the right argument term, so the occur check is not required. Most '=' calls introduced for output unification *do* require the occur check, but these are relatively infrequently executed. Chapter 5 describes how unification calls are compiled into simple instructions including, if necessary, a BIND instruction which performs the occur check.

3.7.3 Unification and matching

The ability of PARLOG to support logical variables does not depend upon unification; it only requires a means of binding variables in input arguments. Indeed, earlier versions of PARLOG (Clark and Gregory, 1983, 1986; Gregory, 1985) did not include full unification as a primitive. Outputs were then performed by assignment: each output argument of a call had to be an unbound variable, which was bound to (rather than unified with) the output term after commitment. An error occurred if it was not an unbound variable. Back communication could be effected by the explicit use of an assignment primitive ':='.

The use of full unification for output – **output** unification – adds some expressive power to the language: a trivial example is that arithmetic primitives can be used in 'checking' mode as well as 'computing' mode, e.g. plus(1,2,3) is a valid call. There is no additional overhead: in the case where an output argument is an unbound variable, the effect of unification is the same as assignment. Only rarely will calls to '=' perform more complex computation.

In implementing the '=' primitive in a PARLOG system (Section 5.2.6), it is probably not worth attempting to incorporate parallelism. In two independent studies (Dwork *et al.*, 1984; Yasuura, 1984), it is shown that full unification is an inherently sequential algorithm. They conclude that significant improvements in the speed of logic programs are unlikely to result from the development of parallel unification algorithms. Moreover, Dwork *et al.* show that there is a special case of unification that *can* be 'solved quickly' in parallel: namely, term matching.

3.7.4   Order-independence of unification

In a parallel logic programming language, an important consideration is whether arguments are unified concurrently or sequentially, and (if sequentially) the order of unification. This decision affects the efficiency and, more importantly, the semantics of the language. The method used in PARLOG is to perform the input matching of the arguments concurrently, and in parallel with the guard evaluation.

Before discussing the merits of this approach, consider the following procedure for the relation or(x,y) which has the logical reading: either x *or* y has the value True:

mode or(?,?).

or(True,y).
or(x,True).   (OR)

This procedure is 'non-strict'. That is, a call or(x,y) will succeed if one of its arguments has the value True, even if the other is not instantiated. This is a consequence of the parallel clause search operator '.' between clauses. If the '.' is changed to ';', the procedure would become semi-strict: a call or(True,y) would succeed whereas or(x,True) would suspend until x is given a value.

The parallel (non-strict) procedure for or seems to be the most natural, since otherwise the behaviour of the procedure would be crucially dependent upon the order of its arguments.

A very similar procedure defines the relation and(x,y): x *and* y both have the value True:

mode and(?,?).

and(True,True).   (AND)

The behaviour of this procedure is clarified by considering the standard form of its clause (Section 3.5). This shows that the two arguments are 'input matched' in parallel:

and(p1,p2) <− True <− p1, True <− p2 :.

This means that and is a non-strict procedure, so the two calls and(False,y) and and(x,False) will both fail. If the input matching were performed sequentially, in left–right order:

and(p1,p2) <− True <= p1 & True <= p2 :.

a call and(False,y) would fail but and(x,False) would suspend until x is given a value.

Having decided that the input matching should be performed concurrently, a natural consequence is that this should proceed in parallel with the guard evaluation. This is because the input matching may be done explicitly by calls in the guard, e.g.:

mode and(?,?).

and(True,y) <− True <= y :.

The standard form of this program is the same as that of program AND: the translation to standard form introduces a '<=' call for the first argument, in parallel with the one already in the guard.

Note that the programmer is not forced to accept the default method of translation to standard form: the input matching of arguments could be done sequentially if that is preferred, by explicitly writing the input matching calls in the guard.

The order of unification is a contentious point in Concurrent Prolog (Ueda, 1985b; Saraswat, 1985; Kusalik, 1985). The original definition of Concurrent Prolog dictates that unification is performed before the guard evaluation begins, but does not specify the order in which arguments are unified. Most implementations (e.g. Levy, 1984) perform the unification sequentially, left to right, presumably for pragmatic reasons. This means that the order of arguments is significant. In addition to programs like the and example above, which may either suspend or fail, it is possible to write programs which suspend or succeed, depending upon the order of arguments. This is a consequence of the properties of the read-only annotation in Concurrent Prolog.

3.7.5 Alternatives to modes

From the programmer's viewpoint, the main purpose of mode declarations in PARLOG is to control the parallel evaluation of a program. In this section, modes are compared with some of the other methods that have been proposed to control logic programs in a parallel or coroutining context.

Some languages allow control information to be given in relation calls, so that different calls to a given relation may behave differently. In others, the control is specified in the definition of the relation. The latter approach is more likely to admit efficient compilation.

Of the proposals in which control information is attached to procedures, some allow different control for each clause. In others, including PARLOG, the control specification applies to the entire procedure, though PARLOG allows individual clauses to override the default control if necessary.

3.7.5.1   Wait declarations

The **wait declarations** of MU-PROLOG (Naish, 1982, 1983) are probably the most closely related to PARLOG's modes. They have a slightly different purpose: to impose a constraint on full unification in a Prolog system.

Like PARLOG's mode declarations, the control is specified for each procedure rather than for each clause or for each relation call. Unlike PARLOG, there may be more than one wait declaration for a relation, or none at all.

Each wait declaration for a relation specifies a set of input arguments, i.e. arguments for which the unification of a call with a clause head *must not* generate an output substitution. If there is an attempt to perform an output substitution for these arguments, the call suspends. This is analogous to the input mode constraint of PARLOG. The other arguments of the call, in MU-PROLOG terminology, may be 'constructed': the unifier may include both input and output substitutions, just as with PARLOG's output arguments.

3.7.5.2   Triggers

A simpler, but less powerful, control mechanism is provided by **triggers** (e.g. Warren, 1979; Moss, 1980). A trigger usually takes the form of a declaration for a relation, stating a set of arguments which must be non-variable for the call to proceed. Naish (1983) shows that this is less powerful than wait declarations, and hence mode declarations. In particular, no trigger declaration can delay the evaluation of a call whose arguments are non-variable terms in the program, such as the recursive call in the third Ord clause of Program 2.3.

3.7.5.3   Thresholds

Wise (1982) proposes an even simpler concept than triggers, which he terms **thresholds**. A threshold states the number of arguments of a call that must be instantiated. If fewer arguments are non-variable, the call is delayed. Clearly, this technique is less general than triggers but, if it is applicable, several trigger declarations can be replaced by a single threshold declaration.

3.7.5.4   Read-only variables

There are several proposals that involve annotating relation *calls* in some manner, to cause the call to suspend in certain circumstances. Sometimes these annotations are permitted in a clause head as well as in a call, in which case they provide control linked to the procedure, as well as 'per call' control. One such annotation is the **delay** annotation (Dausmann *et al.*, 1980; Clark *et al.*, 1982; Wise, 1982) which, placed upon a variable in a call, causes the call to suspend until the variable is instantiated by another call. A variant of this is the **read-only** annotation ('?') of Concurrent Prolog (Shapiro, 1983).

In Concurrent Prolog, a **read-only variable** is an occurrence of a variable marked by the read-only annotation. If unification attempts to bind a read-only occurrence of a variable, the offending call suspends. It is reactivated when the variable is instantiated via some non-read-only occurrence.

The read-only variable appears to be inherently expensive to implement: it requires an elaboration of full unification that recognizes read-only variables. Because the control is attached to a call, some run-time overhead is unavoidable. An advantage of this is that a given procedure can be used in more than one 'mode of use'. However, as in Prolog, Concurrent Prolog procedures that can be used efficiently in more than one way are rare since calls in the clause bodies themselves contain read-only annotations, which fixes the direction of communication between calls.

Recent studies (Ueda, 1985b; Saraswat, 1985; Kusalik, 1985) have revealed serious problems with the semantics of the read-only variable in Concurrent Prolog. Saraswat concludes that the read-only variable is under-defined and that its definition cannot be extended in a consistent, 'reasonable' way.

3.7.5.5 *Global variables*

A new language in the same family as PARLOG and Concurrent Prolog has recently been proposed. This is Guarded Horn Clauses (GHC) (Ueda, 1985a), aptly named because the only variation from Horn clause syntax is the use of the guard. The elegant property of GHC is that its communication constraint coincides with the method of ensuring that call variables are not bound by a guard evaluation. Roughly, if a guard evaluation attempts to bind a call variable (or a body evaluation attempts to bind a guard variable) the attempt suspends.

This control mechanism relies upon a run-time test each time a variable is to be bound: if this variable is global, i.e. belongs to the caller, the call suspends. This test is essentially the same as the test that would be required in PARLOG if the safety of guards is checked at run time. An implementation scheme for GHC is described in Ito *et al.* (1985). The test of whether a variable is global appears to require, in general, special-purpose architectural support or a (possibly expensive) software test.

In contrast, the safety of guards in a PARLOG program is intended to be checked at compile time, so that there is no run-time overhead. The run-time test that PARLOG uses to cause a process suspension is very simple: a test of whether a variable is instantiated. Compile-time and run-time safety checks for PARLOG are discussed in Chapter 5.

3.7.6   Unification-related primitives of PARLOG

Section 3.5.1 introduced the primitives '<=', '==' and '=', which are introduced by the translation from PARLOG to Kernel PARLOG. There are two other primitives related to unification: data and var.

3.7.6.1   *The* data *primitive*

A call data(x) will suspend if x is an unbound variable. As soon as x is instantiated, the call succeeds. A call to data never fails. In the logical reading of a program, data calls should be ignored; they are used merely for control purposes.

A data test used in a guard to test an input argument of a clause acts as a generalized input match. The data test simply waits until the argument is instantiated, whereas an input match *additionally* checks that the argument matches a given pattern.

3.7.6.2   *The* var *primitive*

var is a metalogical primitive, as included in Prolog, to test whether a variable is unbound. A call var(x) will succeed if x is an unbound variable at the time of the call and fail otherwise. A call to var never suspends. This means that a call var(x) might succeed if evaluated at one time, but fail if evaluated later, after x has been instantiated.

Note that data(x) is not the same as a negated call ~ var(x). Both of these succeed if x is a non-variable term. However, if x is an unbound variable, data(x) suspends whereas ~ var(x) fails.

Like data tests, var calls should be ignored in the logical reading of a program; they are included purely for their control effect. *Unlike* data tests, the addition of a var test to a program may cause it to fail, where it would otherwise have succeeded. This does not affect the correctness of a program. If var is called, directly or indirectly, from a guard, its effect will be to potentially reduce the number of candidate clauses.

Nevertheless, var should be used carefully, since it may lead to a situation similar to that described in Section 3.2.6.2, but with a different cause. Namely, some solutions according to the declarative semantics might not be computable, because of the failure of an added var call.

The main use of the var primitive is to impose a priority among evaluation paths, as discussed in the next section.

3.8   Priority

Non-determinism arises in PARLOG when there is more than one candidate clause to solve a call. The solution computed depends upon the choice of candidate clause, to which the evaluation is committed. PARLOG does not specify which candidate clause should be selected if there is a choice.

This underspecification of the control may in some cases be undesirable: an implementation might consistently favour one of the alternatives over another, resulting in 'starvation'. For example, if merge is defined by the procedure in Program 3.2, a process merge(x,y,z) might continually use its first clause, thus accepting items from list x and ignoring those from list y (or vice versa) if there is data available on both arguments. Thus, if an item is available on one input argument list, it may wait indefinitely before appearing on the output list. Whether this happens will depend upon the way in which a particular implementation selects a candidate clause.

The original definition of CSP (Hoare, 1978), which inspired the committed choice non-determinism of PARLOG, left an implementor to decide how to select a command from a set of alternatives if more than one guard is executable. Bernstein (1980) considers that a programmer should have the ability to control the selection of an alternative. For this purpose, he proposes a priority function to be associated with each alternative.

Shapiro (Shapiro, 1983; Shapiro and Mierowsky, 1984) chooses to solve the problem by employing information about the implementation. He defines a 'stable' implementation of Concurrent Prolog as one that always selects the first candidate clause (in textual order). In a stable implementation, given the merge procedure of Program 3.2, the first clause will always be selected if the first and second clauses are both candidates, i.e. if there is data available on both input arguments. Then, the merge program will be *biased* to the first input stream. Shapiro shows how a biased merge can be changed to a *fair* merge procedure simply by interchanging the two input arguments in the recursive call to merge, thus alternating the priority given to each argument:

```
merge([u|x],y,[u|z]) <- merge(y,x,z).
merge(x,[v|y],[v|z]) <- merge(y,x,z).
```

The drawback of the stability assumption is that its validity depends upon the implementation strategy used. For example, Shapiro's (1983) definition of stability applies only to clauses with empty guards. While a particular implementation may well exhibit stability for such programs, others may not.

Therefore, the selection of a candidate clause should be controlled by explicit information in the program, rather than by making assumptions about the implementation. In PARLOG, this control can be achieved by the use of the var primitive, introduced in Section 3.7.6.2. To specify a priority among a number of candidate clauses, their guards can be selectively strengthened by adding var tests to them.

Program 3.14 defines a merge procedure biased to the first argument list. The declarative reading of the biased-merge relation is identical to that of merge (Program 3.2), since the extra var condition (in the second clause) is ignored in the logical reading. However, the programs behave differently. In a process evaluating biased-merge(x,y,z), if data is available on lists x and y, items from the first list x will be consumed in preference to those of y, for the following reason. The first clause is a candidate if the first argument is instantiated to a list pattern, regardless of the state of the second argument. The second clause is a candidate if the second argument is instantiated to a list *and the first argument is uninstantiated*, because of the var test in its guard.

```
mode biased-merge(?,?, ↑ ).

biased-merge([u|x],y,[u|z]) <− biased-merge(x,y,z).
biased-merge(x,[v|y],[v|z]) <− var(x) : biased-merge(x,y,z).
biased-merge([],y,y).
biased-merge(x,[],x).
```

Program 3.14   Biased merge.

The control effect of the added var test is to reduce the number of candidate clauses: the first and second clauses are *almost never* (see below) both candidate clauses in evaluating a call. In the event that both input arguments are instantiated to lists, only the first clause is a candidate because the var test in the second clause guard fails.

A pathological case in evaluating biased-merge(x,y,z) arises when y is already instantiated and x is bound to a list at some time *after* the beginning of the call evaluation but *before* the time of commitment. In this case, the second clause could be a candidate because var(x) succeeds when first evaluated, but when x is instantiated (so that var(x) would fail if evaluated now), the first clause also becomes a candidate. Therefore, either clause may be chosen. This means that an item arriving on the first argument stream during this time interval will not necessarily be consumed in this resolution step; it will, however, certainly be consumed in the next step, i.e. the recursive call to biased-merge.

The biased merge procedure of Program 3.14 could be changed to a fair merge using the above 'argument interchanging' technique. Alternatively, a fair merge can be programmed directly as in Program 3.15. In a call fair-merge(x,y,z), if items are available on *both* input argument lists an item is consumed from each of them in one resolution step; this is done by the third clause. The first and second clauses deal with the situation where there is data on only *one* argument, because of the var tests in their guards.

---

mode fair-merge(?,?, ↑).

fair-merge([u|x],y,[u|z]) <− var(y) : fair-merge(x,y,z).
fair-merge(x,[v|y],[v|z]) <− var(x) : fair-merge(x,y,z).
fair-merge([u|x],[v|y],[u,v|z]) <− fair-merge(x,y,z).
fair-merge([],y,y).
fair-merge(x,[],x).

Program 3.15 Fair merge.

The biased-merge procedure implements 'bounded waiting' for the first argument list: an item arriving on this list will have to wait no more than two resolution steps before it is passed to the output list. fair-merge implements bounded waiting for both input arguments.

This technique for imposing priority or fairness makes no assumptions about the implementation. The programs given here will behave as intended, whether or not the underlying system is 'stable'. The addition of var tests to guards in this manner does not give rise to the incompleteness problem noted at the end of Section 3.7.6.2. For example, in a call biased-merge(x,y,z), it is still the case that the computed value of z can be *any* interleaving of x and y, as specified by the declarative semantics. The added var tests merely make the value computed more dependent upon the behaviour. Hence, var can be regarded as a control 'annotation'.

The use of the var primitive for priority was considered by Broda and Gregory (1984) and Clark and Gregory (1986). It has (independently) been proposed for Concurrent Prolog by Kusalik (1984a) and Takeuchi (1983). Shapiro and Mierowsky (1984) discuss various aspects of fair and biased merge programs, not using the var primitive.

3.9 Metalevel programming

Many declarative programming languages, including Prolog and LISP, provide a metalevel programming facility, whereby a program may construct other programs and evaluate them. In Prolog, the metalevel facility is the **metacall** – a primitive which interprets an argument term as a relation call. A similar, but generalized, metacall is included in PARLOG.

3.9.1 The simple metacall primitive

The call primitive of PARLOG has mode (?). A call call(proc) suspends until proc is instantiated to a term denoting a PARLOG clause body (i.e. a relation call or a conjunction) and then behaves like proc. The logical reading of call(proc) is identical to that of proc. This facility allows a program to evaluate calls determined at run time.

Some form of metalevel facility simplifies the programming of command interpreters for operating systems (e.g. Clark and Gregory, 1983; Shapiro, 1983). Each command is defined by a PARLOG procedure; a stream of commands read from the user is a list of terms denoting calls to these procedures. Program 3.16 shows a simple command interpreter, or 'shell', written in PARLOG. shell(cmds) has the logical reading: cmds is a list of terms of the form BG(proc) or FG(proc), such that each proc is a term denoting a true condition.

```
mode shell(?).

shell([BG(proc)|cmds]) <- call(proc), shell(cmds)..
shell([FG(proc)|cmds]) <- call(proc) & shell(cmds)..
shell([]).
```

Program 3.16   Simple shell.

Operationally, the shell procedure interprets each term on its list argument as either a foreground or background command. For a background command BG(proc), the call denoted by proc is evaluated concurrently with a recursive invocation of shell. A foreground command FG(proc) is evaluated completely, prior to the recursive shell call; note the essential use of the sequential conjunction operator '&'.

There are two shortcomings with this simple shell program. First, if a command, proc, fails for any reason, call(proc) will fail so the shell evaluation will itself fail. Second, there is no way in which the evaluation of each command can be interrupted or otherwise controlled by the shell procedure; the commands must always run to completion. These problems were identified by Shapiro (1984) and solutions suggested, all of which involve evaluating the commands in guards. This technique is inadequate if a command process generates output, because no output is possible from a guard evaluation (see Section 3.2.4 and Chapter 5).

3.9.2   The control metacall primitive

The problems with the shell program of Program 3.16 stem from the fact that the user programs (commands) are evaluated at the same level as systems programs (the shell). Really, the operating system should be regarded as a metalevel program controlling user (object level) programs. An operating system is not concerned with the logical meaning of user programs and a failure of the latter should not cause the operating system to crash. From the viewpoint of the operating system, only the results generated by a user program are significant; they have no logical meaning to the system. Moreover, the system should have the ability to initiate, terminate and otherwise control the evaluation of a user program.

These observations lead to a generalization of the simple single-argument metacall. Two extra arguments are added to the call primitive: one input and one output. The three-argument metacall has mode (?, ↑ ,?): call(proc,status,control). This is the **control metacall**.

A call call(proc,status,control) *always succeeds*. It evaluates its first argument proc (a term denoting a relation call) as in the simple metacall. The result of evaluating proc (normally SUCCEEDED or FAILED) is given explicitly by output unification with the status argument. If another process binds the control argument to STOP, the evaluation of proc is terminated within a 'reasonable' finite time, and status is unified with STOPPED. Any output produced by the evaluation, on shared variables of proc, is made available to other processes immediately, even if the evaluation subsequently fails or is aborted.

Because the evaluation of the control metacall always succeeds, it has no logical reading. In fact, the evaluation can be regarded as a 'black box'; see Fig. 3.5. Any output produced by proc is treated in the same way as data from some external device: it has no logical significance to the metalevel program.

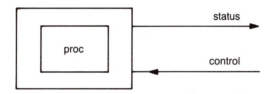

Fig 3.5 Control metacall evaluation.

The control metacall has a logical reading only if the evaluation succeeds; this can be verified by testing that the status argument is SUCCEEDED. For example, the simple metacall, which does have a logical reading, could be defined as follows:

```
mode call(?).

call(proc) <−
    call(proc,SUCCEEDED,control).
```

Program 3.17 is a more elaborate shell procedure, for the abort-shell relation, that uses the control metacall to overcome both of the objections to Program 3.16. In the first clause of abort-shell, a background command is evaluated in parallel with the recursive call to abort-shell. This clause is similar to the first clause of Program 3.16 except that the command is evaluated by the control metacall. Therefore, if the command fails, the shell evaluation will not itself fail. Any output already generated by the command will remain, but may not be complete.

For each foreground command received (the second clause), the command is evaluated in parallel with a process that searches for an ABORT command in the command stream, both evaluated by the control metacall. A third process, arb, monitors the result of both the command process and the search process. If the command terminates with a result of either SUCCEEDED or FAILED (tested by the data call in the guard of the first arb clause), a STOP message is sent to terminate the search process, and abort-shell is called recursively with command stream cmds (the stream beginning immediately after the command). If, instead, an ABORT is found before the command process terminates (the search process has SUCCEEDED), the command is aborted by a STOP message (from the second arb clause) and abort-shell is called recursively with the command stream acmds, beginning immediately following the ABORT. In this case, any commands entered between the current foreground command and the ABORT are ignored.

```
mode abort-shell(?), search(?,?, ↑ ), arb(?,?, ↑ , ↑ ,?,?).

abort-shell([BG(proc)|cmds]) <−
    call(proc,s,c), abort-shell(cmds)..
abort-shell([FG(proc)|cmds]) <−
    call(proc,s1,c1),
    call(search(ABORT,cmds,acmds),s2,c2),
    arb(s1,s2,c1,c2,abort-shell(cmds),abort-shell(acmds))..
abort-shell([]).

search(u,[u|x],x);
search(u,[v|x],y) <− search(u,x,y).

arb(s1,s2,c1,STOP,body1,body2) <− data(s1) : call(body1).
arb(s1,SUCCEEDED,STOP,c2,body1,body2) <− call(body2).
```

Program 3.17   Shell that allows interruption of foreground commands.

Notice that, in the second abort-shell clause of Program 3.17, the search procedure is evaluated via a control metacall:

```
call(search(ABORT,cmds,acmds),s2,c2)
```

Since the first argument of this control metacall is a non-variable, it is not really a metacall; the call primitive is used here only for its ability to control the evaluation. Such a use of the three-argument form of call, with the first argument instantiated, will therefore be given a different name: a **control call**.

It would have been possible to obtain the same effect by *transforming* the search procedure to a procedure with two extra arguments, say gen-search, which gives the result of the search explicitly and responds to a STOP message. Then the control call call(search(ABORT,cmds,acmds),s2,c2) could be replaced by an equivalent call:

gen-search(ABORT,cmds,acmds,s2,c2)

Any control call could, in principle, be replaced in this way by such a transformation, examples of which appear in Chapter 4. The use of the control metacall in the second abort-shell clause is essential, because the relation called is not known until run time.

Further features could be provided in the control call/metacall primitive. For example, the control argument could be generalized to be a stream of SUSPEND and CONTINUE messages, so that an operating system can temporarily suspend the evaluation of individual user programs. The status argument could have the value ERROR, as a means of handling errors. Some of these possibilities are discussed in Clark and Gregory (1984), where the application of the control metacall is discussed in detail.

The control call/metacall is proposed as a *primitive* of a PARLOG implementation. The properties described are believed to be easy to implement efficiently on any reasonable architecture, and sufficiently expressive to enable the programming of realistic operating system behaviour. It has some features in common with the simulate metapredicate earlier proposed for KL1 (Furukawa *et al.*, 1984), but the latter is intended as a powerful, general-purpose metainference predicate, some features of which appear to require an interpretive evaluation.

As well as its use in systems programming, the control call proves useful in compiling PARLOG programs into programs with simpler control. This is motivated in Chapter 4 and described fully in Chapter 5.

3.10   Negation

A negated call $\sim P$ has the logical reading 'not P', i.e. P is false. In PARLOG, as in most logic programming languages, negation is implemented as 'failure to prove'. That is, to evaluate a negated call $\sim P$, P is evaluated: then $\sim P$ succeeds if and only if P fails. This rule, which is usually known as **negation as failure** (Clark, 1978), has the benefit of being amenable to very straightforward implementation. Unfortunately, a failure to prove P cannot, in general, be taken as a proof that P is false.

Clark (1978) discusses the relationship between proof failure and logical falsity. The two concepts are equivalent only under the **closed world assumption**, i.e. the assumption that a program contains a complete definition of its relations. This assumption can be made explicit by adding extra laws to the program. For example, the Parent definition of Program 2.1 is augmented by the implication:

$$(\forall x,y)[\text{Parent}(x,y) \rightarrow [x = \text{Alice} \wedge y = \text{Caspar}] \vee$$
$$[x = \text{Caspar} \wedge y = \text{Eric}] \vee$$
$$[x = \text{Alice} \wedge y = \text{Brian}] \vee$$
$$[x = \text{Alice} \wedge y = \text{Dexter}]]$$

in addition to rules stating the inequality of distinct constants. ('=' has been used here to mean logical equality; it should not be confused with the unification primitive of PARLOG.) The above implication is the **completion law**. It states that the *only* solutions to the Parent relation are those implied by the relation definition. The original definition of Parent together with the completion law is equivalent to an 'if and only if' definition:

$$(\forall x,y)[\text{Parent}(x,y) \leftrightarrow [x = \text{Alice} \wedge y = \text{Caspar}] \vee$$
$$[x = \text{Caspar} \wedge y = \text{Eric}] \vee$$
$$[x = \text{Alice} \wedge y = \text{Brian}] \vee$$
$$[x = \text{Alice} \wedge y = \text{Dexter}]]$$

from which a failure to prove Parent(x,y) can be interpreted as a proof that Parent(x,y) is logically false.

3.10.1 Negation as failure in PARLOG

3.10.1.1 The completion law

To justify negation as failure in PARLOG, the completion law must be implicitly added to the program in the manner outlined above for a general logic program. The completion law for an arbitrary PARLOG program is obtained most easily by considering a PARLOG program in which each clause is in standard form (Section 3.5):

$$R(x_1,\ldots,x_k) <- G_1 : B_1..$$
$$R(x_1,\ldots,x_k) <- G_2 : B_2..$$
$$\ldots$$
$$R(x_1,\ldots,x_k) <- G_n : B_n.$$

Suppose that the guard and body of the ith clause (G_i and B_i) contain, apart from $x_1,\ldots,x_k$, variables $y_{i,1},\ldots,y_{i,mi}$. Then the definition of relation R is strengthened to:

$$(\forall x_1,\ldots,x_k)[R(x_1,\ldots,x_k) \leftrightarrow (\exists y_{1,1},\ldots,y_{1,m1})[G_1 \wedge B_1] \vee$$
$$(\exists y_{2,1},\ldots,y_{2,m2})[G_2 \wedge B_2] \vee$$
$$\ldots$$
$$(\exists y_{n,1},\ldots,y_{n,mn})[G_n \wedge B_n]]$$

of which the 'if half' is the original definition and the 'only if half' is the completion law.

3.10.1.2 *The sufficient guards law*

Because of the committed choice operational semantics of PARLOG, an additional implicit law is necessary to justify negation as failure:

For all i and j such that $1 \leqslant i,j \leqslant n$:
$$(\forall y_{i,1},\dots,y_{i,mi},y_{j,1},\dots,y_{j,mj})[G_i \wedge G_j \to [B_i \leftrightarrow B_j]]$$

This is just a more precise statement of the sufficient guards property stated in Section 3.2.6.1, i.e. if the guard G_i of a clause is true (so the ith clause is a candidate), its body B_i is true if and only if the body of every other candidate clause is true. To state it differently: if guard G_i succeeds but body B_i fails, there is *no* clause that has a successfully terminating guard and body.

The sufficient guards law ensures that, in evaluating a relation call, the commitment to a particular candidate clause (which excludes alternative candidate clauses) will not affect the ultimate success or failure of the call. Hence, the failure of the computation of a relation call can be interpreted as logical falsity.

3.10.2   Implementation of negation

Negation as failure can be implemented in PARLOG in terms of a sequential clause search. The metapredicate '~' can be defined by a metalogical procedure (Program 3.18), very similar to that used to define negation in Prolog. FAIL is a PARLOG primitive which always fails; it has the logical reading *false* but is usually, as here, used only for its control effect. A negated call $\sim P$ is evaluated by running P in the guard of the first clause; if this succeeds, the clause commits and the $\sim P$ call fails. If the P evaluation fails, $\sim P$ succeeds.

```
mode ~ ?.

~ p <- call(p) : FAIL;
~ p.
```

Program 3.18 Definition of negation.

The semantics of negation as failure apply only if the evaluation of a negated call does not bind any variables in the call. Clark (1978) suggests a stronger condition: that the arguments of a negated call should be ground at the time of call. The conventional implementation of negation in Prolog does not enforce any restriction on variable binding, but some more sophisticated logic programming systems do. MU-PROLOG (Naish, 1982) delays the evaluation of a negated call until its arguments are ground. IC-PROLOG does not insist that arguments are ground, but tests at run time that no variables are bound by the evaluation of a negated call; such a test is potentially expensive. The logic programming system described by Hansson *et al.* (1982), based on natural deduction, implements full negation rather than negation as failure, so no restrictions on binding call variables are necessary to ensure correctness.

An interesting property of Program 3.18 is that the prohibition on binding variables in the negated call is identical to the requirement that the guard (of the first clause for '~') is safe; see Section 3.2.4. Therefore, the PARLOG implementation of negation as failure requires no special mechanism to ensure correctness.

The safety of the guard containing call(p) can be guaranteed either by a run-time safety check or by a sophisticated compile-time analysis that checks the possible values that p may take. This analysis must check all calls to '~' to ensure that '~' is only ever called with an argument which is a call, all of whose arguments are strong input arguments. If this property is satisfied, it follows that the guard call(p) is safe. Compile-time and run-time safety checks are discussed in Chapter 5.

Independently, Ueda – in an early draft of (Ueda, 1985a) – has suggested a similar implementation of negation as failure in the new language GHC. That language uses PARLOG's guard safety constraint as its (only) synchronization mechanism, so the GHC equivalent of Program 3.18 will suspend on an attempt to bind variables in a negated call; this requires a run-time safety test.

3.11   Set constructors

Because of the committed choice non-determinism of PARLOG, no more than one solution to a query can be computed by any single evaluation. This makes the language unsuitable for applications such as problem solving programs and deductive databases. In such applications, some or all solutions to a query are required, i.e. don't-know non-determinism (Section 2.5.2).

To allow the use of PARLOG for these applications, the language is extended so that relations may, if desired, be defined using pure Horn clauses, without the guards, mode declarations and other control facilities of PARLOG, e.g. sequential and parallel operators. These **all-solutions relations** are defined by sequences of Prolog-style clauses, like the programs in Chapter 2, and are evaluated using don't-know non-determinism. No relation may be defined by both an all-solutions program and a normal (**single-solution**) PARLOG program.

All-solutions relations may call single-solution PARLOG relations, including primitives such as '<', plus, etc. Calls to these relations compute a single solution in the normal manner.

The interface that enables a PARLOG program to evaluate an all-solutions program is the **set constructor** primitive. In the spirit of the functional logic program interpreter of Section 2.5.4, the output of a set constructor is a single solution which is a *bag*, represented as a list, of some or all of the solutions to an all-solutions program.

As noted in Section 2.5.4.3, the list of solutions may usefully be computed in various ways. PARLOG provides two set constructors, differing in the computation strategy they use. The **eager** set constructor computes all solutions to a query, either sequentially or using some of the forms of parallelism outlined in Section 2.6. The **lazy** set constructor evaluates the solution list by demand, finding as many of the solutions as required; this yields a sequential, Prolog-like, backtracking behaviour. Since the use of the lazy set constructor relies upon a special PARLOG programming technique, to be presented in Chapter 4, its description is deferred to Section 4.4.

Set constructors are an important feature of the lazy functional language KRC (Turner, 1981), which inspired their inclusion in PARLOG. Several recent proposals for integrating functional and logic languages incorporate set constructors as an interface between the two languages, (e.g. Darlington *et al.*, 1985; Reddy, 1985b; Finn, 1985); this is analogous to their role in PARLOG, where they act as an interface between don't-care and don't-know non-determinism. In IC-PROLOG (Clark *et al.*, 1982), a set constructor is provided; this may be evaluated incrementally, using coroutining or parallel control, like any other IC-PROLOG relation. In contrast, Moss (1983) and Kahn (1984) both suggest the addition of a general (possibly lazy) set constructor to Prolog as a means of extending Prolog to allow coroutining or parallel evaluation.

Note that the set constructor primitives, especially the eager one, also provide an appropriate interface between PARLOG and relational databases.

3.11.1   The eager set constructor of PARLOG

The eager set constructor in PARLOG is similar in use to the corresponding primitive of Prolog, sometimes named bagof. The set primitive has the mode ($\uparrow$,?,?):

    set(solutions,term,conjunction)

where conjunction is a conjunction of calls to all-solutions relations. The set call is intended to bind solutions (assuming it is an unbound variable), perhaps incrementally, to a list of the different instantiations of term given by *all* of the successful evaluations of conjunction. The solutions list generated incrementally by the set call can be consumed by another relation call in parallel.

As an example, the Sibling relation of Program 2.1 can be evaluated from a PARLOG program by a call:

set(solutions,x,Sibling(x,Caspar))

This binds solutions to the list [Brian,Dexter] *or* [Dexter,Brian]. The Perm relation of Program 2.3 can be evaluated by a call such as:

set(solutions,z,Perm([3,v,1],z))

Here, solutions is bound to the list of all permutations of the given list:

[[3,v1,1],[3,1,v2],[v3,3,1],[v4,1,3],[1,3,v5],[1,v6,3]]

in some order. Notice that each solution contains a different variable as a copy of v.

Beyond the requirement that all solutions to a query are generated, the operational semantics of set is not precisely specified. This allows a PARLOG system to implement it as in most Prolog systems, by a sequential backtracking search for solutions. However, its implementation provides an opportunity to exploit OR parallelism (Section 2.6.3), perhaps combined with some form of all-solutions AND parallelism (Sections 2.6.1–2.6.2) and restricted AND parallelism (Section 2.6.4). In Clark and Gregory (1985), a possible OR parallel operational semantics for the set 'primitive' is defined by a PARLOG program for set, in which an OR parallel search is realized by the AND parallelism of PARLOG.

To permit an OR parallel implementation of set, the order of solutions in the solution list is deliberately not specified. An effect of this is that a program called from set must not use the cut primitive; the cut has a valid control use only in a sequential evaluation.

3.11.2 Negation for all-solutions relations

Because all-solutions relations are evaluated using don't-know non-determinism, negation as failure has the conventional semantics, discussed by Clark (1978). The negation of a conjunction P is inferred from the failure to prove P. Program 3.19 defines negation for all-solutions relations by a metalogical PARLOG program; this differs from Program 3.18 which defines negation for normal, single-solution, relations. A call not(p) is evaluated by checking that the list of solutions to p – a conjunction of all-solutions relation calls – is empty.

---

mode not(?).

not(p) <− set([],T,p).

Program 3.19 Negation for all-solutions relations.

4
Programming in PARLOG

One purpose of this chapter is to illustrate further the use of PARLOG by means of more substantial example programs than those presented in Chapter 3. In particular, these examples demonstrate techniques whereby PARLOG programs can be transformed to others with different control but the same declarative and operational semantics.

The first section explains how sequential evaluation can be achieved by the use of mode constraints rather than by explicit sequential operators. Section 4.2 demonstrates how an OR parallel evaluation of alternative clause guards can be transformed to AND parallel evaluation.

The operational semantics of PARLOG specifies that processes are evaluated eagerly. In some cases, however, lazy evaluation is desirable. Section 4.3 explains how lazy evaluation can be obtained by a transformation approach: an eager PARLOG program is transformed to another which exhibits 'lazy' behaviour. The final section describes and illustrates PARLOG's lazy set constructor primitive; this can be used to obtain the backtracking behaviour of Prolog.

4.1 Eliminating sequential conjunction

As explained in Section 3.3.3, a PARLOG program that uses a sequential conjunction operator '&' can always be transformed to one with only parallel conjunction by introducing a synchronization flag or 'control token'. This transformation is illustrated here by a program for the quicksort algorithm.

4.1.1 A parallel algorithm

Consider first the sort relation defined in Program 4.1. The logical reading of sort(list,sorted) is: sorted is a list containing the same items as list, but

95

ordered by the '=<' partial ordering relation. The sort relation is defined in terms of qsort, which has the same logical reading but represents the sorted list as a **difference list**.

```
mode sort(?, ↑ ), qsort(?, ↑ ,?), partition(?,?, ↑ , ↑ ).

sort(list,sorted) <−
    qsort(list,sorted,[]).

qsort([u|x],sorted-h,sorted-t) <−
    partition(u,x,x1,x2),
    qsort(x1,sorted-h,[u|sorted]),
    qsort(x2,sorted,sorted-t)..
qsort([],sorted,sorted).
```

Program 4.1   Parallel quicksort.

The logical reading of qsort(list,sorted-h,sorted-t) is: the ordered version of list is the difference between sorted-h and sorted-t, i.e. all elements on the list sorted-h up to the sublist sorted-t. To sort the list [u|x], x is split into two lists x1 and x2 by the partition procedure of Program 3.11 and each of these lists is itself sorted by a recursive qsort call. The sorted versions of x1 and x2 are implicitly concatenated, with u inserted, by the requirement that the sorted x1 is the difference between sorted-h and [u|sorted] *and* the sorted x2 is the difference between sorted and sorted-t.

4.1.1.1   *Difference lists in PARLOG*

The difference list representation as a logic programming technique was first formalized by Clark and Tarnlund (1977). It is widely exploited in Prolog programming since it allows lists to be concatenated in constant time.

In PARLOG programs, a difference list is represented by a pair of arguments: one input and one output. This can be visualized by considering the graphical representation of the program. Fig. 4.1 shows the graphs corresponding to the head and body of the first qsort clause of Program 4.1. A qsort call is a process producing a list on sorted-h (an output argument) whose tail is input on argument sorted-t. The process forks into three processes: a partition call and two recursive qsort calls. Because the output of one qsort process is connected to the input of the other, with the pivot argument u added as the first item of this list, the sorted lists are automatically appended.

4.1.2   **Constraining the parallelism**

As explained in Sections 3.3 and 3.4, PARLOG allows the degree of parallelism in a program to be controlled by the use of sequential

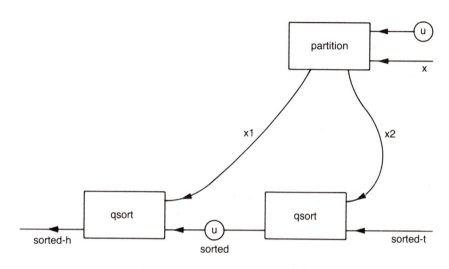

Fig 4.1 Graphical representation of qsort clause.

operators. An alternative version of quicksort is defined in Program 4.2. Here, sort is defined in terms of seq-qsort which has the same logical reading as qsort but different behaviour. Because of the sequential '&' following the partition call in the first seq-qsort clause, a seq-qsort process will not immediately fork. The partition call must terminate before the seq-qsort process forks into two parallel seq-qsort processes.

```
mode sort(?, ↑ ), seq-qsort(?, ↑ ,?), partition(?,?, ↑ , ↑ ).

sort(list,sorted) <−
    seq-qsort(list,sorted,[]).

seq-qsort([u|x],sorted-h,sorted-t) <−
    partition(u,x,x1,x2) &
    (seq-qsort(x1,sorted-h,[u|sorted]),
     seq-qsort(x2,sorted,sorted-t))..
seq-qsort([],sorted,sorted).
```

Program 4.2 Sequential/parallel quicksort.

4.1.3   Transformation to eliminate sequential conjunction

As demonstrated in Section 3.3.3, sequential evaluation can be enforced by the mode constraints of PARLOG. Any uses of the sequential conjunction operator '&' can therefore be removed by transformation to an alternative program in which the same sequencing effect is obtained by modes.

In general, each sequential conjunction of the form:

$$C_1 \ \& \ C_2$$

can be replaced by a *parallel* conjunction:

R1(s), R2(s)

where s is the synchronization flag, a new shared variable. In addition, R1 and R2 must have as arguments any non-local variables used in conjunctions C_1 and C_2 respectively; these are ignored here. R1 has mode ($\uparrow$) and is defined such that it evaluates the conjunction C_1 and, *when C_1 has terminated*, binds its s argument to the constant SUCCEEDED. R2 has mode (?) and simply waits for the s argument to be instantiated to SUCCEEDED before it evaluates C_2. In this way, a synchronization signal sent from R1 to R2 ensures that C_1 is evaluated sequentially before C_2; if C_1 fails, R1 fails and R2 is never evaluated.

The program for R2 can be obtained quite easily and automatically. It takes the form:

mode R2(?).

R2(SUCCEEDED) <− C_2.

(ignoring the extra arguments required to carry shared variables to C_2).

In the procedure for R1, the sequential '&' cannot be used to ensure that the s argument is bound after C_1 has terminated. It must therefore be derived by a transformation of the procedures for the relations called from C_1. This transformation may, in general, require user guidance.

In the first seq-qsort clause of Program 4.2, the evaluation of the partition call must successfully terminate before the remainder of the clause body is evaluated. The alternative seq-qsort procedure in Program 4.3 exhibits the same behaviour (and has the same logical reading). In the first clause of the new seq-qsort procedure, the partition call has been replaced by a call to a new relation partition-s which has an extra argument, s. This call is evaluated in parallel with a call to an auxiliary relation qsort1 which replaces the remainder of the original clause. The arguments of the qsort1 call are s, together with all of the variables that are used in the part of the original clause that the call replaces.

```
mode seq-qsort(?, ↑ ,?), partition-s(?,?, ↑ , ↑ , ↑ ), qsort1(?,?,?,?, ↑ ,?).

seq-qsort([u|x],sorted-h,sorted-t) <−
    partition-s(u,x,x1,x2,s),
    qsort1(s,u,x1,x2,sorted-h,sorted-t)..
seq-qsort([],sorted,sorted).

qsort1(SUCCEEDED,u,x1,x2,sorted-h,sorted-t) <−
    seq-qsort(x1,sorted-h,[u|sorted]),
    seq-qsort(x2,sorted,sorted-t).

partition-s(u,[v|x],[v|x1],x2,s) <− v < u :
    partition-s(u,x,x1,x2,s)..
partition-s(u,[v|x],x1,[v|x2],s) <− u =< v :
    partition-s(u,x,x1,x2,s)..
partition-s(u,[],[],[],SUCCEEDED).
```

Program 4.3   Quicksort using synchronization flag.

The procedure for qsort1 is obtained as described above, so that when its first (input) argument is bound to SUCCEEDED, the two seq-qsort calls will be evaluated in parallel. In this example, the derivation of the partition-s procedure is also quite straightforward. It is identical to the original partition procedure, except for the extra argument, s. Since the only way in which a partition process may terminate successfully is by the use of its third clause (an assertion) this clause is changed so that it unifies the s argument with SUCCEEDED.

It is worth noting that the same effect could be obtained without the need to transform the partition procedure, by using the control call primitive of PARLOG (Section 3.9.2). The control call always unifies its status argument with SUCCEEDED upon the termination of its argument call, so partition-s could be defined as follows:

```
mode partition-s(?,?, ↑ , ↑ , ↑ ).

partition-s(u,x,x1,x2,s) <−
    call(partition(u,x,x1,x2),SUCCEEDED,c).
```

4.2   Eliminating OR parallel search

As explained in Chapter 3, PARLOG requires all clause guards to be 'safe' in order that variables in a call are instantiated only after commitment to a clause, i.e. in the body. As will be discussed in Chapter 5, this property can (and should) be verified by a compile-time check. The knowledge that guards are safe means that no special mechanism is required to support the OR parallel evaluation of guards, which can therefore be transformed to an AND parallel evaluation. The on-tree procedure of Program 3.7 will be used to illustrate this transformation.

4.2.1 Making the result explicit

As a first step, the on-tree procedure is transformed to one for on-tree-s, which *always succeeds* but gives the result of the evaluation (SUCCEEDED or FAILED) as an extra argument. on-tree can then be defined in terms of on-tree-s. The logical reading of on-tree-s(key,value,tree,s) is:

P(key,value) is on tree and s = SUCCEEDED, or
P(key,value) is not on tree and s = FAILED.

---

mode on-tree(?, ↑ ,?), on-tree-s(?, ↑ ,?, ↑).

on-tree(key,value,tree) <−
    on-tree-s(key,value,tree,SUCCEEDED).

on-tree-s(key,value,T(x,P(key,value),y),SUCCEEDED);
on-tree-s(key,value,T(x,P(rkey,rvalue),y),SUCCEEDED) <−
    on-tree(key,value,x) :.
on-tree-s(key,value,T(x,P(rkey,rvalue),y),SUCCEEDED) <−
    on-tree(key,value,y) :;
on-tree-s(key,value,tree,FAILED).

Program 4.4 Tree search program with explicit result.

In Program 4.4, the first clause for on-tree-s handles the case where the pair P(key,value) lies at the root node of the tree; then, the result is SUCCEEDED. Otherwise, the second and third clauses are tried. These clauses search each branch of the tree in parallel, because of the '.' between the clauses. If the search fails, the fourth clause will be used: this unifies the result argument with FAILED.

4.2.2 Transformation to eliminate OR parallel search

To replace OR parallel search by AND parallelism, the second and third clauses of on-tree-s are collapsed into a single clause whose guard performs the function of both of the original guards; see Program 4.5. The new guard contains two on-tree-s calls: one that searches for the given key on the left subtree x and another that searches y; these are evaluated in AND parallel. A third AND parallel call, to combine-s, monitors the result arguments xs and ys.

If both of the on-tree-s calls yields a FAILED result, the combine-s call will fail, thus failing the guard, so the third clause will be used and the overall result will be FAILED. Otherwise, i.e. if one or both of the on-tree-s calls produces a SUCCEEDED result, combine-s will succeed and bind value to the value output by the successful recursive on-tree-s call.

```
mode on-tree-s(?, ↑ ,?, ↑ ), combine-s(?,?,?,?, ↑ ).

on-tree-s(key,value,T(x,P(key,value),y),SUCCEEDED);
on-tree-s(key,value,T(x,P(rkey,rvalue),y),SUCCEEDED) <−
    on-tree-s(key,xvalue,x,xs),
    on-tree-s(key,yvalue,y,ys),
    combine-s(xs,ys,xvalue,yvalue,value) :;
on-tree-s(key,value,tree,FAILED).

combine-s(SUCCEEDED,ys,xvalue,yvalue,xvalue).
combine-s(xs,SUCCEEDED,xvalue,yvalue,yvalue).
```

Program 4.5   Tree search program with AND parallelism.

Program 4.5 still uses the parallel clause search operator '.' in the procedure for combine-s. But notice that the guards of the (Kernel PARLOG) procedure for combine-s contain only matching calls, not calls to programmer-defined relations. That is, the '.' is used only to realize non-determinism, not to exploit OR parallelism. This use of '.' can be implemented by a sequential algorithm such as that described in Chapter 7; there is no need for (real or simulated) parallelism.

4.2.3   Early termination

The on-tree-s procedure in Program 4.5 does not behave exactly like that in Program 4.4. The difference is that, in the second clause, both of the recursive on-tree-s calls will always be evaluated to completion. Moreover, the output unification in the second clause will not be performed until both of the guard calls have terminated. The net effect is that the entire tree must always be searched and the result of this exhaustive search is not known until it is complete.

The desired behaviour, as exhibited by Program 4.4, is that the search should be aborted as soon as the item is found on one of the branches. This can be achieved by a slightly different transformation. Program 4.6 defines a new relation on-tree-sc with an extra argument for control purposes. The logical reading of on-tree-sc(key,value,tree,s,c) is:

P(key,value) is on tree and s = SUCCEEDED, or
P(key,value) is not on tree and s = FAILED, or
s = STOPPED and c = STOP.

```
mode on-tree(?, ↑ ,?), on-tree-sc(?, ↑ ,?, ↑ ,?),
   combine-sc(?,?, ↑ ,?,?, ↑ , ↑ , ↑ ,?).

on-tree(key,value,tree) <−
   on-tree-sc(key,value,tree,SUCCEEDED,c).

on-tree-sc(key,value,tree,STOPPED,STOP).
(on-tree-sc(key,value,T(x,P(key,value),y),SUCCEEDED,c);
 on-tree-sc(key,value,T(x,P(rkey,rvalue),y),s,c) <−
     on-tree-sc(key,xvalue,x,xs,xc),
     on-tree-sc(key,yvalue,y,ys,yc),
     combine-sc(xs,ys,s,xvalue,yvalue,value,xc,yc,c) :;
 on-tree-sc(key,value,tree,FAILED,c)).

combine-sc(xs,ys,STOPPED,xval,yval,val,STOP,STOP,STOP).
combine-sc(SUCCEEDED,ys,SUCCEEDED,xval,yval,xval,xc,STOP,c).
combine-sc(xs,SUCCEEDED,SUCCEEDED,xval,yval,yval,STOP,yc,c).
```

Program 4.6   AND parallel tree search program with early termination.

A call on-tree-sc(key,val,tree,s,c) *may* succeed with s bound to STOPPED, in the event that c is bound to STOP by some other process.

on-tree-sc and combine-sc differ from their counterparts in Program 4.5 in that they each have an extra clause to allow for the possibility of early termination. The first clause for on-tree-sc tests for early termination in parallel with a *sequential* search among the remaining clauses, whose structure reflects that of Program 4.5. In the guard of the third clause for on-tree-sc, a process is created to search each subtree together with a combine-sc process.

Like combine-s of Program 4.5, a combine-sc call monitors xs and ys, the result arguments of the two on-tree-sc processes. It also monitors its c input argument, using the first clause of its procedure. If this c argument is STOP, a STOP message is sent to both of the on-tree-sc processes. If one of the on-tree-sc processes produces the result SUCCEEDED, on xs or ys, combine-sc will send a STOP message to the other on-tree-sc process.

To achieve the same behaviour as Program 4.4, a further small change is necessary. In a call on-tree-sc(key,value,tree,s,c) where c is bound to STOP, the first on-tree-sc clause is a candidate but there is no guarantee that it will be selected, since the other clauses may well also be candidates. To ensure that the process will always terminate when c is STOP, priority must be given to the first clause, using the technique presented in Section 3.8.

An extra call not-STOP(c) must be added to the guard of the second on-tree-sc clause, since this clause is competing with the first clause for candidacy (the third and fourth clauses will not be tested for candidacy until after the second clause has been tried and has failed). The added guard test fails if the c argument is not bound to STOP, i.e. if it is bound to another term or is an unbound variable. The call not-STOP(c) should therefore be added to the guard of the second clause:

    on-tree-sc(key,value,T(x,P(key,value),y),SUCCEEDED,c) <−
        not-STOP(c) :.

not-STOP is defined by the following simple procedure:

    mode not-STOP(?).

    not-STOP(c) <− var(c) :;
    not-STOP(c) <− ~ c == STOP.

This change does not affect the logical reading of on-tree-sc: the call not-STOP(c) should be ignored. It is added for its operational effect: it increases the likelihood of termination by making the second on-tree-sc clause a non-candidate if the first clause is a candidate.

Note that a call:

    on-tree-sc(key,value,tree,s,c)

is identical to the original on-tree relation, called by the control call primitive (Section 3.9.2):

    call(on-tree(key,value,tree),s,c)

Indeed, using the control call primitive, an OR parallel search can be *compiled* to an AND parallel evaluation, without the need for user-guided transformation. Chapter 5 demonstrates how OR parallel search can be eliminated by such a compilation process, again using on-tree as an example.

4.3 Lazy programming

4.3.1 Non-terminating programs

It is quite possible in PARLOG to write programs that construct infinite data structures. As an example, consider the classic problem due to Hamming (Dijkstra, 1976): to 'generate in increasing order the sequence of all numbers divisible by no primes other than 2, 3 or 5'. Program 4.7 defines the hamming relation, whose solution is this (infinite) list of numbers. It is the PARLOG equivalent of the functional program given by Kahn and MacQueen (1977).

```
mode hamming( ↑ ), timeslist(?,?, ↑ ), amerge(?,?, ↑ ).

hamming([1|x]) <−
    timeslist(2,[1|x],x2),
    timeslist(3,[1|x],x3),
    timeslist(5,[1|x],x5),
    amerge(x2,x3,x23), amerge(x23,x5,x).

timeslist(u,[v|y],[w|z]) <−
    times(u,v,w) and timeslist(u,y,z).

amerge([u|x],[u|y],[u|z]) <−
    amerge(x,y,z)..
amerge([u|x],[v|y],[u|z]) <− u < v :
    amerge(x,[v|y],z)..
amerge([u|x],[v|y],[v|z]) <− v < u :
    amerge([u|x],y,z).
```

Program 4.7   Eager program for Hamming's problem.

The hamming procedure of Program 4.7 generates the desired list by multiplying each member of it by 2, 3 and 5 to obtain lists x2, x3 and x5 respectively. The list is then obtained by merging these three lists in arithmetic order, omitting duplicates, and adding the number 1 to the beginning. Because these activities are performed concurrently, the result is constructed incrementally in finite time. To view the solution, the program can be run by a query of the form:

: hamming(h), writelist(h).

so that the list is displayed while it is being generated, Fig. 4.2 depicts the evaluation of Program 4.7. The channel labelled <output> in the figure might be connected to a consumer process such as writelist.

The logical reading of timeslist(u,y,z) is: z contains every member of list y, multiplied by u. amerge(x,y,z) has the logical reading: if x and y are ordered lists, z is an ordered list containing the same members as x and y with duplicates excluded. Because the base clauses have been omitted from the timeslist and amerge procedures, they are defined only for infinite lists. The semantics of non-terminating logic programs are discussed by van Emden and de Lucena (1982).

Although non-terminating procedures such as hamming can be run in PARLOG and produce useful results, they are rarely useful in practical programs, for two reasons.

First, PARLOG processes are eager: the only constraint on their evaluation is the input mode constraint, i.e. a process may suspend waiting for an input argument that is not available. There is nothing to prevent a

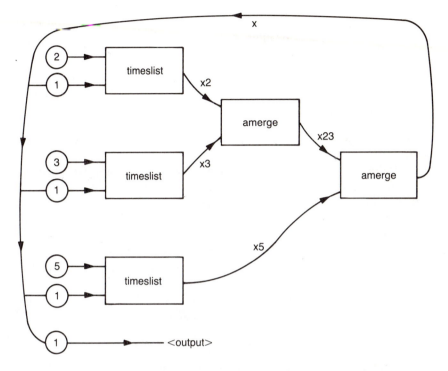

Fig 4.2   Evaluation of hamming program.

producer from running ahead of its consumer processes to an arbitrary extent. For example, hamming has no input arguments so it can never suspend; it may generate items on its output list faster than they can be consumed by other processes, possibly filling all available memory.

Second, there is no way to terminate the evaluation of a process prematurely: an infinite process such as hamming will never terminate unless the entire program is aborted. (The control call primitive (Section 3.9.2) could be used for early termination, but this would destroy the logical reading so it will not be considered here.)

The first problem could be solved by adopting a lazy computation rule (Section 2.4.3.2). This is more natural in functional than logic languages because, in functional programs, an unevaluated (suspended) expression always has a single process responsible for evaluating it; to demand the value of an expression, the associated process is activated. In a logic program, however, an unknown value is represented by an unbound variable. In general, it is not possible to identify automatically a single process that will ultimately bind the variable. Logic programming systems that incorporate demand-driven evaluation, e.g. IC-PROLOG (Clark and McCabe, 1979; Clark *et al.*, 1982) and the system of Hansson *et al.* (1982), therefore usually allow the programmer to designate a single producer call for each variable.

Functional programming languages, with the lazy computation rule, also allow the evaluation of an expression to be prematurely terminated when its value is no longer required. For example, an expression sublist(20,hamming) might evaluate to the list of the first 20 elements of the infinite hamming list; when the first 20 elements of hamming have been demanded, the sublist call is complete, so the hamming expression is automatically terminated. However, in the PARLOG query:

: hamming(h), sublist(20,h,y).

the hamming call would never terminate, regardless of the definition of sublist.

To allow the early termination of a call in a logic programming language, it would be necessary to verify that there are no active consumers of any variables of which the call is the producer. In the presence of back communication (Section 3.6), it is potentially very difficult to determine automatically the variables that might be bound by a particular call.

Also, the termination of the evaluation of a call is logically justifiable only if the relation is known to be total over some domain. In PARLOG, this means that a solution for the output arguments of a call exists for all values of the input arguments. Supposing that the mode declaration for R states that the first i arguments are input and the rest are output, there is an implicit law:

$$\forall x_1,\ldots,x_i \; \exists x_{i+1},\ldots,x_k \; R(x_1,\ldots,x_i,\ldots,x_k)$$

For example, the premature termination of hamming(x) is logically justified only under the assumption:

$\exists x \; \text{hamming(x)}$

Informally, the implicit law ensures that a terminated call would not have failed subsequently if it had not been terminated.

The totality assumption in PARLOG is a generalization of a similar assumption in functional programming: functions are assumed to be total.

The logic programming language of Hansson *et al.* (1982) allows functions to be defined by equational programs. Using a lazy computation rule, the evaluation of such functions is terminated when the consumers have terminated. A similar facility was provided in an early version of PARLOG (Clark and Gregory, 1983). IC-PROLOG allowed the demand-driven, coroutined evaluation of *relation* calls; however, that language does not provide for early termination of calls.

PARLOG does not provide lazy evaluation or early termination of processes at the implementation level, since that would make the language more difficult to implement, especially on a parallel machine. An alternative means of achieving the desired behaviour is by a transformation approach. A PARLOG program that gives eager, possibly non-terminating, behaviour can be *transformed* to another PARLOG program that exhibits the same behaviour as the original program would if evaluated on a system with lazy operational semantics. In the PARLOG program resulting from the transformation, the demand-driven behaviour is made explicit by using messages with variables and the technique of back communication (Section 3.6.1). The transformed program is usually less clear than the original, but can be obtained systematically from the original program.

These techniques for obtaining lazy evaluation were first presented by Takeuchi and Furukawa (1983) in an implementation of bounded-buffer communication in Concurrent Prolog.

The non-terminating procedure of Program 4.7 will be transformed to a lazy equivalent in Section 4.3.3. First, a simpler example is considered in order to introduce some of the techniques involved.

4.3.2   Transformation of a terminating program

Consider the flatten procedure of Program 3.1. A call flatten(tree,list) will *eagerly* flatten the given tree and produce the list of node labels on its output argument. Suppose that it is desired to flatten a tree in a demand-driven manner. That is, another process is to demand successive elements of the label list, one at a time. Each time a demand is received, the flatten process should perform only sufficient computation to obtain the next node label from the argument tree. When the demanding process requires no more labels, the flatten process should terminate.

In order to fully motivate the principles involved, the procedure of Program 3.1 is transformed in several stages. In Section 4.3.2.1, a naive approach is taken. Then, in Section 4.3.2.2, the eager flatten procedure is reformulated to a version which, in Section 4.3.2.3, is transformed to the final lazy flatten procedure.

4.3.2.1   Responding to demands

The first step in the transformation is to reverse the top-level direction of communication: a consumer process becomes the producer of a 'demand' stream, while the producer is transformed to receive these demands and respond to them by binding variables contained in the demand terms. In this example, the flatten procedure is transformed to a procedure for, say, l-flatten, which has mode (?,?). The mode of the second argument has been inverted. A procedure for l-flatten is shown in Program 4.8.

```
mode l-flatten(?,?).

l-flatten(T(T(xx,xu,xy),u,y),DEMAND(r)) <−
    l-flatten(T(xx,xu,T(xy,u,y)),DEMAND(r))..
l-flatten(T(E,u,y),DEMAND(r)) <−
    r = [u|z] and l-flatten(y,z)..
l-flatten(E,DEMAND(r)) <− r = []..
l-flatten(tree,END-DEMAND).
```

Program 4.8   A lazy flatten procedure.

The l-flatten procedure comprises four clauses: one for each clause of the original program, plus an extra clause for termination. In each of the first three clauses, the second argument in the head has been replaced by the term DEMAND(r). The second and third clauses formerly had a non-variable output argument (as second argument), so a unification call ('=') is added to the body of these clauses to bind the request variable r to the head argument of the original clause.

In a query of the form:

: l-flatten(tree,list), user(list).

the l-flatten process is suspended until the list argument is instantiated, to a term DEMAND(r) or END-DEMAND. If the user process binds list to END-DEMAND, the l-flatten process terminates. If, instead, list is bound to DEMAND(r) (with r an unbound variable), the next label on the tree is sought. If the tree is empty, r is bound to the empty list '[]' and the l-flatten process terminates. Otherwise the result is supplied (possibly after several applications of the first clause) by binding r to a list term [u|z], using the second clause. Here, u is the requested tree label and z is the continuation demand stream, which is passed to a recursive call to l-flatten. The consumer process, user, may then demand subsequent items by binding z to DEMAND(r2), and so on, or to the constant END-DEMAND if no more items are required.

Fig. 4.3 shows two possible sequences of bindings to list for a tree with two nodes containing labels 1 and 2. The bindings made by the user and l-flatten processes alternate, with the first binding list=DEMAND(r) in each case made by the user process.

4.3.2.2 *Reformulating the eager producer*

The transformation can be simplified if the output of the producer is a term of a fixed 'type'. Since the flatten relation produces a finite list, its output

user	l-flatten	user	l-flatten
list=DEMAND(r)		list=DEMAND(r)	
	r=[1|z]		r=[1|z]
z=DEMAND(r2)		z=END-DEMAND	
	r2=[2|z2]		
z2=DEMAND(r3)			
	r3=[]		

Fig 4.3   Traces of demand-driven evaluation.

argument is either an empty list '[]' or a non-empty list pattern [u|z]. Suppose, instead, that a finite list [A,B,C] is represented by the term [A,B,C,END], where END is some reserved constant that is not permitted as an element of the list. Program 4.9 shows a procedure for n-flatten; it is an eager procedure identical to flatten except that the empty list is represented by the term [END]. The logical reading of n-flatten(tree,list) is: list is list1 concatenated to the term [END] where flatten(tree,list1).

```
mode n-flatten(?, ↑ ).


n-flatten(T(T(xx,xu,xy),u,y),z) <−
    n-flatten(T(xx,xu,T(xy,u,y)),z)..
n-flatten(T(E,u,y),[u|z]) <−
    n-flatten(y,z)..
n-flatten(E,[END]).
```

Program 4.9   Eager flatten with non-empty lists.

4.3.2.3   *Transformation to a lazy producer*

The output argument of the n-flatten procedure is always a (non-empty) list term, even if this is [END] which represents the empty list. The advantage of this is that the procedure can be transformed to a lazy version in such a way that this list structure is generated by the consumer. When the consumer supplies a list pattern [r|z], this binding acts as a demand for the value of the head of the list, which is eventually returned to the consumer by binding r to the appropriate value. Thus, a (non-empty) list binding replaces the DEMAND term used in the l-flatten procedure. Similarly, if the consumer supplies an empty list, this indicates that no more items are required, replacing the END-DEMAND term of Program 4.8. The lazy variant of n-flatten is the lazy-flatten procedure of Program 4.10.

```
mode lazy-flatten(?,?).


lazy-flatten(T(T(xx,xu,xy),u,y),[r|z]) <−
    lazy-flatten(T(xx,xu,T(xy,u,y)),[r|z])..
lazy-flatten(T(E,u,y),[r|z]) <−
    r = u and lazy-flatten(y,z)..
lazy-flatten(E,[r|z]) <−
    r = END and [] <= z..
lazy-flatten(tree,[]).
```

Program 4.10   Lazy flatten with non-empty lists.

The logical reading of lazy-flatten(tree,list) is: list is an initial sublist of list1 where n-flatten(tree,list1). This can easily be verified by the observation that each clause of lazy-flatten has the same logical reading as the corresponding clause of n-flatten, while the added (fourth) clause allows the output to be a sublist of the output list of n-flatten.

Notice that the structure of Program 4.10 is very similar to the eager version in Program 4.9; there is no need for explicit DEMAND terms as in Program 4.8.

In the second clause, the second head argument is now [r|z] and the call r = u appears in the body. More interestingly, the third clause, instead of generating the term [END], now waits for the input binding [r|z], then binds r to END using '=', and waits for an input binding of z to '[]' using a matching call [] <= z. The traces in Fig. 4.4 show the bindings made by the user and the lazy-flatten processes in the previous example of a tree with two nodes, labelled by 1 and 2.

user	lazy-flatten	user	lazy-flatten
list=[r|z]		list=[r|z]	
	r=1		r=1
z=[r2|z2]		z=[]	
	r2=2		
z2=[r3|z3]			
	r3=END		
z3=[]			

Fig 4.4   Traces of demand-driven evaluation.

4.3.3   Transformation of a non-terminating program

This section returns to the Hamming problem described above. The eager hamming procedure of Program 4.7 will be transformed to one which exhibits lazy behaviour and can be terminated.

The transformation of this example is unusually intricate since the communication is cyclic as shown in Fig. 4.2. The example, although small, has the advantage that it illustrates several generally useful transformation techniques. All communication in the eager version of the program is via *infinite* lists so there is no need to change the list representation as explained in Section 4.3.2.

The aim of the transformation, as usual, is to reverse the direction of communication. The lazy hamming procedure will consume a list of variables, binding each one to the next item in the solution list, and will terminate upon receiving an empty list. Of the three relations comprising the program, all arguments are lists with the exception of the first argument of timeslist. The first requirement, therefore, is to invert the mode of each of these list-valued arguments:

mode lazy-hamming(?), lazy-timeslist(?, ↑ ,?), lazy-amerge(↑ , ↑ ,?).

Whereas the last argument of each of the eager relations is an output argument producing an infinite list, the corresponding argument of each lazy relation is a (possibly finite) input list of request variables. Each lazy relation must be defined in such a way that, upon receiving a request variable, the value of that list member is computed and assigned to the variable; if an empty list is received, the procedure should terminate and, in turn, output an empty list on each of its request list arguments (formerly input arguments). Each of the three procedures of Program 4.7 will be considered in turn.

The timeslist procedure can be transformed very simply: as well as inverting the declared mode, it is necessary to generalize it to handle finite lists by adding a base case clause. The lazy-timeslist procedure is:

mode lazy-timeslist(?, ↑ ,?).

lazy-timeslist(u,[v|y],[w|z]) <−
    times(u,v,w) and lazy-timeslist(u,y,z)..
lazy-timeslist(u,[],[]).

The logical reading of lazy-timeslist(u,y,z) is the same as timeslist(u,y,z) except that y and z may be finite lists, i.e. z contains every member of list y, multiplied by u.

Operationally, a process lazy-timeslist(u,y,z) acts as a lazy producer of a list of numbers on z that are multiples of the numbers on list y of which the process is a consumer. Each time the lazy-timeslist process receives a request variable w on the third argument list, as a demand for the next item of the output list z, the process sends a request variable v on the second argument to demand a value for the next item of the input list y. The call times(u,v,w) in the body of the first clause is suspended until the lazy producer of y binds v to the appropriate value, whereupon the times process binds w to the product of u and v, thus communicating the requested value of w to the process that demanded it.

If the consumer of z requires no more list items, an empty list is received on the third argument. Then the lazy-timeslist process indicates that it requires no more items by sending an empty list to the lazy producer of y, and terminates.

The transformation of the amerge procedure is a little more complex. First, in the second and third clauses, the recursive call to amerge has a non-variable term as one of its input arguments. Since the input arguments of amerge will become output arguments in the lazy version, they should be variables. This can be achieved by a simple change to the eager amerge procedure as follows:

```
mode amerge(?,?,↑).

amerge([u|x],[u|y],[u|z]) <−
    amerge(x,y,z)..
amerge([u|x],[v|y],[u|z]) <− u < v :
    yt = [v|y], amerge(x,yt,z)..
amerge([u|x],[v|y],[v|z]) <− v < u :
    xt = [u|x], amerge(xt,y,z).
```

To transform amerge to a lazy version, it is not sufficient merely to invert the modes and add a base case clause, as before. This is because there are several clauses and the selection of a candidate clause depends upon the values of arguments that are evaluated on demand. That is, the candidate clause is selected by a comparison of the items at the head of the two input lists. In the lazy version, these items will not be available until after their values have been requested by the lazy amerge process. The amerge procedure must therefore be restructured. The resulting lazy-amerge procedure has a base case clause and a single recursive clause, which calls amerge1. The amerge1 procedure has three clauses which correspond to the three recursive clauses of the original amerge procedure:

```
mode lazy-amerge(↑,↑,?), amerge1(?,?,↑,↑,?,↑,?).

lazy-amerge([u|x],[v|y],[w|z]) <−
    amerge1(u,v,w,x,xt,y,yt),
    lazy-amerge(xt,yt,z)..
lazy-amerge([],[],[]).

amerge1(u,u,u,xt,xt,yt,yt)..
amerge1(u,v,u,xt,xt,y,yt) <− u < v :
    buf(yt,v,y)..
amerge1(u,v,v,x,xt,yt,yt) <− v < u :
    buf(xt,u,x).
```

The second clause for lazy-amerge terminates the request lists for the input arguments when the request list on the third argument is terminated. The first clause handles a demand for w by sending demands for the head items u and v of the first two argument lists. The call to amerge1 in the body will suspend until both u and v are instantiated by their respective producers. Then, if u and v are identical, the first amerge1 clause is a candidate and the output variable w is bound to u, x is bound to xt and y is bound to yt. These bindings cause any requests generated on xt and yt by the recursive call to lazy-amerge to be passed directly to x and y, the request lists for the first and second arguments.

If, in the amerge1 call, u is less than v, the second clause is chosen. This again binds x to xt, the continuation request list, but now y and yt become arguments of a call buf(yt,v,y) which corresponds to the call yt = [v|y] in the original eager amerge clause. The role of this buf call is to buffer the value v to satisfy the first demand, if any, generated on list yt by the recursive lazy-amerge call; subsequent demands on yt are passed directly to y. If the request list is empty, y is bound to the empty list. A similar buf call is placed in the third amerge1 clause.

The logical reading of buf(yt,v,y) is: yt is an initial sublist of [v|y], as can be seen by its procedure:

```
mode buf(?,?,↑).

buf([u|x],v,x) <− u = v..
buf([],v,[]).
```

As outlined above, a buf call is introduced for every input argument of a call which is non-variable in the eager procedure and which is therefore to be evaluated on demand in the lazy version.

Finally, the eager hamming procedure (depicted graphically in Fig. 4.2) is transformed. Since the second (input) argument of each timeslist call in the procedure is a non-variable, the first step is to replace each of these arguments by a variable and introduce an appropriate unification call as explained above. It proves useful to do the same to the head output argument of the hamming clause and introduce a call z = [1|x]. The eager hamming procedure is reformulated as follows:

```
mode hamming(↑).

hamming(z) <−
    z = [1|x], z2 = [1|x], z3 = [1|x], z5 = [1|x],
    timeslist(2,z2,x2),
    timeslist(3,z3,x3),
    timeslist(5,z5,x5),
    amerge(x2,x3,x23), amerge(x23,x5,x).
```

Applying the above techniques, the lazy-hamming procedure can now be obtained simply by replacing the timeslist and amerge calls by their lazy equivalents, and by replacing the '=' calls by calls to buf, as in the above transformation of amerge:

```
mode lazy-hamming(?).

lazy-hamming(z) <−
    buf(z,1,x), buf(z2,1,x), buf(z3,1,x), buf(z5,1,x),
    lazy-timeslist(2,z2,x2),
    lazy-timeslist(3,z3,x3),
    lazy-timeslist(5,z5,x5),
    lazy-amerge(x2,x3,x23), lazy-amerge(x23,x5,x).
```

This has the desired effect of reversing the direction of communication: the evaluation of lazy-hamming can be depicted as in Fig. 4.5. The problem with this is that there are now many producers for variable x: the four buf processes. Each of these processes is generating a list of request variables. This is an incorrect PARLOG program since no more than one process is permitted to bind a variable.

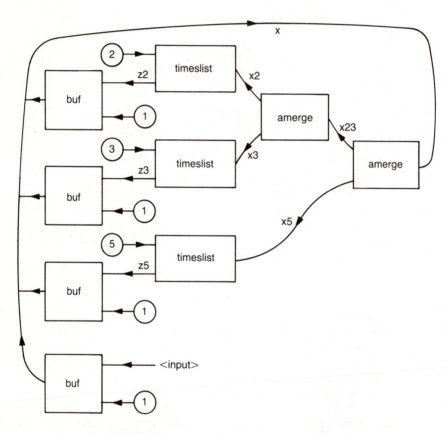

Fig 4.5 Erroneous lazy hamming program.

In such a situation, where a naive transformation results in multiple producers for a variable, a choice must be made: one must decide on *one* process to generate the demand stream. Such a decision is necessary in any demand-driven system (Kahn and MacQueen, 1977). In the present example, the appropriate source of demand is the input argument of lazy-hamming, labelled <input> in Fig. 4.5. The buf process connected to <input> still has x as its output argument, but the outputs of the other buf processes (y2, y3 and y5) are now interfaced to x via sublist processes. This is illustrated in Fig. 4.6.

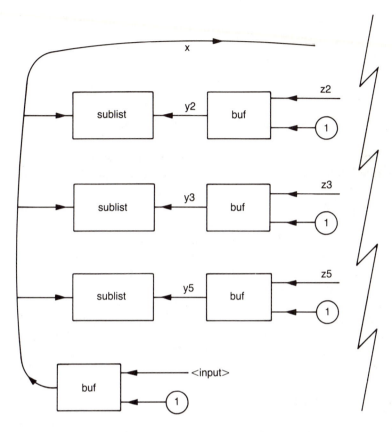

Fig 4.6 Correction to lazy hamming program.

The correct procedure for lazy-hamming is as follows. The logical reading of lazy-hamming(z) is: z is an initial sublist of the infinite list y satisfying hamming(y):

```
mode lazy-hamming(?).

lazy-hamming(z) <−
      buf(z,1,x), buf(z2,1,y2), buf(z3,1,y3), buf(z5,1,y5),
      sublist(y2,x), sublist(y3,x), sublist(y5,x),
      lazy-timeslist(2,z2,x2),
      lazy-timeslist(3,z3,x3),
      lazy-timeslist(5,z5,x5),
      lazy-amerge(x2,x3,x23), lazy-amerge(x23,x5,x).
```

The logical reading of sublist(y,x) is: y is an initial sublist of x. Operationally, y is a list of request variables no longer than the list x; each variable on y is bound to the corresponding value on x:

mode sublist(?,?).

sublist([v|y],[u|x]) <− v = u and sublist(y,x)..
sublist([],x).

4.4   The lazy set constructor of PARLOG

Section 3.11 introduced the set constructor primitives of PARLOG and described in detail the eager set constructor, named set. Recall that a call:

set(solutions,term,conjunction)

binds the *output* variable solutions to a list of the different instances of term given by *all* of the successful evaluations of conjunction (a conjunction of calls to all-solutions relations). The order of individual solutions on the solutions list is not prescribed.

As noted in Sections 2.5.4.3 and 3.11, evaluating a set constructor in a lazy manner results in a backtracking, Prolog-like evaluation, in which successive solutions are obtained one at a time. In PARLOG, a special lazy set constructor primitive, subset, is provided for this purpose. The subset primitive has the mode (?,?,?):

subset(sub-sol,term,conjunction)

where the term and conjunction arguments have the same role as in the set primitive. The first argument, sub-sol, is now an *input* list of request variables to be bound to the solutions. (The members of this list could, in general, be any terms that unify with the computed solutions.)

The use of the subset primitive is analogous to the use of lazy-flatten described above. A process requiring the next element of the solution list sub-sol binds sub-sol to a list pattern [req|reqs], whereupon subset binds the request variable req to the next solution to the conjunction, *or* to the reserved constant END (if there are no more solutions). The requesting process may then request further solutions by binding reqs to a list pattern, or terminate the subset process by binding reqs to the empty list '[]'; it *must* bind reqs to '[]' if req has been bound to END, in order to terminate the subset process.

The logical reading of subset(sub-sol,term,conjunction) is: sub-sol is an initial sublist of all-sol, where all-sol is a list of instances of term corresponding to the successful evaluations of conjunction, terminated by the term END.

Unlike the eager set constructor, subset obtains solutions sequentially, using clauses in their textual order. Therefore, the order of solutions on the list is fixed. For example, the all-solutions relations Sibling (Program 2.1) and Perm (Program 2.3) can be queried as follows:

```
: sol1 = [s1,c2] and
    subset(sol1,x,Sibling(x,Caspar)) and
    writelist(sol1).

: sol2 = [s1,s2,s3] and
    subset(sol2,x,Sibling(x,Caspar)) and
    writelist(sol2).

: sol3 = [s1,s2] and
    subset(sol3,z,Perm([3,v,1],z)) and
    writelist(sol3).
```

The answers displayed for sol1, sol2 and sol3 would be, respectively:

```
[Brian,Dexter]
[Brian,Dexter,END]
[[3,v1,1],[3,1,v2]]
```

Because subset performs a sequential search for solutions, relations called from subset may meaningfully use the cut primitive of Prolog.

The subset primitive is extensively discussed by Clark and Gregory (1985), where it is defined by a program in (the single-solution subset of) PARLOG.

4.4.1 A Prolog query evaluator in PARLOG

Since the subset primitive evaluates queries to all-solutions relations with exactly the backtracking behaviour of Prolog, it can be used as an interface between PARLOG and Prolog. Program 4.11 is a PARLOG program that implements a Prolog 'front-end'. It acts as an evaluator of queries to a Prolog-style database of all-solutions relations.

```
mode prolog( ↑ ), command(?, ↑ ), which(?, ↑ , ↑ ,?), continue(?, ↑ , ↑ ,?).

prolog([REPLY('Command?',cmd)|cmds]) <−
    command(cmd,cmds).

command(Which(term,conj),cmds) <−
    subset([soln|solns],term,conj),
    which(soln,solns,cmds,cmdt),
    prolog(cmdt).
command(End,[]).

which(END,[],['No more solutions'|cmds],cmds);
which(soln,solns,[REPLY(soln,response)|cmds],cmdt) <−
    continue(response,solns,cmds,cmdt).
```

```
continue(CONTINUE,[soln|solns],cmds,cmdt) <−
    which(soln,solns,cmds,cmdt).
continue(STOP,[],[Yes|cmdt],cmdt).
```

Program 4.11 A Prolog query evaluator in PARLOG.

The program is run by a query:

: prolog(cmds), writelist(cmds).

where writelist is as defined in Program 3.13. The prolog(cmds) call produces, on cmds, a list of messages which are consumed by the writelist call. The messages on cmds include ground terms to be displayed, and terms of the form REPLY(prompt,reply) in which reply is a variable to be bound (by writelist) to a term input by the user.

The prolog(cmds) call begins by sending a message REPLY ('Command?',cmd) (cmd an unbound variable) on the cmds stream, causing the 'Command?' prompt to be displayed and a term to be read from the user. The command call in the body of the prolog clause now suspends until the cmd variable is bound to a command: either End or Which(term,conj). If the command is End, the process terminates and sends an empty list to the writelist process to terminate it. A Which(term,conj) command requests the display of the substitution instances of term corresponding to successful evaluations of the all-solutions conjunction conj.

If a Which(term,conj) command is received, the command process forks into three: a subset process, a which process and a (mutually recursive) call to prolog. The first argument of subset is a list beginning with a variable soln, to request the first solution of term satisfying conj. The which process suspends until the soln variable is instantiated by subset. If soln is bound to END (there are no more solutions to conj), the which process terminates, closes the list of variables (solns) sent to subset and sends the message 'No more solutions' to the user.

If soln is bound to any other value by subset, this is a solution which is sent to the user in a message REPLY(soln,response). The continue call in the second which clause suspends until the user enters a response: either CONTINUE or STOP. If the response is STOP, the which process terminates, closes the solns list and sends the message Yes to the user. If it is CONTINUE, a further request variable is sent to the subset process on solns and which is recursively called to await the instantiation of the variable to the next solution.

The principal relations in Program 4.11 are read logically as follows:

- prolog(cmds):

    cmds is a list of terms of the form REPLY(prompt,reply) and other terms, which corresponds to a valid interaction with a Prolog-style database.

- which(s1,solns,cmds,cmdt): either

    a) solns is [s2,...,sn,END] and the difference between cmds and cmdt is the list [REPLY(s1,CONTINUE), REPLY(s2,CONTINUE), ..., REPLY(sn,CONTINUE), 'No more solutions'], or

    b) solns is [s2,...,sn] (sn ≠ END) and the difference between cmds and cmdt is the list [REPLY(s1,CONTINUE), REPLY(s2,CONTINUE), ..., REPLY(sn,STOP), Yes].

5

Implementation of PARLOG

This chapter discusses various aspects of the implementation of PARLOG. It has two main themes. The first part (Section 5.1) describes the analyses that can be performed at compile time to check that a PARLOG program satisfies certain properties. One such analysis can check whether a program is directional; directional programs lack the expressive power provided by the logical variable but automatically have 'safe' guards and also have efficiency advantages, which are briefly discussed. Another analysis, applicable to non-directional programs, checks that all guards are safe; this is an essential property of any PARLOG program.

The second part of the chapter (Section 5.2) considers some general principles for compiling PARLOG programs. The starting point for this compilation is the modeless form of PARLOG (Kernel PARLOG) introduced in Chapter 3. To avoid machine-specific details, all compilation is discussed within the formalism of Kernel PARLOG. This chapter considers general compilation strategies, showing the principles by which a PARLOG program may be manipulated to fit on to an architecture of any particular granularity. Chapters 6 and 7 show how these techniques can be applied to two specific abstract architectures.

This chapter does not consider the implementation of the set constructors, using 'all-solutions' relations, described in Sections 3.11 and 4.4. The lazy set constructor could be implemented as a standard backtracking Prolog evaluator, while the eager set constructor may be implemented with some form of OR parallelism, as discussed in Section 3.11. For a full discussion of the implementation of set constructors, the reader is referred to Clark and Gregory (1985).

5.1 Compile-time analysis of PARLOG programs

As explained in Section 3.2.4, PARLOG requires all clause guards to be safe. That is, a guard evaluation must not bind variables in the invoking call. This property can be verified at compile time by an analysis of the source PARLOG program, thus avoiding the need for a possibly expensive run-time check.

The guard safety check algorithm will be explained in this section. It is best viewed as a generalization of a stronger compile-time analysis that checks that a program is directional, which is presented first.

5.1.1   Directional PARLOG programs

Directional logic programs were defined in Section 2.4.1.3 as programs in which call arguments are always 'strong', i.e. they are terms that are completely constructed by a single relation call in a conjunction, without any contribution from other calls in the conjunction. In a directional PARLOG program, the mode declarations indicate which call constructs the value of each variable: the call in which the variable appears in an output argument position.

There is a simple mode analysis that can be applied to a PARLOG program to check whether it is directional, as follows.

5.1.1.1   *Program directionality check*

A program is directional if, for each variable, there is no more than one call that is able to instantiate it at any time. To guarantee this, the whole program must be checked, including the query and all of the procedures called, directly or indirectly. If the entire program passes the test, the program is directional. Conversely, all directional programs pass the test.

In a query, variables in output arguments of the calls must be *distinct* variables. That is, each variable may occur in no more than one output argument of a call; this call will be the only one that is able to bind that variable.

To ensure the directional property, the procedures for the relations called (directly or indirectly) from the query must also be examined: it must be verified that variables in input arguments of a call cannot be further instantiated by the evaluation of that call, and that each variable in an output argument of a call can be instantiated by only one call in the ensuing evaluation. All clauses in the program are therefore subjected to the following checks:

1. Variables in input argument positions in the clause head must *not* occur in output arguments of calls in the guard or body. (A variable may occur in any number of input arguments in the clause head: this is recognized as a test that the repeated variables are identical, as explained in Chapter 3.)

2. Variables not occurring in head input arguments must *not* occur in the output arguments of more than one call in the guard or body.

These rules can be summarized by stating that, in all clauses and the query, a variable may occur in any number of input arguments of the head (in the case of a clause) *or in one output argument* of a call, but not both.

5.1.1.2 Examples of directional programs

The timeslist procedure of Program 4.7 passes the directionality check. The diagram of Fig. 5.1 illustrates this with an arc for each variable, joining the single occurrence in the clause where the variable will be bound to its other occurrence(s). The two input arguments of timeslist are 'strong' because the variables u, v and y in these arguments in the clause head occur elsewhere only in input arguments of calls in the body, which are, in turn, assumed to be strong. This means that a call to timeslist cannot further instantiate its input argument terms. The clause body includes a single producer call for each of the variables in the third argument of the clause (w and z); each of these variables is an output argument of a call.

mode timeslist(?,?, ↑).

timeslist(u, [v|y], [w|z]) <−

times(u, v, w) and timeslist(u, y, z).

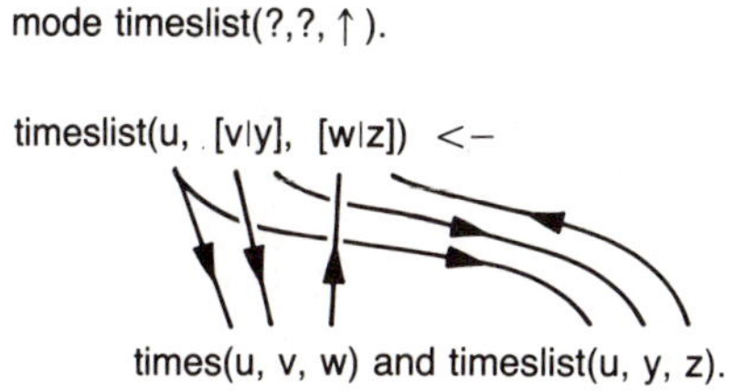

Fig 5.1 Data flow in timeslist clause.

The amerge procedure of Program 4.7 also passes the test. Consider its second clause, where the variables in the input arguments of the head are u, x, v and y. All of these occur only in input arguments in the body, apart from u, which also occurs in an output argument in the head (the third argument term [u|z]). The first and third arguments of amerge are therefore said to be **connected** arguments. This connection is depicted as an arc joining the first and third arguments in the clause head; see Fig. 5.2.

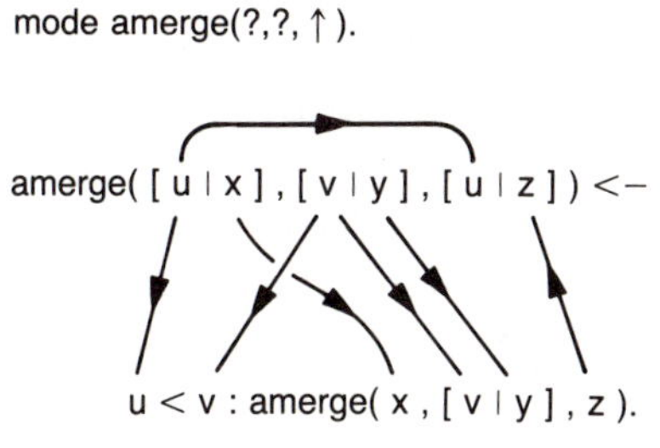

mode amerge(?,?, ↑).

amerge([u | x] , [v | y] , [u | z]) <−

u < v : amerge(x , [v | y] , z).

Fig 5.2 Data flow in amerge clause.

The fact that the first argument is connected to a head output argument in the amerge clause does not affect the directional property: it is still the case that u cannot be bound as a result of evaluating this call. This is because, in the context from which amerge is called, the variable in the third argument position of the amerge call can occur elsewhere only in input arguments of calls and/or in head output arguments. The amerge clause itself (Fig. 5.2) illustrates the second of these possibilities: the third argument of the recursive amerge call is z, which occurs in the output argument of the clause head. The first situation is illustrated by the hamming clause of Program 4.7 where x23, the third argument of one amerge call, occurs otherwise only in an input argument of the other amerge call; see Fig. 5.3.

mode hamming(↑).

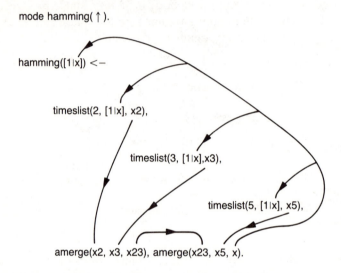

hamming([1|x]) <−

timeslist(2, [1|x], x2),

timeslist(3, [1|x],x3),

timeslist(5, [1|x], x5),

amerge(x2, x3, x23), amerge(x23, x5, x).

Fig 5.3   Data flow in hamming clause.

5.1.1.3   *Guards in directional programs*

Directional programs are guaranteed to have safe guards. In solving a call, no guard may bind any variables in the call because:

1. Bindings to variables in *output* arguments of the call are always performed in the clause body, as explained in Sections 3.2.4 and 3.5. This is true of all PARLOG programs (not only directional programs) and is guaranteed by the translation of each clause to standard form.

2. The checking algorithm of Section 5.1.1.1 ensures that variables in the *input* arguments in the head of a clause cannot occur in output arguments in the guard calls (or even the body calls). They *may* occur in input arguments of such calls but, since these arguments are themselves strong, there is no risk of a guard evaluation binding the input variables.

General PARLOG programs need not be directional, so a more complex check is required to ensure that guards are safe. An algorithm that checks this is presented in Section 5.1.4. It makes use of the concept of 'connected' arguments and 'weak' input arguments, discussed below in Sections 5.1.2 and 5.1.3 respectively.

5.1.2 Connected arguments

Given a (programmer-defined or primitive) relation R, argument i is **connected** to argument j if it is possible that, in a call to R, data input via argument i is output on argument j. As illustrated by the amerge procedure in Section 5.1.1.2, an analysis of variables shared between head arguments of clauses can determine which pairs of arguments are connected. The algorithm presented here does such an analysis.

5.1.2.1 Connected arguments algorithm

Let *arg-pairs* be the set of pairs of arguments for all programmer-defined relations in a program:

arg-pairs =
    $\{(R,i,j) : R$ is an n-ary programmer-defined relation and
        $1 \leqslant i,j \leqslant n\}$

The object of the algorithm is to compute the subset of *arg-pairs* containing just those pairs of arguments that are connected. This set will be named *connected-arg-pairs*:

connected-arg-pairs =
    $\{(R,i,j) : (R,i,j) \in$ *arg-pairs* and argument i of R is connected to
        argument $j\}$

The ith argument of relation R is said to be **connected** to the jth argument of R if argument i is connected to argument j in at least one clause in the procedure for R. Argument i is connected to argument j in a clause C if:

1. the ith and jth head arguments of C contain a common variable x and the ith and jth arguments of R are not both declared input, or
2. the ith and jth head arguments of C contain variables x and y respectively, where x and y occur in connected arguments of a call in the guard or body of the clause, or x and y are indirectly connected in this manner.

The algorithm below makes this more precise. It begins with an empty set as a first approximation to *connected-arg-pairs* and iterates to obtain successively better approximations. At each iteration, the most recent approximation to the set is used to determine whether two arguments are directly or indirectly connected in case 2 above. If the new approximation is identical to the previous one, it is the final solution. The algorithm proceeds as follows:

1. *pairs-so-far* := {}
2. *new-pairs* :=
   {(R,i,j) : (R,i,j) ∈ *arg-pairs* and
                 (R,i,j) ∉ *pairs-so-far* and
                 for some clause C for R:
                     u is a variable in the ith argument
                     of the head of C and
                     v is a variable in the jth argument
                     of the head of C and
                     (u and v are identical or
                         connected-vars(u,v,C,*pairs-so-far*))}
3. if *new-pairs* ≠ {}
       pairs-so-far := *pairs-so-far* ∪ *new-pairs*
       repeat from step 2
   else
       connected-arg-pairs := *pairs-so-far*

Two distinct variables in clause C, u and v, are connected variables if they are either directly connected (i.e. connected by a single call) or indirectly connected (i.e. u is directly connected to a variable w which is connected to v). This is checked relative to *pairs*, the pairs of arguments that are already known to be connected:

connected-vars(u,v,C,*pairs*) iff
    directly-connected-vars(u,v,C,*pairs*) or
    for some variable w:
        directly-connected-vars(u,w,C,*pairs*) and
        connected-vars(w,v,C,*pairs*)

Two variables, u and v, in clause C are directly connected according to *pairs* if u and v occur in two arguments of a call that are known to be connected arguments:

directly-connected-vars(u,v,C,*pairs*) iff
    for some call $R'(t_1,...,t_k)$ in clause C:
        u occurs in t_i (1 ≤ i ≤ k) and
        v occurs in t_j (1 ≤ j ≤ k) and
        ((R'i,j) ∈ *pairs* or
         (R',i,j) ∈ *primitive-connected-arg-pairs*)

primitive-connected-arg-pairs is a predefined set stating the connected arguments of primitive relations:

primitive-connected-arg-pairs =
   $\{(R,i,j) : R$ is an n-ary primitive relation and
            $1 \leqslant i,j \leqslant n$ and
            argument i of R is connected to argument $j\}$

The only primitives used that have connected arguments are the matching and full unification primitives. The arguments of '<=' and '=' are connected, because variables in either argument of a call may be bound to components of the other argument. Hence:

primitive-connected-arg-pairs =
   $\{('<='\text{,}1,2), ('<='\text{,}2,1), ('='\text{,}1,2), ('='\text{,}2,1)\}$

5.1.2.2 Examples of connected arguments

Consider a program which comprises only the merge procedure of Program 3.2. In computing the set of connected arguments, initially empty, the first iteration of the algorithm detects that the first and third arguments are connected because the variable u is shared between these arguments in the head of the first clause. Similarly, the second and third arguments are found to be connected by virtue of the second clause:

   $\{('merge'\text{,}1,3), ('merge'\text{,}3,1), ('merge'\text{,}2,3), ('merge'\text{,}3,2)\}$

The second iteration adds nothing to the set, so this is the final value of connected-arg-pairs.

Program 4.1, comprising procedures for sort and qsort, is slightly more interesting. The first iteration of the algorithm detects only that the second and third arguments of qsort are connected because of the common variable, sorted, in the second qsort clause:

   $\{('qsort'\text{,}2,3), ('qsort'\text{,}3,2)\}$

The second iteration of the algorithm can now determine that the first and second arguments of qsort are connected because these head arguments of the first qsort clause contain variables u and sorted-h, which also occur in the third and second arguments, respectively, of a recursive qsort call. Because ('qsort',2,3) is already in the set, it follows that the first and second arguments of qsort are also connected. The set is now augmented with these new pairs:

   $\{('qsort'\text{,}2,3), ('qsort'\text{,}3,2), ('qsort'\text{,}1,2), ('qsort'\text{,}2,1)\}$

Finally, since the first and second head arguments of the sort clause are the same variables as the first and second arguments of the qsort call, these arguments are also connected. The final value of *connected-arg-pairs* is therefore:

{('qsort',2,3), ('qsort',3,2), ('qsort',1,2), ('qsort',2,1),
('sort',1,2), ('sort',2,1)}

This corresponds to the intuitive knowledge that the output of a call to sort
may contain the data that is input.

5.1.3   Non-directional programs

As explained in Section 3.6, input arguments must be allowed to be 'weak'
in order to realize the logical variable. An example of a clause with a weak
input argument is the first clause of Program 3.12:

```
mode trans(?,?,↑ ).

trans(IN(key,reply),db,db) <−
      on-ord-tree(key,value,db) :
      reply = value.
```

In this case, it is fairly easy to detect that the first argument of trans is weak
because a variable, reply, in the head input argument appears in a weak
input argument of a body call reply = value. In general, a more complex
analysis may be required, such as that described below.

5.1.3.1   *Weak input arguments algorithm*

The object of this algorithm is to compute the set of all weak input
arguments, *weak-input-args*:

> *weak-input-args* =
> {(R,i) : R is a programmer-defined relation and
>   the ith argument of R is declared input and
>   the ith argument of R is weak}

The ith (input) argument of a relation is said to be **weak** if it is weak in
at least one clause in the procedure for the relation. It is weak in a clause C
if the ith head argument of C contains a variable which:

1. occurs in an output argument *or* a weak input argument of a call in
   the guard or body of C, or
2. is connected to another variable which occurs in an output
   argument or a weak input argument of a call in the guard or body
   of C.

Like the connected arguments algorithm of Section 5.1.2.1, the
following algorithm performs a bottom-up analysis of a program,
beginning with an empty set as the first approximation and then iterating.

At each iteration, the algorithm may add new weak input arguments to the set: input argument positions for which an argument of the call might be made weak by a call in the clause:

1. *args-so-far* := {}

2. *new-args* :=
   $\{(R,i) : R$ is a programmer-defined relation and
   the *i*th argument of R is declared input and
   $(R,i) \notin$ *args-so-far* and
   for some clause C for R:
   for some call P in the guard or body of C:
   weak-because(i,C,P,args-so-far)}

3. if *new-args* ≠ {}
   args-so-far := *args-so-far* ∪ *new-args*
   repeat from step 2
   else
   weak-input-args := *args-so-far*

Argument *i* of clause *C* is **weak because of** a call *P* in the guard or body if a variable *u* in the *i*th head argument of *C* occurs in an output argument of *P* or in one of *P*'s input arguments that are already known to be weak, or *u* is connected to another variable *v* that occurs in such a location:

weak-because(i,C,R'($t_1,...,t_k$),args) iff
   u is a variable in the *i*th (input) argument
   of the head of clause *C* and
   v is a variable in t_j and
   (*u* and *v* are identical or
   connected-vars(u,v,C,connected-arg-pairs)) and
   (the *j*th argument of R' is declared output or
   $(R',j) \in$ *args* or
   $(R',j) \in$ *primitive-weak-input-args*)

Finally, it is necessary to state the weak input arguments of primitive relations. The first argument of the (simple and control) metacall primitive call is weak, as is the first argument of the lazy set constructor primitive subset. Some arguments of the unification primitives are also weak:

primitive-weak-input-args =
   {('call',1), ('subset',1), ('<=',1), ('=',1), ('=',2)}

5.1.3.2 *Examples of weak input arguments*

The merge relation as defined in Program 3.2 has only strong input arguments. The above algorithm immediately confirms this because the variables in the first two arguments in the head of each merge clause occur only in the first two arguments of a recursive merge call in the body. Since these are input arguments and have not been found to be weak, the analysis terminates with an empty set of weak input arguments.

Consider the database manager defined in Programs 3.10 and 3.12. In analysing this program, the first iteration of the algorithm detects that the first argument of trans is weak because, in each clause, the reply variable occurs in an input argument in the head and a weak input argument in the body. The first approximation to the *weak-input-args* set is therefore:

{('trans',1)}

The next iteration now determines that the first argument of dbase1 is weak because, in its first clause, the variable cmd occurs in the first head argument and in the first argument of the trans call, which is now known to be weak. The final iteration finds that the only argument of dbase is weak because the variable cmds occurs in the head argument and in the first argument of the dbase1 call in the dbase clause. The final value of *weak-input-args* is therefore:

{('trans',1), ('dbase1',1), ('dbase',1)}

This illustrates how the weakness of an input argument of a relation propagates upward to the arguments of higher-level procedures.

5.1.4   Safe guards

The concept of safe guards is closely related to that of weak input arguments. A weak input argument was defined in Section 5.1.3 as one for which a head argument of a clause contains a variable that is identical to, or is connected to, a variable occurring in a position, in the guard *or* body, where it might be bound. If that position is in the guard, the guard is **potentially unsafe**, i.e. its evaluation *might* bind an input variable.

5.1.4.1   Examples of unsafe guards

Section 3.6.1.1 presented a variant of the first clause of trans (Program 3.12) that has an unsafe guard:

    trans(IN(key,reply),db,db) <−
        on-ord-tree(key,reply,db) :.

The above guard is unsafe because reply (an input variable) occurs in an output argument in the guard. The following variant of this clause also has an unsafe guard. Here, the reply variable occurs in a weak input argument in the guard:

    trans(IN(key,reply),db,db) <−
        on-ord-tree(key,value,db) and reply = value :.

The guard in the following clause is unsafe because the reply variable is connected to r, which occurs in an output argument in the guard:

```
trans(IN(key,reply),db,db) <-
    r <= reply and on-ord-tree(key,r,db) :.
```

5.1.4.2   Guard safety check

A guard G of clause C (for relation R) is **potentially unsafe** iff, for some input argument position i of R and some call P in G:

$$weak\text{-}because(i,C,P,weak\text{-}input\text{-}args)$$

where *weak-input-args* is the set computed by the algorithm of Section 5.1.3.1. Informally, this means that an input variable of the clause occurs in the guard in a position where it might be bound. If a guard is *not* potentially unsafe, as determined by the above analysis, then it is a **safe guard**. The converse – that no safe guards are potentially unsafe – is not necessarily true. This is because the mode analysis described is not sufficiently fine: it may reject a safe guard as potentially unsafe.

It is simple to construct a procedure that has safe guards but is rejected by the described analysis. For example, the following trans clause is similar to the first clause of Program 3.12, except that the first two arguments of the original on-ord-tree call have been grouped into one argument of a call to new-on-ord-tree:

```
trans(IN(key,reply),db,db) <-
    new-on-ord-tree(P(key,value),db) :
    reply = value.

mode new-on-ord-tree(?,?).

new-on-ord-tree(P(key,value),db) <-
    on-ord-tree(key,value,db).
```

The first argument of new-on-ord-tree is weak because the value variable occurs in a head input argument *and* an output argument of the call in the body of its clause. In the above trans clause, the mode analysis will classify the guard as potentially unsafe because the key variable occurs in a head input argument and in the weak input argument of the new-on-ord-tree call. In fact, the guard is safe since key cannot be bound by the new-on-ord-tree call.

In cases such as this, the program can be rewritten to a form in which structured terms occurring as call arguments are split up into separate arguments. The rewritten program then passes the safety check. In some programs, the mode analysis described may still be too coarse; it treats only the worst case. The best way to check the safety of guards may prove to be by some form of symbolic evaluation which would examine the paths that may actually be followed by a possible evaluation in order to check whether a guard is unsafe. This is left as a topic of future research.

Guards that cannot, in general, be proved safe at compile time include those that include metacalls whose first argument is, or is connected to, a variable occurring in a head input argument of the clause:

$$R(...p...) <- ... call(p) ... : ... . \tag{M}$$

If nothing is known about the value input on p in a call to R, the guard must be assumed unsafe. For example, p may be the term plus(1,2,x), in which case x will be bound to the value 3 by the guard.

To avoid the need for a run-time safety check (Section 5.1.4.3), clauses such as M should be rejected by the compiler in general. An exception can be made to allow Program 3.18: to ensure that the first clause for '~' has a safe guard, all *calls* to '~' are checked as described in Section 3.10.2.

Codish (1985) describes a syntactic (compile-time) safety checking algorithm that can be used to verify the safety of a program in Safe Concurrent Prolog, a subset of Concurrent Prolog augmented with annotations.

5.1.4.3 *Run-time checking of guards*

The most general way to check that guards are safe would be by a run-time test. Each time that a variable is bound during a guard evaluation, a test is performed to determine whether the variable belongs to the environment of the call or is a variable local to the guard and body of the clause. In the former case, an error occurs. Some additional action may need to be performed when a clause commits, to enable the clause body to freely bind variables of the call.

The advantage of a run-time safety check is that it would handle programs for which a compile-time check is complex or impossible, such as clause M above. The details of a run-time safety check would depend upon the particular implementation and the representation of variable bindings, etc., but it is likely to present a considerable run-time overhead unless specialized hardware support is provided. It may be possible to find a way to combine the efficiency advantages of a compile-time check with the power of a run-time test where this is required; this is a topic for future research.

The run-time guard safety check is essentially the same as the mechanism proposed by Ueda (1985a) for Guarded Horn Clauses, described in Section 3.7.5.5, and could be implemented using similar techniques (Ito *et al.*, 1985). The crucial difference is that an unsafe guard causes an error in PARLOG, since it should be avoided by the programmer. In GHC, an unsafe guard is a common occurrence because this is the means by which processes suspend: an unsafe guard suspends until it becomes safe (if ever). Ueda suggests that the expense of GHC's run-time test can be avoided in certain cases by adopting a compile-time analysis like that of PARLOG. This is done in FGHC, the subset of GHC in which guards are 'flat'.

Unlike PARLOG and Guarded Horn Clauses, Concurrent Prolog (Shapiro, 1983) places no restrictions upon bindings by a guard evaluation of variables in the invoking call. Instead, a multiple environment mechanism is provided: any bindings made to a call variable by a guard are stored in a local environment until the time of commitment, when they are made public. Some methods of implementing this in a sequential implementation of Concurrent Prolog have been described (e.g. Levy, 1984; Miyazaki et al., 1985), but they all seem to be computationally expensive.

More fundamentally, the multiple environment mechanism has proved to present serious problems in the semantics and implementation of Concurrent Prolog. Some of the problems are related to the semantics of the read-only variable (Section 3.7.5.4). They centre on the coordination between the global environment and the local environment of each guard evaluation, e.g. how incrementally generated input to a call is transmitted from the global environment to the local environment, and how to handle variables which may be instantiated both locally and in the global environment. These issues have been investigated in great detail by Ueda (1985b), Saraswat (1985) and Kusalik (1985).

5.1.5 Shared memory and message passing

The method of communication between processors is one of the most important characteristics of parallel architectures (MacQueen, 1979). There are two main communication methods. In tightly coupled systems, all processors have access to a common memory which they may read and update; in loosely coupled systems, processors communicate by sending messages along physical channels that connect them. As Seitz (1985) points out, various hybrids are possible.

The message-passing approach is often considered more viable for systems with a large number of processors, in which a shared memory would constitute a bottleneck. On the other hand, a shared memory architecture is clearly more powerful since it can easily simulate a message-passing machine using memory buffers for messages; to simulate a shared memory by message passing is potentially very expensive.

In implementing PARLOG on a parallel architecture, different PARLOG processes/calls may (but need not) reside on physically separate processors. If they do, the binding of a variable shared between calls implies some form of communication between the host processors. The manner in which this communication takes place depends upon the nature of the architecture.

If PARLOG is implemented on a shared memory machine, each variable shared between PARLOG processes is implemented as a location in the shared memory. When the variable is bound, the binding is stored in the appropriate memory location. This method of implementation presents no conceptual difficulty. However, to avoid the bottleneck, it would be desirable to implement PARLOG without shared memory communication, especially because the full power of shared memory (such as destructive assignment) is not needed in PARLOG.

In general, to implement PARLOG on a loosely coupled machine is potentially more difficult. If a number of processes have access to a shared variable v, it is not known in advance which process will bind v. When one of them does bind v, the binding might be communicated to all of the processors on which the other processes using v reside. In the absence of a shared memory, this may require a very complex message-passing regime.

On a message passing system, the *directional* form of PARLOG (Section 5.1.1) is likely to be much easier to implement. Since there is never more than one process that can bind a shared variable v, v can be represented by a one-way communication path from the producer processor to the processors on which the consumers of v reside. The earlier version of PARLOG, now referred to as the Relational Language (described in Clark and Gregory, 1981), was directional, primarily to facilitate efficient implementation on a distributed, loosely coupled architecture.

Yuji Matsumoto (personal communication) has suggested a compromise scheme that would allow PARLOG to be implemented on a hybrid architecture with some shared memory. Most PARLOG programs are 'almost directional', i.e. most variables only have a single producer, so a message-passing mechanism can usually be used. Only a variable whose ultimate producer is not known would be represented as an address in shared memory. For example, in the following query involving the dbase process defined in Program 3.10:

```
: produce(cmds), dbase(cmds).
```

the value of cmds generated by the produce call might take the form:

```
[IN(K1,r1),ADD(K2,V2,r2),DELETE(K3,r3),...]
```

Because variables r1, r2, etc., are used for back communication, they would be represented as shared memory addresses. Other variables such as cmds can be handled by message passing.

A PARLOG implementation would need to determine whether each variable needs to be represented by a shared memory address. To do so, a mode analysis algorithm similar to those presented above might be appropriate. The compiler would analyse the program to detect which variables in an output argument of a clause might be bound by another (consumer) process and use a different variable representation for these.

5.2   Compiling PARLOG programs

5.2.1   Kernel PARLOG

In compiling PARLOG programs, the first stage is the translation to Kernel PARLOG described in Section 3.5. In Kernel PARLOG, there are no mode declarations and each clause is in 'standard form', where the input matching and output unification is performed by explicit primitive calls which are added to the guard and body. Kernel PARLOG is the starting point for the subsequent phases of compilation. It is therefore worth summarizing the form of Kernel PARLOG here.

A Kernel PARLOG procedure *KP-proc* is either a single clause or a group of clauses composed using the operators '.' (parallel search), ';' (sequential search) and '..' (neutral, i.e. either parallel or sequential):

> *KP-proc = KP-clause |*
> *KP-proc . KP-proc |*
> *KP-proc ; KP-proc |*
> *KP-proc .. KP-proc*

A Kernel PARLOG clause has a guard and a body conjunction:

> *KP-clause = KP-guard : KP-body |*
> *KP-guard : |*
> *KP-body*

Both guard and body are conjunctions, i.e. a call or a group of calls composed using the operators ',' (parallel conjunction), '&' (sequential conjunction) and 'and' (neutral):

> *KP-guard = KP-conjunction*

> *KP-body = KP-conjunction*

> *KP-conjunction = KP-call |*
> *KP-conjunction , KP-conjunction |*
> *KP-conjunction & KP-conjunction |*
> *KP-conjunction* and *KP-conjunction*

Any call (*KP-call*) in the program may be a call to either a primitive or a programmer-defined relation. The primitives include the unification-related primitives ('<=', '==', '=', data and var), arithmetic relations such as '<' and plus, input and output primitives (read and write), the metacall primitive call and the set and subset primitives. Some calls to the unification-related primitives are introduced by the translation of PARLOG to standard form, but they may also be included in the source PARLOG program, as noted in Chapter 3.

The syntax of a query, and of the first argument of the call primitive, is the same as a *KP-body* of Kernel PARLOG.

5.2.2   Compilation from Kernel PARLOG

The first task of a compiler will be to check a source PARLOG program for safety and transform it to Kernel PARLOG. The Kernel PARLOG program is then compiled to machine code for some target architecture. Parallel architectures that are available or proposed differ widely in their characteristics, so it would be inappropriate to examine the peculiarities of any particular machine in detail. Instead, the approach taken is to consider *abstract* architectures, for which the machine code is a lower-level form of Kernel PARLOG. This target language will be named KP_a, where a identifies the target architecture. Two example abstract architectures will be considered in the next two chapters: a = 'AND/OR tree' and a = 'AND tree'. KP_a is then further compiled to machine code for a specific machine of type a; see Fig. 5.4.

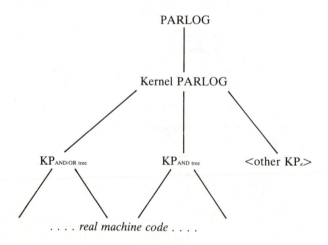

Fig 5.4   PARLOG implementation scheme.

The syntax of each KP_a is a subset of the Kernel PARLOG syntax described in Section 5.2.1. Whereas the Kernel PARLOG form of a program reflects the structure of the source PARLOG program, the KP_a form is oriented to the architecture a. The compilation from Kernel PARLOG to KP_a can be considered in three distinct phases, as follows.

First, the granularity of the program is manipulated to fit onto the target architecture. As explained in Section 3.4.1, a PARLOG program (and hence a Kernel PARLOG program) may be written with sequential, parallel or neutral operators. The first phase of the compilation will replace all uses of neutral operators '..' and 'and' by explicit sequential or parallel operators. It may also decompose large (coarse-grained) sequential sections of program code into smaller pieces which are evaluated in parallel, sequencing being obtained by mode constraints. The program is decomposed to a greater extent for a more fine-grained architecture.

Second, calls to most of the primitive relations will be compiled as far as possible. As described in Section 3.5, the unification in a PARLOG program is performed by explicit calls to unification primitives in the Kernel PARLOG form of the program. All calls to the matching primitive '$<=$' thus introduced are compiled to simple instructions, leaving only calls to the test unification primitive '$==$' and full unification '$=$' to be implemented by recursive procedures. Calls to the unification primitives that appeared in the source program are compiled along with those introduced by the compiler. Because of the single-mode nature of PARLOG programs, calls to many other primitives can also be compiled to sequences of simpler instructions.

The third and final phase of compilation is the optimization of the generated code. This removes any redundant instructions generated by the compilation of primitives.

Sections 5.2.3–5.2.5 demonstrate the principles of each of the three phases of compilation. The way in which these techniques are applied depends upon the nature of the target architecture and is made more specific in Chapters 6 and 7.

5.2.3 Manipulating the granularity

The first phase of compilation may decompose a program into a more fine-grained equivalent. This section illustrates how this might be done by treating the extreme case, for a hypothetical highly parallel architecture, such as a dataflow machine; a dataflow implementation of the GHC language is outlined in Ito *et al.* (1985). Each procedure is compiled to a procedure whose guards, if any, contain *only matching* and which uses only parallel conjunction in the body.

The first step is to replace all neutral operators ('..' and 'and') by either sequential or parallel operators.

5.2.3.1 *Eliminating OR parallel search*

As explained in Section 5.1, a compile-time check can be performed to verify the safety of guards. The knowledge that guards are safe means that no special mechanism, such as a run-time safety check, is required to support the evaluation of guards. This has the important consequence that the OR parallel evaluation of a group of clause guards can be replaced by an AND parallel evaluation, where several guards are evaluated in AND parallel in one compound guard.

The technique used is essentially the same as the transformation approach presented in Section 4.2, except that the control call (Section 3.9.2) is used to obtain the result of an evaluation and to allow an evaluation to be terminated. Recall that the term 'control call' refers to a use of the three-argument call primitive in which the first argument is given in the call at compile time.

Consider a Kernel PARLOG procedure comprising two clauses, to be tried in parallel:

$$R(HVARS) <- G_1 : B_1.$$
$$R(HVARS) <- G_2 : B_2.$$

(Recall that the head arguments, represented here by *HVARS*, are distinct variables.) The first step is to ensure that all variables in G_1, apart from those occurring in the head arguments, are named differently from those in G_2. Let *VARS* denote all of the variables that occur both in the body and elsewhere (i.e. in the head or guard) in each clause. This parallel clause group can then be replaced by a single clause:

$$R(HVARS) <- \text{call}(G_1, s1, c1), \text{call}(G_2, s2, c2),$$
$$\text{or2}(s1, s2, c1, c2) :$$
$$\text{eval-R}(s1, s2, VARS). \tag{PS}$$

The original guards G_1 and G_2 are each evaluated by AND parallel control calls in the guard of clause PS. Since G_1 and G_2 are safe, they are not able to instantiate variables in the head argument terms. The other variables in each guard, which the guard *may* bind, are not shared with the other guards because of the prior renaming of variables noted above.

In the guard of clause PS, the result arguments s1 and s2 of the G_1 and G_2 control calls are monitored by a call to or2. If either G_1 or G_2 succeeds, a STOP message is sent to terminate the evaluation of the other control call and the entire guard then succeeds. If both G_1 and G_2 fail, the or2 call, and hence the guard of clause PS, will fail. The guard of clause PS has the logical reading: G_1 or G_2. Because of the behaviour of the control call (defined in Section 3.9.2), if one guard succeeds, the other will be terminated as soon as possible. or2 is defined by the following simple Kernel PARLOG program:

```
or2(s1,s2,c1,c2) <- SUCCEEDED <= s1 :
    c2 = STOP.
or2(s1,s2,c1,c2) <- SUCCEEDED <= s2 :
    c1 = STOP.
```

In the general case, where *n* clauses are to be tried in parallel, there are *n* control calls and a call to or$_n$ in the compound guard. The or$_n$ relation has *n* input arguments, *n* output arguments and *n* clauses and is defined in a manner analogous to or2. For example, or3 is defined by the Kernel PARLOG procedure:

```
or3(s1,s2,s3,c1,c2,c3) <- SUCCEEDED <= s1 :
    c2 = STOP and c3 = STOP.
or3(s1,s2,s3,c1,c2,c3) <- SUCCEEDED <= s2 :
    c1 = STOP and c3 = STOP.
or3(s1,s2,s3,c1,c2,c3) <- SUCCEEDED <= s3 :
    c1 = STOP and c2 = STOP.
```

The eval-R relation used in the body of clause PS is a new auxiliary relation, which must be defined specially for each parallel group of clauses replaced. In this case, it is defined (in Kernel PARLOG) as:

```
eval-R(s1,s2,VARS) <- SUCCEEDED <= s1 : B₁.
eval-R(s1,s2,VARS) <- SUCCEEDED <= s2 : B₂.
```

The call to eval-R in the body of clause PS will evaluate the appropriate body B_1 or B_2 corresponding to the guard (G_1 or G_2) that succeeded. For example, if G_1 succeeds, s1 is SUCCEEDED and so the eval-R call in the body reduces to B_1. The *VARS* argument of eval-R allows values to be communicated from the successful guard evaluation to the corresponding body. In general, eval-R has *n* input arguments plus an argument for each member of *VARS*, where *n* is the number of clauses in the parallel clause group replaced.

A program compiled in this manner has no remaining OR parallel search; the '.' operator is still used in the procedures for or_n and each auxiliary relation eval-R, but the guards of these procedures contain only matching calls, not calls to programmer-defined relations. This simple 'OR parallel' search can be implemented by a sequential mechanism; such a mechanism is described in Chapter 7.

As an example of the above transformation, consider the on-tree procedure of Program 3.7 whose Kernel PARLOG form appears in Section 3.5.2. The compiled version of this, after the elimination of OR parallel search, is shown below; it uses an auxiliary relation eval-on-tree:

```
on-tree(p1,p2,p3) <-
    T(x,P(q1,value),y) <= p3, p1 == q1 :
    p2 = value;
on-tree(p1,p2,p3) <-
    call((T(x1,P(rkey1,rvalue1),y1) <= p3,
        on-tree(p1,value1,x1)),s1,c1),
    call((T(x2,P(rkey2,rvalue2),y2) <= p3,
        on-tree(p1,value2,y2)),s2,c2),
```

```
      or2(s1,s2,c1,c2) :
      eval-on-tree(s1,s2,p2,value1,value2).

    eval-on-tree(s1,s2,p2,value1,value2) <- SUCCEEDED <= s1 :
      p2 = value1.
    eval-on-tree(s1,s2,p2,value1,value2) <- SUCCEEDED <= s2 :
      p2 = value2.
```

Finally, because no guard is necessary in a clause which is the only clause of
a procedure, or the last of a *sequence* of clauses comprising a procedure
(Section 3.3.3.1), the ':' can be omitted from the second on-tree clause.

5.2.3.2 *Eliminating sequential search*

Having eliminated OR parallel search, each procedure comprises a
sequence of clauses. Again invoking the property that guards are safe, such
a procedure can be collapsed into an equivalent single-clause procedure.
Consider a procedure comprising a sequence of two clauses:

$$R(HVARS) <- G_1 : B_1;$$
$$R(HVARS) <- B_2.$$

(As noted above, a guard is never required in the final clause of a
sequence.) This procedure can be replaced by the clause:

$$R(HVARS) <- \text{call}(G_1,s,c) \text{ and choose-R}(s,BVARS,VARS). \qquad \text{(SS)}$$

where *BVARS* denotes the variables among the head argument variables
HVARS that occur in one or both of the bodies B_1 and B_2. *VARS* denotes
the variables that do not occur in *HVARS* but *do* occur in the body of the
first clause, B_1.

choose-R is an auxiliary relation which must be defined each time a pair
of clauses is replaced by a single clause. Its procedure takes the form:

```
    choose-R(s,BVARS,VARS) <- SUCCEEDED <= s : B₁..
    choose-R(s,BVARS,VARS) <- FAILED <= s : B₂.
```

Sequential search can be removed from the above on-tree procedure by
this technique. The final variant of this procedure, together with the above
auxiliary procedure eval-on-tree, is shown below. It has been simplified to a
single clause, together with an auxiliary procedure for choose-on-tree whose
guards contain only matching calls. All of the former guards are now
evaluated by control calls:

```
    on-tree(p1,p2,p3) <-
        call((T(x,P(q1,value),y) <= p3, p1 == q1 ),s,c) and
        choose-on-tree(s,p1,p2,p3,value).
```

```
choose-on-tree(s,p1,p2,p3,value) <- SUCCEEDED <= s :
    p2 = value..
choose-on-tree(s,p1,p2,p3,value) <- FAILED <= s :
    call((T(x1,P(rkey1,rvalue1),y1) <= p3,
        on-tree(p1,value1,x1)),s1,c1),
    call((T(x2,P(rkey2,rvalue2),y2) <= p3,
        on-tree(p1,value2,y2)),s2,c2),
    or2(s1,s2,c1,c2),
    eval-on-tree(s1,s2,p2,value1,value2).

eval-on-tree(s1,s2,p2,value1,value2) <- SUCCEEDED <= s1 :
    p2 = value1.
eval-on-tree(s1,s2,p2,value1,value2) <- SUCCEEDED <= s2 :
    p2 = value2.
```

To remove sequential search from a general procedure comprising a sequence of n clauses, this technique must be applied repeatedly. That is, a sequence of n clauses for R:

$$R(HVARS) <- G_1 : B_1;$$
$$R(HVARS) <- G_2 : B_2;$$
$$\dots$$
$$R(HVARS) <- B_n.$$

is treated as a two-clause procedure for R together with an $(n - 1)$-clause procedure for R', which can then be further processed in the same way:

$$R(HVARS) <- G_1 : B_1;$$
$$R(HVARS) <- R'(HVARS).$$

$$R'(HVARS) <- G_2 : B_2;$$
$$\dots$$
$$R'(HVARS) <- B_n.$$

5.2.3.3 Eliminating sequential conjunction

Finally, uses of the sequential conjunction operator '&' can be removed by a method based on the 'synchronization flag' approach of Section 4.1, but utilizing the control call primitive. Each occurrence of C_1 & C_2 is replaced by:

```
call(C₁,s,c), next-C(s,VARS)
```

$VARS$ comprises the variables of the second call or conjunction, C_2. The auxiliary relation next-C must be defined specially for the purpose, and contains a single clause:

next-C(s,*VARS*) <− SUCCEEDED <= s & C_2.   (SC)

The new clause uses '&', but only following a matching call. This is much simpler to implement than general conjunction C_1 & C_2 in which C_1 may involve programmer-defined relations.

5.2.3.4   Example: alternative definition of negation

Another example that illustrates the elimination of sequential search is the negation procedure of Program 3.18 (in PARLOG or Kernel PARLOG):

```
~ p <− call(p) : FAIL;
~ p.
```

Applying the above rules, the procedure compiles to the following:

```
~ p <− call(call(p),s,c) and choose-not(s).

choose-not(s) <− SUCCEEDED <= s : FAIL..
choose-not(s) <− FAILED <= s :.
```

There are two optimizations that can be made to this procedure. First, observe that the nested metacall call(call(p),s,c) is identical to call(p,s,c). Second, as can be seen from the choose-not procedure, a call choose-not(s) succeeds if and only if s is FAILED, and therefore is equivalent to the call FAILED <= s. An alternative definition of the '~' relation is therefore:

```
~ p <− call(p,s,c) and FAILED <= s.
```

Note that this is equivalent to Program 3.18 because a compile-time analysis (Section 3.10.2) has verified that the guard call(p) of Program 3.18 is safe, i.e. that p contains no variables that will be bound by its evaluation.

5.2.4   Compiling primitive calls

A significant advantage afforded by the use of modes as the communication constraint of PARLOG is that much of the unification can be compiled. All calls to the one-way unification (term matching) primitive '<=' that are introduced for input matching can be compiled into in-line groups of simple instructions. This is because matching is a deterministic algorithm, owing to its directional nature. Moreover, the way in which these '<=' calls are compiled exposes the parallelism exhibited by the term-matching algorithm (Section 3.7.3). The fact that PARLOG relations are used in a single mode also enables many other primitive calls to be compiled into simple in-line instructions.

In this section, the following notational conventions are used: v, v_1, etc., are variables; K, K_1, etc., are constants; t, t_1, etc., are arbitrary terms; and nt, nt_1, etc., are arbitrary non-variable terms.

As explained in Section 3.5, the translation of a clause to standard form introduces some calls to the unification primitives. These take a certain simple syntactic form: both arguments of a '==' call are variables, the left argument of a '=' call is a variable, while the '<=' primitive is called with a non-variable term on the left and a variable on the right. These can be summarized as:

$$nt <= v$$
$$v_1 == v_2$$
$$v = t$$

Moreover, in the introduced calls of the form $nt <= v$, any variables in nt are guaranteed to be unbound at the time of the call, because of the guard safety property.

In general, the unification primitives are allowed in a source PARLOG program so they may be called with arguments of any form. The compilation scheme presented below therefore caters for all possible uses.

5.2.4.1 Simplifying calls to '='

Any call to the full unification primitive that has non-variable terms as both arguments can be simplified by a partial evaluation of the '=' procedure in Section 5.2.6. Both arguments must be the same constant, or they must both be lists, or structured terms with the same function name and arity. If this is the case, the following simplifications can be made, otherwise the call is illegal and causes a compile-time error:

- $K = K$

  A call whose arguments are two constants, which must be identical, is removed. The empty list '[]' is treated as a constant.

- $[t_1|t_2] = [t'_1|t'_2]$

  This is replaced by a conjunction of two simpler '=' calls:

  $$t_1 = t'_1 \text{ and } t_2 = t'_2$$

- $F(t_1,\dots,t_j) = F(t'_1,\dots,t'_j)$

  This is replaced by the conjunction:

  $$t_1 = t'_1 \text{ and } \dots \text{ and } t_j = t'_j$$

The above simplification steps are repeated until every '=' call has a variable as one or both of its arguments. As an example, the call:

```
F(K1,[v1|K2],G(v2),v3) = F(K1,[[]|v4],v5,v6)
```

is simplified to the conjunction:

```
v1 = [] and K2 = v4 and G(v2) = v5 and v3 = v6
```

Note the use of the neutral operator 'and', indicating that the components can be performed either sequentially or in parallel. (However, even if 'and' is interpreted as parallel conjunction, the data dependencies between the components may constrain the actual degree of parallelism; see Section 3.7.3.)

As a result of this simplification, all calls to '=' have a variable as either the left or right argument, or both. Because '=' is symmetric, it can be assumed that the resulting calls to '=' are all of the form $v = t$. Further, if it is known that v will be unbound at the time of the call, $v = t$ can be replaced by a simpler call, BIND(v,t); this is one of the optimizations described in Section 5.2.5.

5.2.4.2   *Simplifying calls to '=='*

A call to the test unification primitive '==' whose arguments are both non-variable terms can be simplified in much the same way as described above for '='. A call of the form $K == K$ is removed, while other forms of call are simplified to conjunctions as follows:

$$[t_1|t_2] == [t'_1|t'_2] \qquad \Rightarrow \quad t_1 == t'_1, t_2 == t'_2$$

$$F(t_1,...,t_j) == F(t'_1,...,t'_j) \Rightarrow \quad t_1 == t'_1, ..., t_j == t'_j$$

Note that the use of the parallel conjunction operator ',' is essential here, as in the '==' procedure of Section 5.2.6. This ensures that, for example, F(1,2) == F(x,3) fails; if sequential conjunction were used, the call would suspend waiting for a value for x (see Section 3.7.4).

These simplification steps are applied repeatedly until at least one argument of every '==' call is a variable. Since '==' is symmetric, the resulting calls can all be considered to be of the form $t == v$. In fact, calls to '==' that have a non-variable as one argument (i.e. $nt == v$) can be further simplified. If nt is a ground term, the call $nt = v$ is replaced by a matching call $nt <= v$. More generally, if nt contains variables $v_1,...,v_i$, these are substituted in nt by $u_1,...,u_i$ to obtain another term nt'. Then, $nt == v$ is replaced by the conjunction:

$$nt' <= v \text{ and } (u_1 == v_1, ..., u_i == v_i)$$

(The call $nt' <= v$ introduced above can be completely compiled, because it is the only call that can bind $u_1,...,u_i$, the variables in nt'. This compilation is explained in detail below.)

After this simplification, all calls to '==' have a variable as *both* arguments, i.e. they take the form $v_1 == v_2$. These '==' calls must be implemented by a recursive procedure that might suspend internally, depending upon the terms to which v_1 and v_2 are bound at run time. A PARLOG procedure for '==' is presented in Section 5.2.6.

5.2.4.3 *Compiling calls to '<='*

The first step in compiling '<=' calls is the simplification of any calls with non-variable terms as both arguments. This is handled in the same way as the simplification of '==' calls. A call of the form $K <= K$ is removed, and the following transformations are made:

$$[t_1|t_2] <= [t'_1|t'_2] \quad\Rightarrow\quad t_1 <= t'_1, \ t_2 <= t'_2$$

$$F(t_1,...,t_j) <= F(t'_1,...,t'_j) \quad\Rightarrow\quad t_1 <= t'_1, \ ..., \ t_j <= t'_j$$

(Again, the parallel conjunction operator ',' is used, to ensure non-strict behaviour.)

Repeated application of these steps ensures that all '<=' calls are of the form $v <= t$ or $t <= v$. The next phase compiles all matching calls of the form $nt <= v$ to groups of simpler instructions. This form of call is very common since it is introduced for the input matching of every non-variable head argument. The ability to compile such calls is therefore very important for efficiency.

- $K <= v$

   A match of a variable v with a constant K consists of two steps, performed sequentially. First, ensure that v is instantiated, then check that it is bound to constant K. This is expressed as a *sequence* of calls: to DATA and GET-CONSTANT:

   DATA(v) & GET-CONSTANT(K,v)

- $[t_1|t_2] <= v$

   A match of a variable v with a list $[t_1|t_2]$ again begins with a check that v is instantiated, expressed as a DATA call, followed by a GET-LIST call to check that v is a list. Then the head and tail of the list to which v is bound (v_1 and v_2) are matched with the terms t_1 and t_2, respectively, by subsequent '<=' calls:

   DATA(v) & GET-LIST(v,v_1,v_2) & ($t_1 <= v_1, \ t_2 <= v_2$)

- $F(t_1,...,t_j) <= v$

   A match of a variable v with a structured term $F(t_1,...,t_j)$ begins with a DATA call, followed by a GET-STRUCTURE call to check that v is bound to a structured term with function name F and arity j. Then the arguments of this term ($v_1,...,v_j$) are matched with terms $t_1,...,t_j$, by subsequent '<=' calls:

   DATA(v) & GET-STRUCTURE($F/j,v,v_1,...,v_j$) &
   ($t_1 <= v_1, \ ..., \ t_j <= v_j$)

The relations DATA, GET-CONSTANT, GET-LIST and GET-STRUCTURE can be regarded as instructions of the target abstract machine; hence, they are written in upper-case. The only instruction that can suspend is DATA;

its only purpose is to suspend until its argument variable is instantiated. The suspension effect of the '$<=$' primitive is achieved in each case by the use of DATA *sequentially preceding* the rest of the code.

Because of the preceding DATA instructions, each GET-... instruction proceeds in the knowledge that its v argument is instantiated. Each may either succeed or fail, depending upon the type of v. If a GET-LIST or GET-STRUCTURE call succeeds, because the v argument is bound to a list or a structured term respectively, v_1, v_2, etc., are bound to the subterms of v. Note that the last two arguments of GET-LIST and the last j arguments of GET-STRUCTURE are **first occurrences** of variables v_1, v_2, etc. That is, the GET-LIST or GET-STRUCTURE call sequentially precedes all other calls (in this case '$<=$' calls) that use these variables. This property means that the output arguments of the GET instructions are guaranteed to be unbound, non-shared variables (see Section 5.2.5).

After repeated application of the above compilation steps, the only matching calls that remain are of the form $v <= t$. In general, v *may* be instantiated at the time of the call, so the '$<=$' primitive must be implemented by a recursive procedure that might suspend internally until t is a substitution instance of v; a suitable definition of '$<=$', in PARLOG, appears in Section 5.2.6.

In the (very common) special case where it is known that v will be unbound at the time of the call, a call $v <= t$ can be replaced by a simple assignment instruction, BIND(v,t). Furthermore, if v is not shared with any other, parallel, process, the call can be removed and v identified with t at compile time. These optimizations are important because they can always be performed for all '$<=$' calls that are introduced by the compiler. The optimizations are described fully in Section 5.2.5.

The output argument of a BIND(v,t) call (its first argument) is known to be an unbound variable at the time of the call, but it is *not* guaranteed to be the first occurrence of v; v may also occur in a call that sequentially precedes BIND(v,t), or in a call that is in parallel with it. If the output argument of BIND(v,t) is a variable that is shared with an AND parallel call, the binding of v to t may involve communication between parallel processes, depending upon the nature of the architecture (Section 5.1.5). BIND is the only primitive that has to perform such communication. Also, BIND(v,t) is the instruction that performs an occur check if one is required (see Section 3.7.2). The occur check causes the instruction to fail if v occurs in the term t. The BIND instruction is also used in the procedures that implement the '$<=$' and '$=$' primitives, to bind variables; see Section 5.2.6.

5.2.4.4 Compiling other primitive calls

As noted in Sections 5.2.4.2 and 5.2.4.3, all remaining calls to the '$==$' and '$<=$' primitives that remain after compilation must be implemented by recursive, suspending, procedures (which could be expressed in PARLOG, as in Section 5.2.6). These primitives are therefore not considered instructions of any abstract machine for PARLOG. The full unification primitive ('=') must also be implemented by a recursive procedure but, unlike the other unification primitives, a '=' call never suspends. Whether '=' should be considered an instruction will therefore depend upon the nature of the target architecture, i.e. the ability of a processor to perform non-suspending recursive computations. In the following, '=' is (fairly arbitrarily) classified as an instruction (though a PARLOG procedure for '=' is included in Section 5.2.6 for completeness).

Other primitives that have been used so far, and their modes, include:

```
mode data(?), var(?),
     write(?), ? < ?, ? =< ?,
     plus(?,?, ↑ ), times(?,?, ↑ ), read( ↑ ),
     call(?), call(?, ↑ ,?), set( ↑ ,?,?), subset(?,?,?).
```

A call to the data primitive of PARLOG compiles to a DATA instruction (the same instruction that begins the compiled code for matching calls):

$$\text{data}(v) \qquad\qquad \Rightarrow \quad \text{DATA}(v)$$

The instruction corresponding to the var primitive is VAR:

$$\text{var}(v) \qquad\qquad \Rightarrow \quad \text{VAR}(v)$$

The write primitive has been used to print an arbitrary (even non-ground) term without suspension. It is intended to be used in conjunction with data tests to construct higher-level stream output procedures. A write call therefore compiles to a single instruction:

$$\text{write}(t) \qquad\qquad \Rightarrow \quad \text{WRITE}(t)$$

All other primitives that have input arguments are compiled to sequences beginning with DATA instructions, to wait for the arguments to be instantiated:

$$t_1 < t_2 \qquad\qquad \Rightarrow \quad (\text{DATA}(t_1) \text{ and } \text{DATA}(t_2)) \ \& \\ \text{LESS}(t_1,t_2)$$

$$t_1 =< t_2 \qquad\qquad \Rightarrow \quad (\text{DATA}(t_1) \text{ and } \text{DATA}(t_2)) \ \& \\ \text{LESSEQ}(t_1,t_2)$$

LESS and LESSEQ are instructions that simply perform the required test and either succeed or fail; they do not suspend.

All primitives with output arguments compile to sequences of code ending with '=' calls which perform the output unification:

read(t)	$\Rightarrow$	READ(v) & $t = v$
plus(t_1,t_2,t)	$\Rightarrow$	(DATA(t_1) and DATA(t_2)) & PLUS(t_1,t_2,v) & $t = v$
times(t_1,t_2,t)	$\Rightarrow$	(DATA(t_1) and DATA(t_2)) & TIMES(t_1,t_2,v) & $t = v$

Like the GET-... instructions, instructions like PLUS and TIMES are always called with instantiated input arguments, and their output arguments are always first occurrences of variables (which therefore are uninstantiated and non-shared).

The set, subset and call primitives are not considered instructions since they may, in general, require recursive procedures that may suspend internally. These may be implemented wholly or partly as PARLOG programs, such as the set and subset programs presented in Clark and Gregory (1985). The simple metacall (Section 3.9.1) requires that the PARLOG compiler is invoked on the argument term. The implementation of the control metacall (Section 3.9.2) is discussed in Chapters 6 and 7.

5.2.4.5　Summary of instructions

Several instruction primitives have been introduced in this section. Since they are of importance in Chapters 6 and 7, they are listed below:

$v = t$
VAR(v)
DATA(v)
BIND(v,t)
GET-CONSTANT(K,v)
GET-LIST(v,v_1,v_2)
GET-STRUCTURE($F/n,v,v_1,\ldots,v_n$)
LESS(t_1,t_2)
LESSEQ(t_1,t_2)
PLUS(t_1,t_2,v)
TIMES(t_1,t_2,v)
READ(v)
WRITE(t)
NL
FAIL

5.2.5　Optimization

Some of the code generated by the compilation of primitives may be unnecessarily complex. This is remedied by an optimization phase, described here, that replaces some primitive calls by simpler instructions and removes other instructions from the KP_a form of a program. The scope for optimization will be greater if *a* is of a more sequential nature. This is because many of the instructions are introduced only to allow for the possibility of parallel evaluation; if the evaluation is sequential they can often be removed. This section illustrates some of the most common types of optimization that are possible; others are possible and could be made by an optimizing compiler.

5.2.5.1 Definition: first occurrence of a variable
In a Kernel PARLOG (or KP_a) clause:

$$R(p_1,...,p_k) <- G : B.$$

a call *P*, in *G* or *B*, is the **first occurrence** of a variable *v* if:

1. *v* occurs in an argument of *P*, and
2. *v* is not one of the head variables $p_1,...,p_k$, and
3. for every other call P' in which *v* occurs in an argument, *P* sequentially precedes P' in the conjunction *G* & *B*.

A variable *v* can be treated as local to a call that is the first occurrence of *v*. That is, at the time of the call, *v* is guaranteed to be uninstantiated and not shared with any other, parallel, process.

5.2.5.2 Definition: first-write occurrence of a variable
In a Kernel PARLOG (or KP_a) clause:

$$R(p_1,...,p_k) <- G : B.$$

a call *P*, in *G* or *B*, is the **first-write occurrence** of a variable *v* if:

1. *v* occurs in an argument of *P*, and
2. *v* is not one of the head variables $p_1,...,p_k$, and
3. for every other call P' in which *v* occurs in an argument, *P* sequentially precedes P' in the conjunction *G* & *B*, *or* the evaluation of P' does not bind *v*.

This property is a weaker one than the 'first occurrence' property: every call that is a first occurrence of a variable *v* is also a first-write occurrence of *v*. At the time of executing a call that is a first-write occurrence of *v*, *v* is guaranteed to be unbound; however, *v* *may* be shared with another, parallel, process. Clearly, to detect whether a use of a variable is a first-write occurrence requires more than a syntactic check.

5.2.5.3 Definition: sequentially preceding calls
A call P_1 **sequentially precedes** a call P_2 in a sequential conjunction *A* & *B* if:

1. P_1 is in *A* and P_2 is in *B*, or

2. P_1 sequentially precedes P_2 in A, or

3. P_1 sequentially precedes P_2 in B.

P_1 sequentially precedes P_2 in a parallel conjunction A , B if:

1. P_1 sequentially precedes P_2 in A, or

2. P_1 sequentially precedes P_2 in B.

5.2.5.4   *Simplifying '<=' and '=' calls*

Any call of the form:

$$v <= t$$
$$v = t$$
$$t = v$$

which is the first-write occurrence of v, can be replaced by a BIND(v,t) call, because then v is guaranteed to be uninstantiated. Moreover, because a BIND call cannot suspend, a parallel conjunction containing one:

$$P_1, \ldots, P_i, \text{BIND}(v,t), P_{i+1}, \ldots, P_k$$

can be reorganized to:

$$\text{BIND}(v,t) \text{ and } (P_1, \ldots, P_k)$$

That is, a BIND call in a parallel conjunction may, if desired, be performed sequentially before the remainder of the conjunction. This is important because it introduces more scope for sequential optimizations.

As an application of this transformation, suppose that a matching call:

$$F(u_1,\ldots,u_i,t_{i+1},\ldots,t_j) <= v$$

is a first-write occurrence of variables $u_1,\ldots,u_i$. The call compiles to:

$$\text{DATA}(v) \ \& \ \text{GET-STRUCTURE}(F/j,v,v_1,\ldots,v_j) \ \&$$
$$(\text{BIND}(u_1,v_1) \text{ and } \ldots \text{ and } \text{BIND}(u_i,v_i) \text{ and }$$
$$(t_{i+1} <= v_{i+1}, \ldots, t_j <= v_j))$$

As an example, consider the first on-tree clause of Program 3.7, whose Kernel PARLOG form is:

```
on-tree(p1,p2,p3) <-
    T(x,P(q1,value),y) <= p3, p1 == q1 :
    p2 = value.
```

Compiling the matching call as explained in Section 5.2.4.3 yields the following:

```
on-tree(p1,p2,p3) <-
    (DATA(p3) & GET-STRUCTURE(T/3,p3,v1,v2,v3) &
    (x <= v1,
      (DATA(v2) & GET-STRUCTURE(P/2,v2,v4,v5) &
      (q1 <= v4, value <= v5)),
      y <= v3)),
    p1 == q1 :
    p2 = value.
```

The structure of this procedure is quite complex. It can be simplified as explained above: every '<=' call is a first-write occurrence of its left argument variable, so is replaced by a corresponding BIND call. The resulting conjunction is then reorganized using 'and', which is interpreted as '&':

```
on-tree(p1,p2,p3) <-
    (DATA(p3) & GET-STRUCTURE(T/3,p3,v1,v2,v3) &
    BIND(x,v1) & BIND(y,v3) &
    DATA(v2) & GET-STRUCTURE(P/2,v2,v4,v5) &
    BIND(q1,v4) & BIND(value,v5)),
    p1 == q1 :
    p2 = value.
```

5.2.5.5 *Removing redundant* BIND *calls*

If a BIND(v,t) call is the first occurrence of v in a clause, it can be removed and v replaced by t throughout the clause. This is because v is guaranteed to be an uninstantiated variable with no other uses at the time of the call. Of the four BIND calls in the above clause, three can be removed because they are the first (or only) occurrences of a variable (x, y and value). All that remains is BIND(q1,v4) because q1 occurs in an AND parallel call (a '==' call):

```
on-tree(p1,p2,p3) <-
    (DATA(p3) & GET-STRUCTURE(T/3,p3,x,v2,y) &
    DATA(v2) & GET-STRUCTURE(P/2,v2,v4,value) &
    BIND(q1,v4)),
    p1 == q1 :
    p2 = value.
```

5.2.5.6 *Introduced matching can be compiled*

It is easy to see that all matching ('<=') calls that are introduced by the compiler can be completely compiled to groups of instructions, so that no calls to the recursive '<=' procedure remain. Consider a general PARLOG clause:

$$R(t_1,...,t_k) <- G : B.$$

Assuming that the first i arguments of R are input, the standard form of this clause, shown in Section 3.5.1, is:

$R(p_1,...,p_i,p_{i+1},...,p_k) <-$
    $t'_1 <= p_1, ..., t'_i <= p_i,$
    <test unifications for repeated variables of $t_1,...,t_i$>,
    G :
    $p_{i+1} = t_{i+1}$ and ... and $p_k = t_k$ and
    B.

where $t'_1,...,t'_i$ are $t_1,...,t_i$ with duplicated variables replaced by new variables.

By the rules given in Section 5.2.4.3, each '$<=$' call in the guard, $t'_j <= p_j$, is reduced to a conjunction in which the only '$<=$' calls have a variable as left argument, i.e. $u <= v$, where u is a variable occurring in the term t'_j. Now, u must be either a variable in the original head argument t_j or one of the introduced variables. In either case, u may occur in one of the '$==$' calls in the guard; by definition, such a call cannot bind u. If u is a variable of t_j, it may occur in G but, because of the guard safety property, u cannot be bound by G. Therefore, the call $u <= v$ is a first-write occurrence of u, and can be replaced by the instruction $\text{BIND}(v,u)$, or removed (if a first occurrence).

5.2.5.7   *Removing redundant* DATA *calls*

The DATA instruction is used to test whether a variable is instantiated. A $\text{DATA}(v)$ instruction can be removed if used in a context where v is known to be instantiated already. One example of this is where a $\text{DATA}(v)$ call sequentially precedes another $\text{DATA}(v)$ call in a clause: then the second call can be omitted.

A more common situation where this optimization can be applied is in a sequence of clauses, the first of which has a guard which is a sequence of calls beginning with a $\text{DATA}(p_i)$ call, where p_i is one of the head arguments of the clause. Then, no $\text{DATA}(p_i)$ call is necessary in the guards of subsequent clauses. As an example, consider the qsort procedure of Program 4.1, of which the Kernel PARLOG form is:

```
qsort(p1,p2,p3) <- [u|x] <= p1 :
    partition(u,x,x1,x2),
    qsort(x1,p2,[u|sorted]),
    qsort(x2,sorted,p3)..
qsort(p1,p2,p3) <- [] <= p1 :
    p2 = p3.
```

Each matching call can be compiled as in Section 5.2.4.3 and the guards optimized as explained in Section 5.2.5.5. Because no calls to BIND remain in the guards, no occur check is performed; this is an example of '<=' calls that do not require an occur check (see Section 3.7.2). Now, if the '..' operator is interpreted as ';', the DATA(p1) call can be omitted from the beginning of the second clause guard:

```
qsort(p1,p2,p3) <- DATA(p1) & GET-LIST(p1,u,x) :
    partition(u,x,x1,x2),
    qsort(x1,p2,[u|sorted]),
    qsort(x2,sorted,p3);
qsort(p1,p2,p3) <- GET-CONSTANT([],p1) :
    p2 = p3.
```

5.2.6 Procedures for the unification primitives

The three unification primitives can be expressed partly in PARLOG, in terms of a few special-purpose instructions:

mode ? $==$?, ? $<=$?, ? $=$?.

5.2.6.1 *The '$==$' primitive*

A call $t_1 == t_2$ succeeds if t_1 and t_2 are the same constant, the same variable, or a pair of lists or structured terms whose arguments can be unified, in parallel, by '$==$' calls:

```
c1 == c2 <- EQCONST(c1,c2) :;
v1 == v2 <- EQVAR(v1,v2) :;
str1 == str2 <- (DATA(str1) & STRLIST(str1,list1)),
                (DATA(str2) & STRLIST(str2,list2)) :
    list1 == list2;
[h1|t1] == [h2|t2] <-
    h1 == h2, t1 == t2.
```

The above procedure uses two new instructions, EQCONST and EQVAR, which succeed if both arguments are the same constant or variable, respectively. It also uses a STRLIST instruction, which outputs a list containing the function name and arguments of the structured term given as its first (input) argument; STRLIST fails if its first argument is not a structured term.

5.2.6.2 *The '$<=$' primitive*

The procedure for the matching primitive is very similar to that for '$==$'. An extra clause, the third, handles the case where the left argument is an unbound variable. In this case, the variable is bound by a call to BIND in the body:

```
c1 <= c2 <- EQCONST(c1,c2) :;
v1 <= v2 <- EQVAR(v1,v2) :;
v <= t <- LOCKVAR(v) : BIND(v,t);
str1 <= str2 <- (DATA(str1) & STRLIST(str1,list1)),
                (DATA(str2) & STRLIST(str2,list2)) :
    list1 <= list2;
[h1|t1] <= [h2|t2] <-
    h1 <= h2, t1 <= t2.
```

In order to prevent simultaneous binding of a variable by several processes, the concept of **locking** is introduced. An unbound variable may now be in either locked or unlocked state; this locking is transparent, except for its effect on the BIND and LOCKVAR instructions.

The LOCKVAR instruction is used at entry to a 'critical section', prior to an attempt to bind a variable. $LOCKVAR(v)$ suspends if v is a *locked*, unbound variable; this indicates that another process has locked v and will eventually either unlock v or bind it. If v is bound to a non-variable term, $LOCKVAR(v)$ fails; if v is an unlocked, unbound variable, $LOCKVAR(v)$ succeeds *and* locks v in the same atomic action.

The BIND instruction must be changed slightly. If $BIND(v,t)$ leaves v as an unbound variable, the call must unlock v. This is a rare event, occurring only when BIND fails, perhaps as a result of an occur check failure (see Section 5.2.4.3).

Keith Clark (personal communication) has suggested a more complex, but more general, locking scheme whereby a call that locks a variable returns a unique key. This may then be handled like any other term, and must be used by any BIND instruction in order to bind the locked variable.

5.2.6.3   The '=' primitive

In the procedure for full unification, another new clause is introduced: the third clause for '=' handles the case where the right argument is an unbound variable:

```
c1 = c2 <- EQCONST(c1,c2) :;
v1 = v2 <- EQVAR(v1,v2) :;
t = v <- LOCKVAR(v) : BIND(v,t);
v = t <- LOCKVAR(v) : BIND(v,t);
str1 = str2 <- STRLIST(str1,list1) and STRLIST(str2,list2) :
    list1 = list2;
p1 = p2 <-
    GET-LIST(p1,h1,t1) and GET-LIST(p2,h2,t2) and
    h1 = h2 and t1 = t2.
```

After the failure of the first four clauses for '=', both arguments are known to be non-variable terms, so no DATA tests are needed in the last two clauses.

6
The AND/OR tree model of PARLOG implementation

This chapter presents a model for PARLOG evaluation based on a tree of AND and OR processes: the **AND/OR tree** model. This is an abstract architecture that can directly support the control structure of a Kernel PARLOG program. The model itself is described in Section 6.3.

The first section outlines the compilation from Kernel PARLOG to a form specific to the AND/OR tree model: $KP_{AND/OR\ tree}$. Examples of programs in $KP_{AND/OR\ tree}$ appear in Section 6.2. The final section outlines how the AND/OR tree model might act as the basis of implementations of PARLOG.

6.1   Compiling Kernel PARLOG to $KP_{AND/OR\ tree}$

As explained in Sections 5.2.2 and 5.2.3, the first phase of compilation of a Kernel PARLOG program is to manipulate the granularity of the program to fit on to the target architecture. The AND/OR tree model described in this chapter can support full Kernel PARLOG as described in Section 5.2.1, so there is no need to change the structure of the program. All that is required is to replace the neutral operators '..' and 'and' by explicit parallel or sequential operators.

Whether the neutral operators should be replaced by parallel or sequential operators depends upon the nature of the target machine. For example, if the AND/OR tree model is chosen as the basis of a PARLOG implementation on a sequential (uniprocessor) machine, the best choice will be to replace '..' and 'and' by ';' and '&', respectively. This allows maximum scope for optimization, as explained in Section 5.2.5.

The compilation proceeds by compiling primitive calls as described in Section 5.2.4, and then optimizing the generated code as in Section 5.2.5. The resulting code, the 'machine code' for the AND/OR tree model, will be named $KP_{AND/OR\ tree}$.

6.2   Examples of KP$_{AND/OR\ tree}$ programs

6.2.1   Example: merge

The Kernel PARLOG form of the merge procedure of Program 3.2 is:

```
merge(p1,p2,p3) <- [u|x] <= p1 :
    p3 = [u|z] and merge(x,p2,z).
merge(p1,p2,p3) <- [v|y] <= p2 :
    p3 = [v|z] and merge(p1,y,z).
merge(p1,p2,p3) <- [] <= p1 :
    p3 = p2.
merge(p1,p2,p3) <- [] <= p2 :
    p3 = p1.
```

To compile this to KP$_{AND/OR\ tree}$, each 'and' is replaced by the sequential '&' and each matching call is compiled as explained in Section 5.2.4.3:

```
merge(p1,p2,p3) <- DATA(p1) & GET-LIST(p1,u,x) :
    p3 = [u|z] & merge(x,p2,z).
merge(p1,p2,p3) <- DATA(p2) & GET-LIST(p2,v,y) :
    p3 = [v|z] & merge(p1,y,z).
merge(p1,p2,p3) <- DATA(p1) & GET-CONSTANT([],p1) :
    p3 = p2.
merge(p1,p2,p3) <- DATA(p2) & GET-CONSTANT([],p2) :
    p3 = p1.
```

6.2.2   Example: timeslist

The timeslist procedure of Program 4.7 has the following Kernel PARLOG form:

```
timeslist(p1,p2,p3) <- [v|y] <= p2 :
    p3 = [w|z] and times(p1,v,w) and timeslist(p1,y,z).
```

First, the 'and' operators are replaced by '&', as is the ':' (because this is the only clause of the procedure). Then the matching call is compiled as in the merge example, and the call to the times primitive is compiled to a sequence of instructions as explained in Section 5.2.4.4:

```
timeslist(p1,p2,p3) <- DATA(p2) & GET-LIST(p2,v,y) &
    p3 = [w|z] &
    DATA(p1) & DATA(v) & TIMES(p1,v,u) & w = u &
    timeslist(p1,y,z).
```

6.2.3 Example: on-tree

The Kernel PARLOG form of the on-tree procedure of Program 3.7 appeared in Section 3.5.2. Using the techniques of Section 5.2.4.3, the matching calls are compiled, and then optimized as explained in Section 5.2.5. The resulting $KP_{AND/OR\ tree}$ procedure is:

```
on-tree(p1,p2,p3) <−
    (DATA(p3) & GET-STRUCTURE(T/3,p3,x,v2,y) &
     DATA(v2) & GET-STRUCTURE(P/2,v2,v4,value) &
     BIND(q1,v4)),
    p1 == q1 :
    p2 = value;
on-tree(p1,p2,p3) <−
    (DATA(p3) & GET-STRUCTURE(T/3,p3,v1,v2,y) & BIND(x,v1) &
     DATA(v2) & GET-STRUCTURE(P/2,v2,rkey,rvalue)),
    on-tree(p1,value,x) :
    p2 = value.
on-tree(p1,p2,p3) <−
    (DATA(p3) & GET-STRUCTURE(T/3,p3,x,v2,v3) & BIND(y,v3) &
     DATA(v2) & GET-STRUCTURE(P/2,v2,rkey,rvalue)),
    on-tree(p1,value,y) :
    p2 = value.
```

6.3 The AND/OR tree model

The model centres on a **process tree**, a process structure whose state at any time records the state of a PARLOG evaluation. The nodes in the tree are processes, of which each leaf process is either **runnable** or **suspended** (on some variable). The non-leaf processes are not runnable; these have a **process type** (AND or OR) and are awaiting the outcome of their offspring process(es).

Each process has the ability to internally execute a *sequence* of instructions (the primitives DATA, BIND, '=', GET-CONSTANT, PLUS, etc., listed in Section 5.2.4.5). This defines the granularity of the model. If a sequential conjunction begins with a programmer-defined relation call or a call to a non-compilable primitive ('<=', '==', call, set and subset), the process **forks**, spawning an offspring process to evaluate the call; see Section 6.3.1. Similarly, if a relation R is defined by a sequence of clauses, the process evaluating a call to R spawns an offspring process to evaluate the guard of each clause (Section 6.3.3). For each parallel group of calls in a conjunction, or of clauses in a procedure, the process spawns several offspring processes which are evaluated in parallel (Sections 6.3.2 and 6.3.4).

The instructions of Section 5.2.4.5 affect only the binding environment of variables, not the control structure (i.e. the process tree). The state of the process tree *is* changed as a result of the operators '&', ',', ';' and '.' in a $KP_{AND/OR\ tree}$ program, so these can be regarded as control instructions of the model; they are described in Sections 6.3.1–6.3.4. There are three other such control instructions: success, corresponding to the end of a conjunction (Section 6.3.5); commitment, corresponding to the ':' operator of $KP_{AND/OR\ tree}$ (Section 6.3.6); and failure, corresponding to the FAIL instruction which is usually called implicitly upon the failure of other instructions (Section 6.3.7).

To evaluate a PARLOG query : Q, a tree is created with a single process, whose state is simply Q. If the query Q begins with a sequence of instructions, they will be evaluated by the process itself. For any other form of query, new processes are spawned.

6.3.1 Sequential conjunction

To evaluate a sequential conjunction beginning with a call to a non-instruction relation (i.e. a programmer-defined relation or the primitives '<=', '==', call, set and subset), an offspring process is created to evaluate the call. The process type of the current process is set to AND, and its state is changed to the 'continuation': the code to be executed if and when the call eventually succeeds.

Suppose that the state of a process is the conjunction P & B, where P is a call. The process tree changes as shown in Fig. 6.1. The process evaluating P & B becomes an 'AND process', and its continuation is set to the remainder of the conjunction, B. The contents of the AND process preceding the continuation are underlined in the figure. B is the code to be evaluated after P has successfully been evaluated by the new offspring process; Section 6.3.5 explains the effects of P succeeding.

Fig 6.1   Sequential conjunction.

6.3.2 Parallel conjunction

A parallel conjunction is handled in the same way as a sequential conjunction, except that there may be more than one offspring process. For example, to evaluate the conjunction (P1, P2) & B the process tree changes as shown in Fig. 6.2. B is the code to be evaluated when both offspring processes (P1 and P2) have succeeded.

Fig 6.2 Parallel conjunction.

6.3.2.1 Tail forking

A special case of parallel conjunction is the occurrence of a parallel conjunction at the end of a clause body. This is a quite common situation; for example, the qsort procedure of Program 4.1 and the seq-qsort procedure of Program 4.2. Suppose that the P1 call above has reduced using a candidate clause of the form:

P1 <− G : B1 &...& Bn & (P11, P12).

Then, following the successful evaluation of B1 &...& Bn, the state of the process tree is as shown in Fig. 6.3(a).

(a)
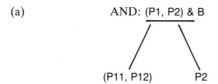

(b)
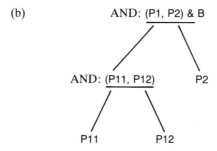

(c)
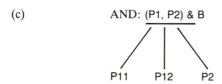

Fig 6.3 Tail forking optimization: (a) before fork; (b) naive fork;
(c) optimized fork.

One way to proceed would be to spawn a new offspring process to evaluate each of P11 and P12, as in Fig. 6.3(b). However, there is no need to increase the depth of the tree. Because the process evaluating (P11, P12) already has a parent which is an AND process, this process can fork *at the same level*. A sibling process is created for each of the members of the parallel conjunction. The resulting tree is shown in Fig. 6.3(c).

This optimization, **tail forking**, is a generalization of the tail recursion optimization applicable to sequential logic programs. It is very important since it prevents the process tree from increasing in depth during a long evaluation.

6.3.3   Sequential clause search

Clause search is handled analogously to conjunction, except that the tail forking optimization is not applicable. A sequential procedure:

    H <- G1 : B1;
    H <- G2 : B2;
    H <- B.

is evaluated by spawning an offspring process to evaluate the guard, G1, of the first clause. The original process becomes an 'OR process', i.e. its process type is set to OR, and its continuation is set to the code to execute in the event that the guard of G1 fails; see Fig. 6.4.

Fig 6.4   Sequential clause search.

6.3.4   Parallel clause search

In a parallel clause search, an offspring process is created to evaluate the guard of each clause in the parallel group. The continuation of the parent process is the code to execute if the guards of all clauses in the parallel group fail. Consider the procedure:

    H <- G1 : B1.
    H <- G2 : B2;
    H <- B.

The process tree changes as shown in Fig. 6.5.

(G1:B1. G2:B2); B   ⇒   OR: (G1:B1. G2:B2); B

G1:B1   G2:B2

Fig 6.5   Parallel clause search.

A procedure that comprises just a parallel group of clauses:

    H <- G1 : B1.
    H <- G2 : B2.

is treated as though it were sequentially followed by a clause that fails:

    H <- G1 : B1.
    H <- G2 : B2;
    H <- FAIL.

That is, if all guards (G1 and G2) fail, the parent will continue and immediately fail itself, by executing the FAIL instruction.

6.3.5   Success

A process that was created to evaluate a conjunction will terminate when all instructions or calls in its conjunction have been evaluated. This termination represents the **success** of the conjunction. The parent of a succeeding process always has a process type of AND.

There are two possibilities. If the succeeding process has no siblings in the process tree, the process is disposed of and its parent is reactivated at the stored continuation point. Fig. 6.6 shows the change to the process tree when P succeeds. If the successful process has siblings, the process is simply disposed of; the parent process is *not* reactivated. For example, if P1 and P2 are evaluating in parallel and P1 succeeds, the process tree changes as shown in Fig. 6.7.

AND: P & B   ⇒   P & B

P

Fig 6.6   Success.

Fig 6.7   Success.

6.3.6   Commitment

A process that was created to evaluate a clause guard will always have a parent with a process type of OR. Such a process will evaluate the guard and, if the guard succeeds, will **commit** (provided no other clause has committed). Upon commitment, the contents of the committed process are promoted to overwrite the parent process, which now proceeds by evaluating the body of the successful clause. If the committed process has no siblings, the process tree changes as shown in Fig. 6.8. If there are siblings, the commitment causes them to be disposed of. For example, if guard G1 succeeds, the body B1 is promoted to the parent node *and* the evaluation of G2 is terminated; see Fig. 6.9.

Fig 6.8   Commitment.

Fig 6.9   Commitment.

6.3.7   Failure

Any process may fail, because of the failure of an instruction such as GET-CONSTANT(K,[v_1|v_2]) or by the explicit use of a FAIL instruction (as in the negation procedure of Program 3.18). The effect of such a failure depends upon the type of the parent process; indeed, the purpose of the process type is to determine the action to be taken upon failure.

If the parent's type is OR, the failure is of a clause guard. If there are other (sibling) guard processes active, the failing guard process is simply disposed of. The process tree changes as shown in Fig. 6.10 (in the case where guard G1 fails). If the last remaining offspring of an OR process fails, the parent is reactivated at its continuation point. For example, upon the failure of G1, the guard of the first clause in a sequence, the process tree changes as shown in Fig. 6.11. In this example, the parent will now spawn another process to evaluate the next guard, G2.

Fig 6.10 Failure of a guard.

Fig 6.11 Failure of a guard.

The failure of a process whose parent has type AND represents the failure of a call in a conjunction. Such a failure must cause the failure of the entire conjunction. In this case, all sibling processes are disposed of and the parent process is explicitly failed, as though it had executed a FAIL instruction; see Fig. 6.12.

Fig 6.12 Failure of a conjunction.

6.3.8 Suspension

As explained above, each process internally executes a sequence of instructions: those listed in Section 5.2.4.5. Two of these, DATA and BIND, are of particular importance since they effect the suspension and reactivation of processes.

A DATA(v) instruction tests whether v is instantiated. If not, the process executing the instruction **suspends** on v. The process cannot proceed further until v is bound. The only way that v can be bound is by some other (parallel) process executing a BIND instruction for the same variable, i.e. BIND(v,t). Since there may be any number of consumer processes for a variable, a single BIND instruction may result in several other processes being reactivated; i.e. those that had executed a DATA instruction for that variable.

There are at least two ways to implement process suspension. The simplest, though potentially computationally expensive, is the **busy-waiting** scheme. Here, a process that suspends on a variable v (because of a DATA(v) instruction) continually tests whether v is bound. When it finds that v is instantiated, the process proceeds by executing the next instruction.

An alternative, **non-busy-waiting**, scheme avoids the expense inherent in repeatedly testing a variable. In such a scheme, if a process executes a DATA(v) instruction, the process is descheduled (i.e. becomes non-runnable) and is entered on a list associated with the variable v so that, when v is instantiated, the process can be scheduled. In the non-busy-waiting scheme, not all leaf processes will necessarily be runnable: they may instead be suspended on a variable.

The **suspension list** associated with a variable v contains an identifier of each process that is suspended on v; there may be any number of processes on the list, but each process will be on no more than one list. This is because, as noted above, each process executes a *sequence* of instructions (including DATA instructions) so will only suspend on one variable at a time. In a parallel conjunction such as

DATA(u), DATA(v)

each DATA call is invoked from a different process: one may suspend on u and the other on v.

The instruction BIND(v,t) must now, as well as binding v to t, activate all processes (if any) that are on v's suspension list. In the non-busy-waiting scheme, there is an additional action associated with the garbage collection of processes. Whenever a process is disposed of (as shown in Sections 6.3.5–6.3.7), it must be removed from any suspension list of which it is a member. If the system maintains a list of the scheduled (runnable) processes, a disposed process will need to be removed from exactly one list: the scheduled list *or* the suspension list of some variable.

6.3.9   The control metacall

For the sake of completeness, the implementation of the control metacall primitive (Section 3.9.2) should be considered. Section 5.2.3 discusses how the use of the control metacall, combined with mode constraints, can replace several control structures of PARLOG: sequential conjunction and clause search, and OR parallel clause search. Indeed, this is one of the purposes of this primitive.

However, the AND/OR tree model of PARLOG implementation directly supports the above control structures. This allows the opposite approach to be taken: the control metacall can be defined by a PARLOG program which exploits sequential and parallel clause search. The following Kernel PARLOG program approximates the desired behaviour:

```
call(p,s,c) <- STOP <= c : s = STOPPED.
(call(p,s,c) <- call(p) : s = SUCCEEDED;
 call(p,s,c) <- s = FAILED ).
```

The evaluation of call(p,s,c) invokes two processes: one suspended until c is bound to STOP, and another which begins by evaluating p in a guard. The result argument s is eventually unified with SUCCEEDED or FAILED according to the result of p, or STOPPED if c is bound to STOP, in which case the evaluation of p is aborted by the commitment mechanism.

The most notable feature of the above program is that the guard of the second clause might not be safe: variables in p might be bound. In fact, it is essential to allow this guard to be unsafe in order to obtain the defined behaviour of the control metacall. The program would be illegal if guard safety is always checked.

The shortcoming of the above definition of call is that it fails to express the property that the evaluation should terminate 'reasonably soon' after the control argument is bound to STOP. This places a constraint upon the scheduling strategy used. First, the guard of the second clause should not be allowed to run indefinitely to the exclusion of other processes. Second, the first clause should commit soon after its guard is able to succeed.

6.4 Implementations of the AND/OR tree model

The AND/OR tree model is a natural implementation scheme for PARLOG, since the process structure directly reflects the structure of the language. In a concrete implementation, the AND/OR process structure must be mapped on to the target architecture in some way. It should be noted that the granularity of the model is quite fine: there is a branch in the tree to evaluate each clause guard, even if this contains only (for example) a matching call, like the merge procedure (Section 6.2.1). Similarly, within a clause guard, a process is created to perform the input matching of each of the input arguments of the clause.

To distinguish the processes of the AND/OR tree model from the processes implemented by the various architectures, the former will sometimes be termed **nodes** in the following discussion.

6.4.1   ALICE

The first implementation of PARLOG was one on ALICE, a parallel reduction architecture (Darlington and Reeve, 1981) primarily designed to support HOPE (Burstall *et al.*, 1980) and related functional languages, but augmented with a facility to support the logical variable. This implementation (completed in 1982) comprised a compiler from PARLOG to ALICE CTL (Compiler Target Language) (Reeve, 1981).

ALICE treats processes as 'rewritable' packets, whose contents represent the state of the process. The evaluation of a process (of which there may be an arbitrary number) is achieved by a sequence of rewrite steps performed by the finite number of 'agents', or processing elements. Processes may be linked into structures by means of argument fields in the corresponding packets, pointing to other packets; the packet identifiers are globally unique. Data is represented in a uniform manner: by structures of 'constructor' packets.

This early implementation of PARLOG on ALICE was based on the AND/OR tree model: the AND/OR process tree was represented by a tree of rewritable packets. Each leaf packet contained a call that was being evaluated, while non-leaf packets were processes monitoring the results of their offspring processes.

In tests, the implementation proved to be inefficient, compared with a compiled HOPE implementation running similar programs. The inefficiency took the form of a high turnover of packets, i.e. process creation and deletion, and hence a low speed. The reason was that, whereas HOPE was directly supported by the ALICE architecture, PARLOG required an extra layer of interpretation: the non-leaf processes in the packet structure representing the AND/OR tree. In a sense, the granularity of the AND/OR tree model is unsuited to ALICE: the AND/OR tree contains many processes, most of which are very trivial.

For greater efficiency, there should be fewer processes (rewritable packets) and these should make greater use of the power of the architecture. These considerations resulted in an alternative implementation scheme for PARLOG on ALICE, described in Chapter 7.

6.4.2   Crammond and Miller

Crammond and Miller (1984) present a design for a special-purpose parallel architecture to support PARLOG. It comprises a control structure which directly implements the AND/OR tree model, together with a parallel unification algorithm which is claimed to provide support for Concurrent Prolog. In their machine, each node in the AND/OR tree is implemented by a process; these processes are allocated to a fixed number of physical processors by a scheduler.

A possible cause of computational expense in this architecture is that every AND/OR tree node is implemented by a process. For example, a process is created to evaluate a guard even if the guard is very simple, as in the merge example. In such cases, the process handling overhead might outweigh the benefits of parallel evaluation. On the other hand, the degree of parallel forking is not as great in Crammond and Miller's machine as that advocated here, because unification of arguments is performed sequentially, left to right. For semantic reasons, discussed in Section 3.7.4, it is preferable to unify arguments (at least conceptually) in parallel.

An improved design, with optimizations, has recently been described (Crammond, 1986).

6.4.3 The Sequential PARLOG Machine

The Sequential PARLOG Machine (SPM) (Gregory, 1986) is an abstract instruction set designed for the sequential implementation of PARLOG. The SPM is based on the AND/OR tree model but incorporates features that enhance its efficiency in a sequential implementation.

Since the intention is to optimize the performance of PARLOG on a sequential machine, Warren's (1983) abstract Prolog instruction set (the 'Warren Machine') was used as a starting point. In a sequential implementation of PARLOG, the AND/OR process tree is simply a data structure used to record the progress of the evaluation, just as Prolog implementations use one or more stacks.

If only sequential operators ('&' and ';') are used in a PARLOG program, its behaviour is very similar to Prolog. The AND/OR tree representing the PARLOG evaluation is then linear: each node has just one offspring, except the leaf which is the only runnable process; the non-leaf nodes are AND or OR processes, not necessarily alternating. This linear AND/OR tree is analogous to the stack used in the Warren Machine, which contains two kinds of object: environments (corresponding to the AND nodes in PARLOG's tree) and choice points (corresponding to the OR nodes). (Some Prolog systems such as McCabe's Sigma Machine (McCabe, 1984b) use two separate stacks: one for environments and another for choice points.)

The Warren Machine seeks to avoid continually growing and popping the stack by buffering the most recent values in registers. For example, upon a relation call, the return address is saved in a register but the stack is not grown. The stack is grown only if the called procedure itself executes a call. This buffering enhances the speed of calls to relations which are defined by assertions.

Whenever parallel operators (',' and '.') are used in a PARLOG program, there may be more than one runnable process. These can be kept on a **runnable list** and evaluated in turn by some timesharing mechanism.

The SPM features two techniques for minimizing the expense of process creation. First, a depth-first scheduling strategy is always used. That is, if several processes are to be evaluated in parallel, they are actually evaluated one at a time, in textual order. This differs from PARLOG's sequential evaluation in that, if a process suspends, control continues with the next process to the right (after placing the suspended process on a suspension list; see Section 6.3.8). To avoid problems caused by a non-terminating process, the current process can be scheduled (i.e. placed on the runnable list) at any time, and another process on the runnable list made current.

Second, the current process is buffered using techniques analogous to (but different from) the buffering used in the Warren Machine. The contents of a new process node are kept only in registers and the node is added to the process tree only if the process forks *or* suspends.

An effect of these optimizations is that simple, non-forking processes (which are very common in PARLOG) are evaluated very inexpensively if they do not suspend; only if they suspend (which is relatively infrequent) are they added to the tree. For example, if merge (Program 3.2) is called with its arguments instantiated to ground lists, it will run without modifying the process tree, just as a list concatenation program can be run on the Warren Machine without growing the stack.

6.4.4   Other parallel implementations

It would appear that the most effective way to implement PARLOG on an arbitrary, reasonably coarse-grained, parallel architecture is by an extension of the Sequential PARLOG Machine. That is, the evaluation of an AND/OR tree begins on one processor using the depth-first method of the SPM. When other processors are available, any process in the runnable list can be evaluated on another processor, in the same way as the SPM.

The AND/OR tree model might provide a suitable basis for a dataflow implementation of PARLOG because of its relatively fine granularity. Then, the compilation from Kernel PARLOG to $KP_{AND/OR\ tree}$ (Section 6.1) might replace neutral operators by the parallel operators (',' and '.') for greater concurrency.

7

The AND tree model of PARLOG implementation

This chapter presents an alternative implementation scheme for PARLOG: the **AND tree** model. Unlike the abstract architecture described in Chapter 6, the AND tree model does not directly support the structure of Kernel PARLOG; as its name implies, there are only AND processes in the tree. This model is more coarse-grained than the AND/OR tree model. The motivation for the AND tree model is that it corresponds to the 'term rewrite' mechanism embodied by functional reduction architectures such as ALICE (Darlington and Reeve, 1981). The model is described in Section 7.4.

The first section describes the 'machine code' for the AND tree model: $KP_{AND\ tree}$. This differs from Kernel PARLOG mainly in that all clause guards must take a certain simple form. The compilation from Kernel PARLOG to $KP_{AND\ tree}$ is explained in Section 7.2, while examples of $KP_{AND\ tree}$ programs appear in Section 7.3. The final section outlines how the AND tree model can act as the basis of implementations of PARLOG.

7.1 $KP_{AND\ tree}$

The form of a $KP_{AND\ tree}$ procedure is summarized below. Like a Kernel PARLOG procedure, it is built from clauses using the parallel and sequential clause search operators '.' and ';':

> $KPat\text{-}proc$ = $KPat\text{-}clause$ |
> $\quad\quad KPat\text{-}proc$. $KPat\text{-}proc$ |
> $\quad\quad KPat\text{-}proc$; $KPat\text{-}proc$

As in Kernel PARLOG, a $KP_{AND\ tree}$ clause comprises a guard and body, either of which may be omitted:

169

> *KPat-clause = KPat-guard : KPat-body |*
> *KPat-guard : |*
> *KPat-body*

A guard is a conjunction of **guard instructions** (see below), composed using the parallel and sequential conjunction operators ',' and '&':

> *KPat-guard = guard-instruction |*
> *KPat-guard , KPat-guard |*
> *KPat-guard & KPat-guard*

A body is a *sequence* of **body instructions** (see below), possibly sequentially followed by a body fork:

> *KPat-body = body-fork |*
> *body-instruction |*
> *body-instruction & KPat-body*

A body fork is a *parallel* conjunction of **body calls** (see below):

> *body-fork = body-call |*
> *body-call , body-fork*

A $KP_{AND\ tree}$ query has the same syntax as *KPat-body*, as does the first argument of the call primitive.

Notice that the syntax of $KP_{AND\ tree}$ differs from that of Kernel PARLOG in several respects. First, each guard may contain only 'guard instructions'. These are the instructions listed in Section 5.2.4.5, with the exception of those that cause side-effects, such as READ and WRITE.

Second, $KP_{AND\ tree}$ clause bodies are restricted to the form:

> *body-instruction &...& body-instruction &*
> *(body-call,...,body-call)*

A 'body instruction' is any instruction (Section 5.2.4.5) except DATA, while a 'body call' is a call to a programmer-defined relation or to a non-instruction primitive ('<=', '==', call, set and subset).

The reasons for the restriction of $KP_{AND\ tree}$ to the above form will become clear from the description of the evaluation mechanism in Section 7.4, but may be summarized as follows.

Because the guards contain only instructions, not programmer-defined relation calls, they may be evaluated internally by the process that is solving a call. This process may evaluate all or some of the guards in an attempt to find a candidate clause. In doing so, any parallelism within a guard or between alternative clause guards is handled by a sequential mechanism: alternative OR parallel guards are evaluated sequentially, one at a time, in such a way that if one guard suspends, the next one is tried. This mechanism achieves the required non-determinism between guards without actual concurrency and is acceptable because of the simple nature of guards.

If, in evaluating a call $R(t_1,...,t_k)$, all guards are suspended, the search for a candidate clause suspends. There is no need to save the state of such a suspended search: the call $R(t_1,...,t_k)$ may be saved and re-evaluated at a later time, repeating the search for a candidate clause from the beginning. This is possible because the guards exclude side-effects.

When the process finds a candidate clause, it can internally execute the sequence of instructions in the body (which cannot suspend, since DATA is excluded). Any non-instruction calls in the body occur in a parallel group at the end, in the form of a tail fork (cf. Section 6.3.2.1). If there is such a tail fork, the final action of a process will be to spawn several sibling processes: one for each body call.

7.2   Compiling Kernel PARLOG to $KP_{AND\ tree}$

The first phase in the compilation of any Kernel PARLOG program involves manipulating the granularity of the program to fit on to the target architecture. The abstract architecture described in this chapter requires a substantial restructuring of the program, described here.

7.2.1   Simple guards

$KP_{AND\ tree}$ requires all clause guards to contain only certain types of call, namely instructions that do not cause side-effects. To ensure this, the Kernel PARLOG program is processed so that its guards include only calls to primitives that will be compiled to guard instructions. These include those calls to the matching primitive '$<=$' that are introduced by the compilation to standard form (Section 3.7.2), as well as all calls to data, var, plus, times, '$<$', '$=<$', etc. A **simple guard** in a Kernel PARLOG program is one that only includes such calls. The compiler must ensure that all guards are simple, by applying the techniques presented in Sections 5.2.3.1 and 5.2.3.2. The reader is referred to Chapter 5 for an explanation of the principles involved, and examples.

First, all uses of the neutral clause search operator '..' must be replaced by either '.' or ';'. The best choice is to use the sequential operator ';' since this allows greater scope for optimization. Then, non-simple guards are eliminated by the following steps.

7.2.1.1   *Simple guards in a parallel clause group*

In each parallel group of clauses, all clauses with *non-simple* guards are collapsed into a single clause, as explained in Section 5.2.3.1. Suppose that the following parallel group of clauses occurs as, or in, a procedure for R:

$R(HVARS) <- G'_1 : B'_1.$
...
$R(HVARS) <- G'_n : B'_n.$
$R(HVARS) <- G_1 : B_1.$
...
$R(HVARS) <- G_m : B_m.$

where $G'_1,...,G'_n$ are simple guards and $G_1,...,G_m$ are non-simple guards. Since the order of clauses is not significant, this represents the general case of a procedure with n clauses with simple guards and m with non-simple guards.

The above group of clauses is replaced by a single clause, in which the non-simple guards are evaluated by AND parallel control calls, along with a control call to an auxiliary relation simple-R:

$R(HVARS) <-$ call$(G_1,$s1,c1$)$, ..., call$(G_m,$sm,cm$)$,
    call(simple-R$($s$'1,...,$s$'n,SVARS)$,s,c$)$,
    or$_{m+1}($s1$,...,$sm,s,c1$,...,$cm,c$)$:
    eval-R$($s1$,...,$sm,s$'1,...,$s$'n,SVARS,NSVARS)$.   (C)

SVARS denotes the variables that are used in both the guard and body of each of the first n clauses (those with simple guards); *NSVARS* denotes those used in the guards and bodies of the last m clauses. The purpose of these arguments is to allow values to be communicated between the guard and body of each clause.

Two auxiliary relations are introduced. The procedure for simple-R is defined to evaluate each of the simple guards $G'_1,...,G'_n$ in a separate guard, and unify the corresponding result argument (of s$'1,...,$s$'n$) with SUCCEEDED:

simple-R$($s$'1,...,$s$'n,SVARS) <- G'_1 :$ s$'1$ = SUCCEEDED.
...
simple-R$($s$'1,...,$s$'n,SVARS) <- G'_n :$ s$'n$ = SUCCEEDED.

In the guard of clause C above, the result of the simple-R call is monitored, along with the results of the other control calls, by a call to or$_{m+1}$; procedures for or$_{m+1}$ are explained in Section 5.2.3.1. If one of $G'_1,...,G'_n$ succeeds, the simple-R call will succeed and so all of the other guard evaluations including $G_1,...,G_m$ will be terminated. If one of $G_1,...,G_m$ succeeds, all others will be terminated, as will the simple-R call.

The other introduced relation is eval-R, which is defined as described in Section 5.2.3.1. It simply evaluates the body corresponding to the successful guard evaluation, which it determines by a test of the result variables s1,...,sm and s$'1,...,$s$'n$:

eval-R$($s1$,...,$sm,s$'1,...,$s$'n,SVARS,NSVARS) <-$
    SUCCEEDED <= s1 : $B_1.$

...

eval-R(s1,...,sm,s'1,...,s'n,*SVARS,NSVARS*) $<-$
    SUCCEEDED $<=$ sm : B_m.

eval-R(s1,...,sm,s'1,...,s'n,*SVARS,NSVARS*) $<-$
    SUCCEEDED $<=$ s'1 : B'_1.

...

eval-R(s1,...,sm,s'1,...,s'n,*SVARS,NSVARS*) $<-$
    SUCCEEDED $<=$ s'n : B'_n.

This method is a refinement of that in Section 5.2.3.1, in which *all* guards in a parallel clause group are evaluated by AND parallel control calls. Here, this is done only for the non-simple guards; simple guards are evaluated as the guards of an auxiliary relation, for efficiency reasons. As a result of the compilation, the procedures for simple-R and eval-R have only simple guards. The compound clause C for R has a non-simple guard but this will be removed by a subsequent step, described below.

7.2.1.2 *Simple guards in a sequence of clauses*

In the last (or only) clause of a sequential procedure, the guard is unnecessary so if the guard is non-simple it can be moved into the body; this applies to clause C above. If a clause with a non-simple guard is not the last in a sequence, the procedure is compiled by applying the technique of Section 5.2.3.2. Consider the general case: a sequence of $m+n+1$ clauses, of which the first n clauses have simple guards and the $(n+1)$th has a non-simple guard:

$R(HVARS) <- G'_1 : B'_1$;
...
$R(HVARS) <- G'_n : B'_n$;
$R(HVARS) <- G : B$;
$R(HVARS) <- G_1 : B_1$;
...
$R(HVARS) <- B_m$.

This is replaced by the sequence:

$R(HVARS) <- G'_1 : B'_1$;
...
$R(HVARS) <- G'_n : B'_n$;
$R(HVARS) <-$ call(G,s,c), choose-R(s,*HVARS,VARS*).

where *VARS* represents the variables not in *HVARS* that occur in the body B. The choose-R procedure simply evaluates the body B if the guard G has succeeded, and evaluates $R'(HVARS)$ otherwise:

choose-R(s,*HVARS,VARS*) $<-$ SUCCEEDED $<=$ s : B;
choose-R(s,*HVARS,VARS*) $<-$ $R'(HVARS)$.

R' is an auxiliary relation defined by the last m clauses of R:

$$R'(HVARS) <- G_1 : B_1;$$
...
$$R'(HVARS) <- B_m.$$

7.2.2 Restructuring guards

Having ensured that guards are simple, it only remains to replace any uses of the neutral conjunction operator 'and' in guards by either ',' or '&'. The use of '&' is recommended since more optimizations are then possible (Section 5.2.5).

7.2.3 Restructuring bodies

The form of a clause body in $KP_{AND\ tree}$ was described in Section 7.1. A clause body may comprise a sequence of body instructions (i.e. any instruction except DATA) followed by a parallel group of non-instruction relation calls, termed body calls. To ensure that this is the case, the body of each Kernel PARLOG clause is processed so that it consists of a sequence of **body primitive calls** followed by a parallel group of body calls:

> *body-primitive-call* &...& *body-primitive-call* &
>   (*body-call* ,..., *body-call*)

7.2.3.1 *Body primitives*

A body primitive call is defined as a call to a PARLOG primitive which compiles only to body instructions. Examples of body primitive calls, and the sequences of body instructions into which they compile, are:

$v = t$	$\Rightarrow$	$v = t$
var(v)	$\Rightarrow$	VAR(v)
write(t)	$\Rightarrow$	WRITE(t)
read(t)	$\Rightarrow$	READ(v) & $t = v$

The primitives that are *not* considered body primitives include '<=', '==', call, set and subset, and 'suspendable' primitives. These suspendable primitive calls are those that would compile to sequences which include DATA instructions, e.g. data, '<' and times.

Calls to suspendable primitives that occur in the body are treated as calls to programmer-defined relations of the same name. The Kernel PARLOG procedures defining these relations use the same primitive calls in their guards, where they *can* be compiled:

data(p1) <- data(p1) :.

p1 < p2 <− p1 < p2 :.

times(p1,p2,p3) <− times(p1,p2,d) : p3 = d.

Following the rules of Section 5.2.4, the $KP_{AND\ tree}$ code for these procedures is:

data(p1) <− DATA(p1) :.

p1 < p2 <− DATA(p1) & DATA(p2) & LESS(p1,p2) :.

times(p1,p2,p3) <−
    DATA(p1) & DATA(p2) & TIMES(p1,p2,u) & d = u :
    p3 = d.

The times procedure can now be optimized (Section 5.2.5) by removing a redundant '=' call:

times(p1,p2,p3) <−
    DATA(p1) & DATA(p2) & TIMES(p1,p2,d) :
    p3 = d.

Calls to the unification primitives '==' and '<=' that occur in a clause body are treated as calls to programmer-defined relations because they are recursive programs that may suspend internally. Procedures for '==' and '<=' appear in Section 5.2.6.

7.2.3.2 *Simplifying sequential conjunction*

In the body of each Kernel PARLOG clause, it must be ensured that a body call never sequentially precedes any other call. The following changes are made where *A* is not a body primitive call:

A and *B*	⇒	*A*, *B*	(B1)
A & *B*	⇒	call(*A*,s,c), next-B(s,*VARS*)	(B2)

where *VARS* denotes the variables in *B*, and next-B is defined by the procedure:

next-B(s,*VARS*) <− SUCCEEDED <= s & *B*.

Note that, after rule B2 is applied, conjunctions *A* (in the control call) and *B* (in the body of next-B) must each be further compiled in the same manner.

Rule B1 above illustrates a case where it is desirable to replace a neutral 'and' operator by a parallel ','. It contrasts with the implementation scheme of Chapter 6, in which 'and' is always replaced by '&'. Rule B2 handles the case where *A must* be performed before *B*; this is handled using the technique of Section 5.2.3.3.

7.2.3.3   Flattening clause bodies

Finally, each clause body is 'flattened' by moving body primitive calls to the beginning of the body. If A is a body primitive call, the following changes can be made:

$$A \text{ and } B \quad \Rightarrow \quad A, B \tag{F1}$$
$$A, B \quad \Rightarrow \quad A \& B \tag{F2}$$
$$(A \& B), C \Rightarrow \quad A \& (B, C) \tag{F3}$$

These rules, together with the commutativity of ',', are sufficient to transform each body into the correct form shown in Section 7.1. Rules F2 and F3 are valid because of the properties of body primitives: because they do not suspend or perform substantial computation, it is always safe to change such a parallel conjunction to a sequential one.

Following all restructuring of guards and bodies, the primitive calls are compiled and the resulting code optimized, as described in Sections 5.2.4 and 5.2.5, respectively.

7.3   Examples of KP$_{\text{AND tree}}$ programs

7.3.1   Example: merge

The code generated for the merge procedure is the same as for the AND/OR tree model, presented in Section 6.2.1. This is because the guards contain only matching calls and the body contains just one (recursive) programmer-defined relation call, which can be preceded by the output unification call in the body.

7.3.2   Example: timeslist

The Kernel PARLOG form of the timeslist procedure of Program 4.7 appeared in Section 6.2.2. It is:

```
timeslist(p1,p2,p3) <- [v|y] <= p2 :
    p3 = [w|z] and times(p1,v,w) and timeslist(p1,y,z).
```

Because the body of the clause contains a call to a 'suspendable' primitive (times), this must be treated as a programmer-defined relation call, as explained in Section 7.2.3.1.

To compile the body of the timeslist clause into a valid $KP_{AND\ tree}$ clause, it is only necessary to replace the first 'and' by '&' and the second 'and' by ','. Then, the matching call can be compiled in the usual manner:

```
timeslist(p1,p2,p3) <- DATA(p2) & GET-LIST(p2,v,y) :
    p3 = [w|z] & (times(p1,v,w), timeslist(p1,y,z)).
```

7.3.3 Example: on-tree

The Kernel PARLOG form of the on-tree procedure of Program 3.7 was presented in Section 3.5.2. All clauses of on-tree have non-simple guards, so the procedure must be restructured as explained in Section 7.2.1. The restructured on-tree procedure is that presented in Section 5.2.3.2.

The final $KP_{AND\ tree}$ procedure is now obtained simply by compiling the matching calls and replacing the neutral operators. Note that the '<=' calls inside control calls are not compiled since '<=' is not a body primitive:

```
on-tree(p1,p2,p3) <-
    call((T(x,P(q1,value),y) <= p3, p1 == q1),s,c),
    choose-on-tree(s,p1,p2,p3,value).

choose-on-tree(s,p1,p2,p3,value) <-
    DATA(s) & GET-CONSTANT(SUCCEEDED,s) :
    p2 = value;
choose-on-tree(s,p1,p2,p3,value) <- GET-CONSTANT(FAILED,s) :
    call((T(x1,P(rkey1,rvalue1),y1) <= p3,
        on-tree(p1,value1,x1)),s1,c1),
    call((T(x2,P(rkey2,rvalue2),y2) <= p3,
        on-tree(p1,value2,y2)),s2,c2),
    or2(s1,s2,c1,c2),
    eval-on-tree(s1,s2,p2,value1,value2).

eval-on-tree(s1,s2,p2,value1,value2) <-
    DATA(s1) & GET-CONSTANT(SUCCEEDED,s1) :
    p2 = value1.
eval-on-tree(s1,s2,p2,value1,value2) <-
    DATA(s2) & GET-CONSTANT(SUCCEEDED,s2) :
    p2 = value2.
```

7.4 The AND tree model

The basis of the model is the **AND tree**: a tree of processes in which branches represent calls in a conjunction. Unlike the AND/OR tree model of Chapter 6, there is no OR branching. In this sense, an AND tree is similar to a proof tree (Section 2.6.5). The difference is that the hierarchy in an AND tree corresponds to the control call structure of a PARLOG evaluation, rather than the history of a proof. Consider the qsort procedure (Program 4.1) of which the Kernel PARLOG and $KP_{AND\ tree}$ forms appear in Section 5.2.5.7. Fig. 7.1 shows a partially constructed proof tree for an evaluation of the call qsort([2,1],y,[]), while Fig. 7.2 shows the corresponding AND tree.

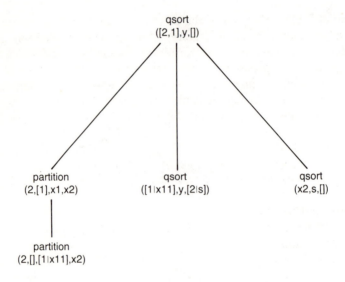

Fig 7.1   Proof tree for a qsort evaluation.

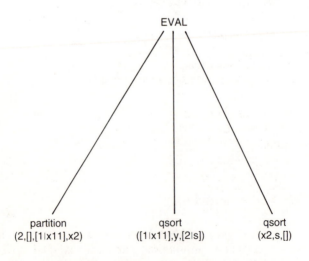

Fig 7.2   AND tree for a qsort evaluation.

Note that the AND tree is flat: it has one node for each *leaf* node of the proof tree, together with an EVAL node at the root. There is no need to retain the non-leaf nodes of the proof tree in the AND tree, since these correspond to previous states of the evaluation. If control calls are used, the AND tree will not be flat; see Section 7.4.2. In every AND tree, each non-leaf node is an EVAL process and each leaf node has a call (to a programmer-defined relation or '<=', '==', call, set or subset) associated with it. All processes in the tree run in parallel.

7.4.1   Evaluation mechanism

Recall that a query takes the same form as a clause body, i.e. a sequence of body instructions followed by a parallel group of body calls. To evaluate a query, the body instructions (if any) are first executed. By definition, these instructions cannot suspend; if any of them fails, the query fails. Otherwise, an initial AND tree is created comprising a process for each body call in the query, and an EVAL process at the root. The **state** of each leaf process is the call associated with it. For example, the initial AND tree for the query : qsort([2,1],y,[]) is shown in Fig. 7.3.

EVAL

qsort
([2,1],y,[])

Fig 7.3   Initial AND tree for a qsort evaluation.

The *leaf* processes in the tree then run independently, each performing a sequence of evaluation steps. Suppose that a process contains the call $R(t_1,...,t_k)$, which represents the state of the process. The next evaluation step comprises the following actions:

1. A candidate clause for the call $R(t_1,...,t_k)$ is sought from among the clauses for R. The search is performed entirely by this process. This is feasible because the guards contain only simple instructions which can be evaluated internally by a process. Any parallelism within guards and in the clause search is simulated by the process; the search for a candidate clause is described in Section 7.4.3. The result of the search will be either: (a) a candidate clause is found; or (b) the call fails; or (c) the call is suspended.

2. Depending upon the result of the search, one of the following actions is performed:

a) If a candidate clause is found, the process executes the sequence of body instructions (if any) at the beginning of the body of the selected clause; the body instructions, by definition, cannot suspend. If any of the instructions fails, the call fails. Otherwise, the process then forks: it is replaced in the tree by several processes (possibly none): one process for each 'body call' in the body.

b) If all clauses are non-candidates (or a body instruction fails, as in (a) above), the call fails. This failure is communicated to the parent EVAL process, which kills all of its offspring processes; see Section 7.4.2.

c) If no candidate clause is found but there are suspended clauses, the process suspends. Note that the suspended process still has the original call $R(t_1,...,t_k)$ associated with it; any computation performed by the process prior to detecting suspension is lost. The details of process suspension are discussed in Section 7.4.4.

7.4.2   Hierarchy of processes

7.4.2.1   *The control metacall*

As explained in Section 3.9.2, the term 'control call' is used to refer to a use of the three-argument call primitive in which the first argument is known at compile time. The control call is considered a *primitive* of the AND tree model; it is used to implement the other control structures of PARLOG, as demonstrated in Section 7.2.

The control *metacall* call(p,s,c), whose first argument is a variable at compile time, is treated as a control call with a simple metacall as argument:

call(call(p),s,c)

Hence, the three-argument call is always a control call in the AND tree model, and is handled specially.

An AND tree is normally flat, i.e. there is just one non-leaf process: the root node in the tree. It is no longer flat if the control call primitive is used; there is then a new subtree for each control call evaluation, rooted at an EVAL process.

7.4.2.2   *Example*

Consider the evaluation of a call on-tree(A,v,T(t1,P(RK,RV),t2)), where t1 and t2 are both large trees. Using the program of Section 7.3.3, the AND tree after one evaluation step is as shown in Fig. 7.4. In the figure, p3 abbreviates the tree T(t1,P(RK,RV),t2).

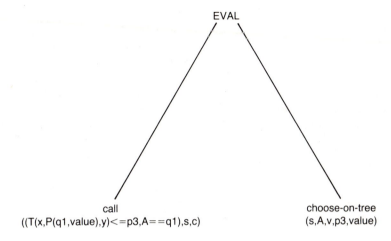

Fig 7.4 AND tree for an on-tree evaluation.

Any process whose state is a control call call(B,s,c) (B is a clause body) begins by evaluating any body instructions at the beginning of B. Then the process node is replaced in the AND tree by a subtree whose root is EVAL(s,c) and whose offspring processes are the body calls in B. The AND tree of Fig. 7.4 therefore changes to that of Fig. 7.5.

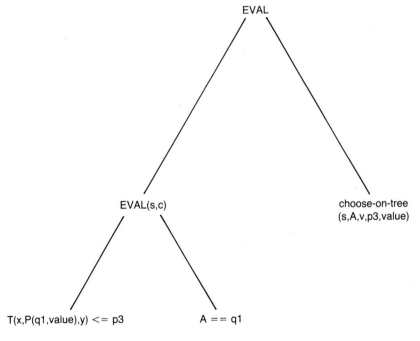

Fig 7.5 AND tree for an on-tree evaluation.

In the example, the T(x,P(q1,value),y) <= p3 process will succeed, binding q1 to the root key RK. This binding causes the A == q1 process to fail, so the subtree rooted at the EVAL(s,c) node is removed from the tree and s is bound to FAILED. The choose-on-tree process can then find a candidate clause (the second one) with which to reduce its call choose-on-tree(FAILED,A,v,p3,value). This call reduces to the body of the second clause: four body calls, each corresponding to a branch in the AND tree. Two of these calls are control calls which become new EVAL subtrees; see Fig. 7.6.

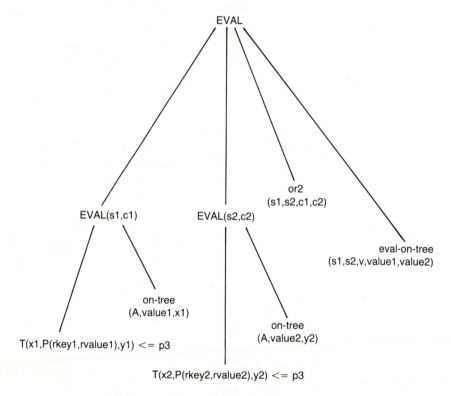

Fig 7.6   AND tree for an on-tree evaluation.

The '<=' processes immediately succeed, binding x1 to t1 and y2 to t2 (the left and right subtrees of the given tree). Fig. 7.7 depicts the resulting AND tree.

7.4.2.3 *EVAL processes*

EVAL processes in the AND tree do not obey the evaluation mechanism described in Section 7.4.1; they have a special function.

The role of each EVAL process is to monitor the evaluation of its offspring processes and the value of its control argument (the control

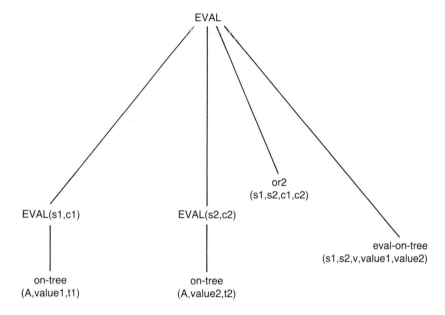

Fig 7.7   AND tree for an on-tree evaluation.

argument of the invoking control call). If all offspring processes succeed, the EVAL process succeeds after unifying its status argument with SUCCEEDED. If any offspring process fails, the EVAL process succeeds after unifying the status argument with FAILED, and garbage collects all active offspring processes. If the control argument of EVAL is bound to STOP, the EVAL process garbage collects its offspring processes and succeeds, unifying its status argument with STOPPED.

It is not necessary for an EVAL process to actively monitor its offspring processes and control argument. If each process has access to its parent in the AND tree (depending upon the particular implementation), a process that fails or succeeds can explicitly activate the parent EVAL process so that it can perform the necessary action. By additionally using a non-busy-waiting scheme to handle suspension on variables (discussed in Section 7.4.4) the EVAL processes can remain idle until required.

7.4.3   Searching for a candidate clause

As noted in Section 7.4.1, the search for a candidate clause with which to reduce a call is part of an evaluation step performed by a single process. An algorithm that performs this search is described here as an interpreter.

7.4.3.1   An algorithm to search for a candidate clause

Given a call $R(t_1,\dots,t_k)$, the algorithm searches the $KP_{AND\ tree}$ procedure for R, in which the head argument variables of all clauses are bound to $t_1,\dots,t_k$, respectively. A search among this procedure, P, is performed by an interpreter invoked by *search(P,r)*. The result of the search, r, will be either:

    CANDIDATE(B)

or

    FAILED

or

    SUSPENDED

A result *CANDIDATE(B)* returns the body of a candidate clause that was found. A *FAILED* result indicates that all clauses are non-candidates. *SUSPENDED* indicates that no candidate clause was found but some clauses are suspended.

    To search a sequence of clauses (or a sequence of clause groups) $A;B$, the first member of the sequence, A, is searched. If a candidate clause is found, this is returned. If A is suspended, so is $A;B$. Only if the search of A fails will the search proceed among B, the remainder of the sequence:

    search((A;B),r):
        search(A,rA).
        if $rA = FAILED$
            search(B,r)
        else
            $r := rA$.   (S1)

    A search among a parallel group of clauses or clause groups $A.B$ begins by searching among A. If a candidate clause is found, it is returned; otherwise (if failed or suspended), the search proceeds among B. Then, if A was suspended and B fails, $A.B$ is suspended. In any other case where A was suspended or failed, the result of $A.B$ is the same as the result of B:

    search((A.B),r):
        search(A,rA).
        if $rA = CANDIDATE(c)$
            $r := CANDIDATE(c)$
        else
            search(B,rB).
            if $rA = SUSPENDED$ and $rB = FAILED$
                $r := SUSPENDED$
            else
                $r := rB$.   (S2)

A search of a single clause evaluates the guard and returns the result of this evaluation. A *SUCCEEDED* result from the guard evaluation is returned as a *CANDIDATE(B)* result, where *B* is the corresponding body:

search((H<−G:B),r):
    guard(G,rG).
    if *rG = SUCCEEDED*
        r := CANDIDATE(B)
    else
        r := rG.   (S3)

The evaluation of a guard is analogous to the search for a candidate clause among a clause group. The result of a guard evaluation is either *SUCCEEDED*, *FAILED* or *SUSPENDED*.

To evaluate a sequential conjunction *A&B* in the guard, the first member of the sequence, *A*, is evaluated. If *A* fails or suspends, so does *A&B*. If *A* succeeds, the result of *A&B* is the result of evaluating *B*:

guard((A&B),r):
    guard(A,rA).
    if *rA = SUCCEEDED*
        guard(B,r)
    else
        r := rA.   (G1)

Evaluating a parallel conjunction *A,B* in the guard is analogous to searching for a candidate clause among a parallel clause group. If *A* fails, the result of *A,B* is *FAILED*, otherwise *B* is evaluated. Then, if *A* was suspended and *B* succeeds, *A,B* is suspended, otherwise the result of *A,B* is the same as the result of *B*:

guard((A,B),r):
    guard(A,rA).
    if *rA = FAILED*
        r := FAILED
    else
        guard(B,rB).
        if *rA = SUSPENDED* and *rB = SUCCEEDED*
            r := SUSPENDED
        else
            r := rB.   (G2)

The result of evaluating a DATA(v) instruction is *SUCCEEDED* if *v* is instantiated, or *SUSPENDED* if *v* is an unbound variable:

guard(DATA(v),r):
    if VAR(v)

$$r := SUSPENDED$$
   else
$$r := SUCCEEDED. \tag{G3}$$

The result of evaluating any guard instruction other than DATA is either *SUCCEEDED* or *FAILED*:

guard(A,r):
   if *A* succeeds
$$r := SUCCEEDED$$
   else
$$r := FAILED. \tag{G4}$$

7.4.3.2 Suspension variables

The above algorithm can easily be extended so that, if the result of a clause search is *SUSPENDED*, a set of **suspension variables** is returned. These are the variables that were unbound and thereby caused a suspension. In the interests of efficient implementation, this set will be constructed by side-effects to global variables. The global variable *susvars* is the set of suspension variables for the search; *gsusvars* is used to accumulate a set of suspension variables for each guard.

The search algorithm begins by initializing *susvars* to the empty set:

$$susvars := \{\}.$$

Rule S3 is changed so that, prior to evaluating a guard, the *gsusvars* set is emptied. If the result of the guard evaluation is suspended, the variables that caused the suspension of the guard are added to the suspension variables set for the whole procedure:

search((H<−G:B),r):
   gsusvars := {}.
   guard(G,rG).
   if *rG* = *SUCCEEDED*
      r := *CANDIDATE(B)*
   else
      r := *rG*.
      if *rG* = *SUSPENDED*
$$susvars := susvars \cup gsusvars. \tag{S3'}$$

Finally, rule G3 is changed so that, if the argument of a DATA instruction is an unbound variable, this variable is added to the guard's suspension variables set:

guard(DATA(v),r):
   if VAR(*v*)

$$gsusvars := gsusvars \cup \{v\}.$$
$$r := SUSPENDED$$
else
$$r := SUCCEEDED. \hspace{4cm} (G3')$$

The final value of *susvars* computed during this search records the reasons for the suspension of each suspended guard. It will be pointless to retry the search until at least one of the variables in *susvars* is bound. This fact can be exploited in implementing a non-busy-waiting suspension scheme; see Section 7.4.4.

7.4.3.3 Compiling the search

For pedagogical reasons, the algorithm above is presented as an interpreter. However, the search for a candidate clause can easily be compiled, treating the rules S1, S2, S3', G1, G2, G3' and G4 as macros rather than functions, and introducing appropriate global variables to replace local result variables. Possible result values are $CANDIDATE(n)$, *FAILED* or *SUSPENDED*, where n is a number identifying the candidate clause.

For example, the and program of Section 3.7.4 compiles as follows. The $KP_{AND\ tree}$ form of this is:

```
and(p1,p2) <−
    (DATA(p1) & GET-CONSTANT(True,p1)),
    (DATA(p2) & GET-CONSTANT(True,p2)) :.
```

This can be compiled to the algorithmic code:

$$susvars := \{\}.$$
$$result := CANDIDATE(1).$$
if VAR(p1)
   $$susvars := susvars \cup \{p1\}.$$
   $$rA := SUSPENDED$$
else
   if GET-CONSTANT(True,p1)
      $$rA := SUCCEEDED$$
   else
      $$result := FAILED.$$
if $result \neq FAILED$
   if VAR(p2)
      $$susvars := susvars \cup \{p2\}.$$
      $$result := SUSPENDED$$
   else
      if GET-CONSTANT(True,p2)
         if $rA = SUSPENDED$
            $$result := SUSPENDED$$

else
        result := FAILED.

In evaluating a call to and, if both arguments are the constant True, the result of *search* will be *CANDIDATE*(1), indicating that the first and only clause is a candidate. If one or both arguments is bound to something other than True, the result will be *FAILED*. In any other case, the result is *SUSPENDED*, meaning that the call is suspended on the variables in *susvars*. The value of *susvars* computed for the calls and(x,True), and(True,y) and and(x,y) are {x}, {y} and {x,y}, respectively.

The or procedure of Section 3.7.4 can be compiled as follows. Its $KP_{AND\ tree}$ form is:

```
or(p1,p2) <- DATA(p1) & GET-CONSTANT(True,p1) :.
or(p1,p2) <- DATA(p2) & GET-CONSTANT(True,p2) :.
```

and the compiled algorithmic code for the search is:

susvars := {}.
result := FAILED.
if VAR(p1)
    susvars := susvars ∪ {p1}.
    rA := SUSPENDED
else
    if GET-CONSTANT(True,p1)
        result := CANDIDATE(1)
    else
        rA := FAILED.
if *result = FAILED*
    if VAR(p2)
        susvars := susvars ∪ {p2}.
        result := SUSPENDED
    else
        if GET-CONSTANT(True,p2)
            result := CANDIDATE(2)
        else
            if *rA = SUSPENDED*
                result := SUSPENDED.

A call or(True,y) or or(x,True) will yield a result of *CANDIDATE*(1) or *CANDIDATE*(2), respectively. A call in which both arguments are bound to something other than True will yield a *FAILED* result. The result of calls or(x,False), or(False,y) and or(x,y) is *SUSPENDED*, with *susvars* computed as {x}, {y} and {x,y}, respectively.

A set of suspension variables can be represented by several boolean flags: one flag for each variable that could be a member of the set; these variables are known at compile time. The action of adding a single variable to the set as required in the algorithm, e.g. *susvars* := *susvars* ∪ {x}, is then very simple.

7.4.4 Suspension

In the AND tree model, a process suspends whenever the search for a candidate clause yields a *SUSPENDED* result. The suspension variables set indicates the variables on which the call suspends. The call will remain suspended until *at least one* of the variables in the set is instantiated. For example, the call and(x,y), where x and y are unbound, suspends on x and y. The call will fail if *either* x *or* y is bound to False. If, however, x or y is bound to True, the call will remain suspended until the other variable is bound.

As in the AND/OR tree model of Chapter 6, suspension can be implemented by a busy-waiting scheme. A process that suspends could repeat the search for a candidate clause, until it no longer gives a *SUSPENDED* result. In this case, the suspension variables set is ignored.

The computational expense of busy-waiting can be avoided by a non-busy-waiting scheme. In such a scheme, a suspended process is descheduled in such a manner that, if *any* of the variables in the suspension variables set is subsequently instantiated, the process is reactivated. The reactivated process will then retry the clause search, whereupon it will either: fail, find a candidate clause, or suspend again (because values of other variables are required). This scheme can be implemented, as in the AND/OR tree model, by associating a **suspension list** with each variable. A process that suspends is placed on the suspension list of *every* variable in the suspension variables set. This contrasts with the AND/OR tree model, in which a process may be on at most one suspension list.

When a variable v is bound, by a BIND(v,t) instruction, all processes on v's suspension list must be activated and removed from v's suspension list. There is an additional complication (compared with the AND/OR tree model) in that each process activated may occur on other suspension lists. There are at least two possible solutions:

1. When a process is activated upon the instantiation of v, remove the process from the suspension list of any other variables on which it is suspended. This requires some means of accessing, for each suspended process, all variables on which the process is suspended.

2. Do not remove the process from other suspension lists. In this case, the record of the process on the other suspension lists must be marked in some way to ensure that the process will not be activated when these other variables are instantiated.

In the non-busy-waiting scheme, a process might be on several suspension lists when it is garbage collected (by its parent EVAL process, as described in Section 7.4.2.3). Corresponding to the above methods of handling process activation, there are two possible methods of handling garbage collection of processes:

1. If there is a means of accessing all variables on which a given process is suspended, garbage collection may remove the process from the suspension list of each of them.

2. Alternatively, a process suspended on the variables $x_1,...,x_n$ can be marked in some way so that, when each of $x_1,...,x_n$ is instantiated the process will not be activated but, when *all* of $x_1,...,x_n$ are bound, the process will be disposed of.

7.5   Implementations of the AND tree model

7.5.1   ALICE

The main motivation for the design of the AND tree model was that it can be directly implemented on the ALICE architecture (Darlington and Reeve, 1981). To state it differently, the granularity of an ALICE agent matches that of a $KP_{AND\ tree}$ program.

The AND tree process structure is represented on ALICE by a tree structure of rewritable packets. The non-leaf nodes (EVAL processes) are represented by packets whose argument fields reference the offspring packets. Each leaf node is a packet containing the call which the process is evaluating; argument fields of such a packet reference the arguments of the call (terms are structures of constructor packets and variable packets).

The evaluation mechanism of ALICE, described in Darlington and Reeve (1981), was originally designed to implement reduction (Section 2.4.1) for functional languages but is sufficiently general to support that of Section 7.4.1. The evaluation of a leaf packet containing a call $R(t_1,...,t_k)$ begins by performing a search for a candidate clause as in Section 7.4.3.

If a candidate clause is found, any body instructions (Section 7.1) in the clause body are executed. These may include assignments to variable packets which are in the arguments $t_1,...,t_k$; this is reminiscent of narrowing (Section 2.4.2). Then the packet is rewritten to a constructor packet SUCCEEDED (if there are no body calls in the body); or a rewritable packet containing a single call (if the body contains one body call); or a structure AND(P1,P2) where P1 and P2 are packets containing body calls, and so on. If, instead, the call $R(t_1,...,t_k)$ fails, the packet is rewritten to a constructor packet FAILED.

In the event that the search for a candidate clause suspends, the search algorithm of Section 7.4.3 computes a set of the variables responsible. The ALICE architecture provides a non-busy-waiting mechanism whereby a rewritable packet can be suspended on variable packets, to be reactivated when one of the variables is subsequently assigned to a constructor packet. This mechanism is used to suspend a leaf packet on all of the variables in the suspension variables set. Of the two alternative methods of non-busy-waiting outlined in Section 7.4.4, ALICE implements the second.

As noted in Section 7.4.2, the non-leaf nodes in the AND tree are EVAL processes, each of which monitors its offspring processes and its control argument (initially a variable). ALICE's non-busy-waiting mechanism allows a packet to suspend awaiting the value of rewritable packets in the same manner as waiting for variables; this is used to ensure that each EVAL packet is idle until required. An EVAL packet is activated when its control argument variable is bound to STOP, or one of its offspring rewritable packets is rewritten to a constructor packet. There are several possibilities, as follows.

A packet that is rewritten to SUCCEEDED is simply removed from the tree, as in Fig. 7.8. If a packet becomes an AND structure (the body of a clause contains more than one body call), the EVAL packet adopts the calls as offsprings; see Fig. 7.9.

Fig 7.8 Success.

Fig 7.9 Forking.

If a packet is rewritten to FAILED, all sibling packets are garbage collected. The same garbage collection occurs if the control argument, c, is bound to STOP. As well as the garbage collection, the status argument, s, of the EVAL packet is unified with FAILED or STOPPED, respectively, and the EVAL packet is rewritten to the constructor SUCCEEDED. Garbage collection in ALICE, of both rewritable and constructor packets, is handled by a uniform reference count method: when the reference count of a packet reaches zero, it is disposed of.

7.5.2 Sequential implementations

The AND tree model can be used as the basis of a sequential implementation of PARLOG, in which the AND tree is a run-time data structure. Gregory (1984b) is a detailed study of such an implementation on a sequential Prolog architecture: McCabe's (1984a) Abstract Prolog Machine (APM). The techniques described by Gregory (1984b) were adapted to the Warren Machine (Warren, 1983) by Moens and Yu (1985).

8
Conclusion

8.1 Past and present research

8.1.1 A brief history of PARLOG

Although Chapter 1 contained an outline of the background to, and objectives of, this research, it is worth recording here the ancestry of PARLOG.

The immediate predecessor of this research was the work on IC-PROLOG (Clark and McCabe, 1979; Clark *et al.*, 1982). IC-PROLOG was an experimental logic programming language incorporating several novel control concepts. The features of IC-PROLOG most relevant to the present discussion are its two forms of non-sequential evaluation: 'dataflow coroutining' and pseudo-parallel evaluation of calls in a conjunction. The former was an attempt to adapt lazy evaluation (Henderson and Morris, 1976; Friedman and Wise, 1976) (Section 2.4.3.2) to logic programming; the latter was the logic programming equivalent of Kahn and MacQueen's (1977) model of parallel evaluation (Section 2.4.3.3). In both cases, the direction of communication between processes is specified by means of annotations on variables.

IC-PROLOG did not feature committed choice non-determinism. Instead, as in Prolog, a backtracking facility was implemented to handle failure. This was more complex and expensive than in Prolog because of the pseudo-parallel evaluation. The scheme chosen to implement backtracking was a global one: upon the failure of a process, the *entire* evaluation (even that of other processes) is undone back to the last choice point of the failed process. This global backtracking scheme is often wasteful because even successful processes were backtracked upon failure of one process; a more selective backtracking scheme proved impossible to implement efficiently.

IC-PROLOG, like MU-PROLOG (Naish, 1982) and the language of Hansson *et al.* (1982), had the advantage of providing stream AND parallelism, even the non-deterministic incremental communication of Section 2.6.6. However, the global backtracking scheme appeared to be suited only to a single-processor implementation. For a parallel implementation of the language, it would be necessary to devise a 'distributed backtracking' scheme, which is likely to be very complex; see Section 2.6.6.

In designing an efficient parallel logic programming language – the objective of the present research – it appeared to be essential to eliminate, or at least localize, backtracking so that a process never attempts to undo its last interaction with other processes. This was achieved by incorporating committed choice non-determinism, an idea inspired directly by its elegant use for parallel programming in Hoare's CSP language (Hoare, 1978). The result of this decision was the so-called Relational Language (Clark and Gregory, 1981), which also introduced mode declarations (inspired by functional programming languages) as a means of constraining the communication between processes.

The mode constraints in the Relational Language were very strong. That is, Relational Language programs are directional, as defined in Section 2.4.1.3: the communication between processes on a shared variable is unidirectional. The reason for this was a desire to implement the language efficiently on a loosely coupled, message-passing architecture, as explained in Section 5.1.5.

The major difference between the Relational Language and the next version of the language, now named PARLOG (Clark and Gregory, 1983), is that the mode constraints were relaxed, to allow 'weak' arguments (Section 3.6). PARLOG programs need not be directional: bidirectional communication on a single channel can be achieved by sending messages containing variables. This change was made for two reasons.

First, the logical variable is easy to implement on a tightly coupled parallel architecture such as ALICE (Darlington and Reeve, 1981) which was the target of the first implementation of the language. Second, the logical variable was found greatly to increase the expressive power of the language when writing the compiler for the language in itself; this is an extension of Warren's (1980) techniques for compiler writing in Prolog. The relaxation of modes was also prompted by the elegant use of 'back communication' (Section 3.6.1) in the (then) new language Concurrent Prolog (Shapiro, 1983).

Subsequent changes to PARLOG have mainly consisted of simplification and removal of redundant language features, together with a small number of additional features that have been found necessary. The resulting language is described by Clark and Gregory (1986) and, with further enhancements, in the present work.

8.1.2 Implementations of PARLOG

The first implementation of the language described in this book is one that runs 'on top of' a Prolog system (Gregory, 1984a). This comprises a compiler (written in Prolog) from PARLOG programs to Prolog clauses. A small interpreter written in Prolog simulates AND parallel evaluation by either a breadth-first or a depth-first scheduling strategy. PARLOG programs of a sequential nature can be run at a speed of up to 20% of that of the host Prolog system. This implementation of PARLOG is based on the AND tree model of Chapter 7.

The implementation of PARLOG on abstract instruction sets designed for Prolog has been investigated. Gregory (1984b) presents a design for an implementation of the AND tree model (Chapter 7) on McCabe's (1984a) Abstract Prolog Machine (APM). These techniques have since been adapted by Moens and Yu (1985) to the implementation of PARLOG on Warren's (1983) abstract Prolog instruction set.

Current implementation work in PARLOG is directed towards both parallel and sequential architectures. A sequential PARLOG system has been constructed, and is being used to develop realistic applications. This system (Foster *et al.*, 1986) is an implementation of the Sequential PARLOG Machine (SPM) (Gregory, 1986), described in Section 6.4.3. It comprises a SPM emulator, written in C, and a compiler from PARLOG to SPM instructions, written in PARLOG.

In a collaborative project between Imperial College, Manchester University, Swedish Institute of Computer Science and Argonne National Laboratory, a parallel logic programming system is being developed to exploit the parallelism of shared-memory multiprocessors. This project aims to combine PARLOG with Prolog, and other forms of parallel evaluation. It is a development of a parallel implementation of the Warren Machine, developed at Argonne (Butler *et al.*, 1986b).

An early version of PARLOG was implemented on the ALICE architecture, but this was not very efficient, as noted in Section 6.4.1. The AND tree model is much better suited to ALICE (Section 7.5.1) and acts as the basis of a new implementation which is being completed in association with the Alvey 'Flagship' project; see Section 8.3. This implementation (Lam and Gregory, 1986) comprises a compiler from PARLOG to the current version of ALICE Compiler Target Language, defined in Reeve (1985).

As noted in Section 6.4.2, Crammond and Miller (1984) have proposed a special-purpose parallel architecture for PARLOG; these ideas have since been revised by Crammond (1986). Another research (Halim, 1984) has investigated some aspects of the implementation of PARLOG on the Manchester dataflow machine (Gurd *et al.*, 1980, 1985).

In addition, it should be noted that several commercial organizations are constructing their own implementations of PARLOG, many of them based on the SPM.

8.1.3   Applications of PARLOG

An obvious application of PARLOG is as a language for systems programming. Some experimental operating systems programs have been written, based on the techniques in Clark and Gregory (1984). Further work in this area has been pursued by Foster and Kusalik (1986) and Foster (1986a). Foster (1986b) has constructed a programming environment for PARLOG: the PPS (PARLOG Programming System).

PARLOG has been investigated as a language for writing runnable specifications of parallel, communicating systems. A specification written in PARLOG can be evaluated in a variety of ways. By running it in the normal manner, the specified system is *simulated*, and so exhibits a single evaluation history. The simulation can be controlled by discrete event-driven time, as considered in Broda and Gregory (1984).

Alternatively, by combining PARLOG with a special backtracking facility to retain previous states of an evaluation, more than one of the possible non-deterministic evaluation histories can be obtained. This allows a user to *browse* (step-by-step) through several possible evaluations to explore alternative behaviours, or to obtain all possible histories in order to *verify* that the specification satisfies certain operational properties. These topics are treated in Gregory *et al.* (1985) where the techniques are applied to the specification of communication protocols.

Natural language is another application area for PARLOG. Matsumoto (1986) has rewritten a bottom-up parser, originally written in Prolog, as a PARLOG program. Alternative solutions to the Prolog version of the parser correspond to alternative candidate parsings of a natural language sentence. In order to explore alternative parsings in parallel, the Prolog parser is transformed to a PARLOG program, whose AND parallel evaluation simulates an OR parallel evaluation of the original program.

An interesting use of PARLOG is reported by Butler *et al.* (1986a). They propose a bilingual approach to programming numerical algorithms on parallel machines: PARLOG is used to express the concurrency and communication, while procedures in a low-level language (e.g. C or FORTRAN) perform the computationally intensive parts of the algorithm. The low-level procedures are sequential processes and their interaction is controlled by a PARLOG program. The hypothesis explored in this paper is that logic programming can ease the task of programming parallel numerical applications without losing the 'number crunching' efficiency of low-level languages.

8.2   Related research

Chapter 2 described in context many of the proposals for parallel logic programming. Therefore, this section concentrates on a few items of closely related research that share PARLOG's objective: to express parallel systems of communicating processes as logic programs.

An excellent survey of parallel logic programming languages can be found in Takeuchi and Furukawa (1986).

8.2.1 Concurrent Prolog

Concurrent Prolog (Shapiro, 1983) is a language very closely related to PARLOG. Like PARLOG, it is a development of the Relational Language (Clark and Gregory, 1981) and shares with these languages the features of guarded clauses and committed choice non-determinism, to implement stream AND parallelism. The specific differences between PARLOG and Concurrent Prolog have been noted at various points throughout the preceding chapters, and are summarized here.

There are perhaps two major differences between PARLOG and Concurrent Prolog. The first is the way in which the communication constraints are expressed. In PARLOG, each procedure has a fixed mode of use: a process suspends if an input mode constraint is not satisfied (because an input argument of a call is not sufficiently instantiated). In Concurrent Prolog, the mode of use is not determined by the procedure but by the call: read-only annotations on variables (usually variables in the call) specify the communication constraint.

Concurrent Prolog uses an elaborate variant of unification which suspends on an attempt to bind a read-only variable to a non-variable term. Hence, an argument of a call can be made an input argument by placing read-only annotations on the variables in the call argument; if read-only annotations are omitted, the argument can be used for input or output (or both). The advantages and disadvantages of the read-only variable are discussed in Section 3.7.5.4.

The other major difference between the two languages is that Concurrent Prolog, as described by Shapiro (1983), requires a 'multiple environment' mechanism: a local binding environment is provided for each guard evaluation, and a given variable might have a different value in each environment. Variables occurring in a call are copied to a local environment during the evaluation of each guard and copied back to the global environment upon commitment to a clause. In contrast, PARLOG maintains only one binding for each variable: guard evaluations are not allowed to bind call variables, so there is no need to keep a local copy of them. These issues are discussed in detail in Section 5.1.4.

The read-only variable and the multiple environment mechanism of Concurrent Prolog were criticized from the viewpoints of both semantics and efficiency (Ueda, 1985b; Saraswat, 1985; Kusalik, 1985). For these reasons, serious implementation efforts were limited to a simpler variant of the language: Flat Concurrent Prolog (FCP) (Mierowsky *et al.*, 1985). FCP avoids the need for multiple environments by prohibiting calls to general, programmer-defined relations in guards. Further, it imposes some restrictions upon the use of the read-only annotation, thus avoiding its semantic problems.

Another subset of Concurrent Prolog that does not require multiple environments has been investigated: Safe Concurrent Prolog (Codish, 1985) is a subset of the language in which guards are safe in the same sense as in PARLOG.

8.2.2   Guarded Horn Clauses and KL1

KL1 (Kernel Language version 1) is a logic programming language intended for implementation on the Parallel Inference Machines currently being designed at ICOT. An earlier version of the language was described by Furukawa *et al.* (1984) while subsequent developments were outlined by Ito *et al.* (1985) which also discussed a dataflow implementation of the language. The design of KL1 was strongly influenced by both PARLOG and Concurrent Prolog.

At the time of writing, KL1 is viewed as comprising a logical 'user language' KL1-u, on top of a core language KL1-c augmented with pragmas (KL1-p). While KL1-u has yet to be designed, KL1-c is synonymous with FGHC, the 'flat' subset of GHC (Guarded Horn Clauses) (Ueda, 1985a, 1986a, 1986b). Like PARLOG and Concurrent Prolog, GHC implements stream AND parallelism by using guarded clauses and the operational semantics of committed choice non-determinism.

GHC features a communication constraint (described in Section 3.7.5.5) different from those of PARLOG and Concurrent Prolog: a guard evaluation suspends upon an attempt to bind a variable belonging to the environment of the call. One consequence of this is that, like PARLOG, the mode of use of a procedure is determined by the procedure itself rather than by the call. Another consequence is that only one environment is required. This is ensured by the run-time check that is performed by GHC's unification upon binding a variable; in PARLOG the same property is guaranteed by a compile-time check on each guard. In general, GHC's run-time check may be computationally expensive unless special-purpose architectural support is provided; see Section 5.1.4.3.

FGHC avoids the need for an expensive run-time safety check by restricting guards to certain only primitive calls. With this restriction, the scope of a variable can be determined at compile time. This means that unification is essentially matching and can be compiled, as in PARLOG. Indeed, FGHC is identical to 'Flat PARLOG', as Takeuchi and Furukawa (1986) observe.

8.2.3   P-Prolog

P-Prolog (Yang and Aiso, 1986) is a parallel logic programming language which seeks to combine stream AND parallelism with 'don't-know' non-determinism. This language has a 'committed choice' subset, which is similar to PARLOG, Concurrent Prolog and GHC, but features a novel communication constraint: if clauses are declared to be 'expected exclusive', a relation call suspends if there is more than one candidate clause, committing to a candidate clause when only one remains. This mechanism leads to an interesting style of programming and has the advantage that programs can be written more logically than is possible in PARLOG and GHC; consequently, relations can often be run in multiple 'modes'.

'Don't-care' and 'don't-know' non-determinism are combined more powerfully and elegantly in P-Prolog than in PARLOG. A procedure may contain non-exclusive groups of clauses, in which case multiple solutions can be computed; that is, non-deterministic incremental communication (Section 2.6.6) is possible. Yang (1986) describes in detail how this is implemented.

It remains to be seen how efficiently the language can be implemented, and whether its increased expressiveness will outweigh any implementation overhead.

8.2.4 Delta-Prolog

A quite different approach to parallel logic programming is taken in the design of Delta-Prolog (Pereira and Nasr, 1984; Pereira *et al.* 1986). This language is an *extension* of Prolog: it augments Prolog with primitives that allow the creation of processes and communication between processes. Each process is an arbitrary Prolog program and is evaluated sequentially.

Communication between processes is handled in a manner reminiscent of CSP (Hoare, 1983): a call of the form S!E:SC suspends until another process executes a 'complementary' call R?E:RC, and vice versa. In these calls, E (the 'event name', similar to a CSP channel name) is a constant and hence of global significance. When both of the above events occur, R and S are unified, provided that the conditions RC and SC are both true. To avoid the need for a shared memory, it appears that an output term S (in S!E:SC) must be ground at the time of the call. The '?' and '!' primitives implement synchronized communication; buffered communication is provided by analogous primitives '??' and '↑↑', which acts as a 'non-blocking' output primitive.

Unlike PARLOG, Concurrent Prolog and GHC, Delta-Prolog programs (at least those which use the process creation and communication primitives) do not have a declarative reading as Horn clauses. Instead, the foundation of the language is the theory of 'Distributed Logic' (Monteiro, 1984).

Delta-Prolog is implemented as an extension to a standard Prolog system (C-Prolog) and makes use of facilities provided by the host operating system for running concurrent processes (on a single machine or distributed around a network) and interprocess communication.

8.3   Future research

Many of the areas upon which future research effort will be expended are extensions of the current research outlined in Sections 8.1.2 and 8.1.3.

Regarding implementation, more work will be required to develop the implementation of PARLOG on the ALICE machine. The first version of the compiler uses ALICE CTL (Reeve, 1985) as a target language. Eventually, it may be modified to compile to the Declarative Alvey Compiler Target Language (DACTL) (Glauert *et al.*, 1985) currently being designed; DACTL is intended as a common target for the various declarative languages to be supported on the architectures being developed in the Alvey 'Flagship' project.

The Sequential PARLOG Machine, currently implemented in C on a single processor, will be extended to run on a coarse-grained parallel architecture with shared memory. This will require the development of efficient techniques for concurrently accessing, or distributing, the shared control and data structures of the SPM.

An issue related to implementation is the provision of program development tools for PARLOG programming. In this regard, the 'browsing' technique developed for running PARLOG specifications (Section 8.1.3) might usefully be extended to implement a debugging facility for general PARLOG programming. This would require an implementation to retain backtracking information and to allow single-step evaluation.

The formal semantics of PARLOG have hardly been studied in the research to date. Such issues as termination, deadlock and livelock need to be considered in the future.

In the area of language design, perhaps the most urgent topic to be investigated is the guard 'safety check'. As noted in Section 5.1.4, the given compile-time algorithm is insufficiently discriminating: it often rejects a program that actually has safe guards. While it seems to be impossible to devise an algorithm which accepts all programs that have safe guards, it would be desirable to approach this objective as closely as possible.

Even a perfect compile-time algorithm to check the safety of guards would have the disadvantage of being global: it potentially has to analyse the entire program. This makes it difficult to compile different parts of a program separately or to compile programs constructed at run time. These objections could be overcome by using a run-time safety check, as noted in Section 5.1.4.3; this would also be the most discriminating.

References

Arvind and Brock, J.D. 1982. 'Streams and managers'. In *Operating Systems Engineering*; *LNCS 143*, M. Makegawa and L.A. Belady (Eds.), New York: Springer-Verlag, pp. 452–465.

Arvind, Gostelow, K.P. and Plouffe, W. 1978. 'An asynchronous programming language and computing machine'. Technical report, Department of Information and Computer Science, University of California, Irvine, December.

Backus, J. 1978. 'Can programming be liberated from the von Neumann style? – a functional style and its algebra of programs'. *Communications of the ACM,* **21(8)**, 613–641.

Bernstein, A.J. 1980. 'Output guards and nondeterminism in "Communicating Sequential Processes"', *ACM Transactions on Programming Languages and Systems*, **2(2)**, 234–238.

Bowen, D.L., Byrd, L., Pereira, F.C.N., Pereira, L.M. and Warren, D.H.D. 1982. 'DECsystem-10 Prolog user's manual'. Department of Artificial Intelligence, University of Edinburgh, November.

Brock, J.D. and Ackerman, W.B. 1981. 'Scenarios: a model of nondeterminate computation'. In *Proceedings of the International Colloquium on Formalization of Programming Concepts*; *LNCS 107* (Peniscola, Spain, April), New York: Springer-Verlag, pp. 252–259.

Broda, K. and Gregory, S. 1984. 'PARLOG for discrete event simulation'. In *Proceedings of the 2nd International Logic Programming Conference* (Uppsala, July), S.A. Tarnlund (Ed.), Uppsala: Uppsala University Press, pp. 301–312.

Burstall, R.M. and Darlington, J. 1977. 'A transformation system for developing recursive programs'. *Journal of the ACM,* **24(1)**, 44–67.

Burstall, R.M., MacQueen, D.B. and Sannella, D.T. 1980. 'HOPE: an experimental applicative language'. Internal report CSR-62-80, Department of Computer Science, University of Edinburgh, May.

Butler, R., Lusk, E., McCune, W. and Overbeek, R.A. 1986a. 'Parallel logic programming for numeric applications'. In *Proceedings of the 3rd International Logic Programming Conference* (London, July), New York: Springer-Verlag, pp. 375–388.

Butler, R., Lusk, E., Olson, R. and Overbeek, R.A. 1986b. 'ANLWAM: a parallel implementation of the Warren abstract machine'. Unpublished report, Mathematics and Computer Science Division, Argonne National Laboratory, Argonne, Illinois, August.

Church, A. 1941. 'The calculi of lambda conversion'. In *Annals of Mathematics Studies 6*, Princeton, NJ: Princeton University Press.

Ciepielewski, A. 1984. 'Towards a computer architecture for or-parallel execution of logic programs'. PhD thesis, Technical report TRITA-CS-8401, Department of Computer Systems, Royal Institute of Technology, Stockholm, May.

Clark, K.L. 1978. 'Negation as failure'. In *Logic and Databases*, H. Gallaire and J. Minker (Eds.), New York: Plenum Press, pp. 293–322.

Clark, K.L. 1979. 'Predicate logic as a computational formalism'. Research monograph, Department of Computing, Imperial College, London, December.

Clark, K.L. and Darlington, J. 1980. 'Algorithm classification through synthesis'. *Computer Journal*, **23(1)**, 61–65.

Clark, K.L. and Gregory, S. 1981. 'A relational language for parallel programming'. In *Proceedings of the ACM Conference on Functional Programming Languages and Computer Architecture* (Portsmouth, New Hampshire, October), Arvind and J. Dennis (Eds.), New York: ACM, pp. 171–178.

Clark, K.L. and Gregory, S. 1983. 'PARLOG: a parallel logic programming language'. Research report DOC 83/5, Department of Computing, Imperial College, London, May.

Clark, K.L. and Gregory, S. 1984. 'Notes on systems programming in PARLOG'. In *Proceedings of the International Conference on Fifth Generation Computer Systems* (Tokyo, November), H. Aiso (Ed.), Amsterdam: Elsevier/North-Holland, pp. 299–306.

Clark, K.L. and Gregory, S. 1985. 'Notes on the implementation of PARLOG'. *Journal of Logic Programming*, **2(1)**, 17–42.

Clark, K.L. and Gregory, S. 1986. 'PARLOG: parallel programming in logic'. *ACM Transactions on Programming Languages and Systems*, **8(1)**, 1–49.

Clark, K.L. and McCabe, F.G. 1979. 'The control facilities of IC-PROLOG'. In *Expert Systems in the Micro-electronic age*, D. Michie (Ed.), Edinburgh: Edinburgh University Press, pp. 122–149.

Clark, K.L. and McCabe, F.G. 1984. *micro-PROLOG: Programming in Logic*. Englewood Cliffs, N.J.: Prentice-Hall.

Clark, K.L., McCabe, F.G. and Gregory, S. 1982. 'IC-PROLOG language features'. In *Logic Programming*, K.L. Clark and S.A. Tarnlund (Eds.), London: Academic Press, pp. 253–266.

Clark, K.L. and Tarnlund, S.A. 1977. 'A first order theory of data and programs'. In *Information Processing 77*; *Proceedings of the IFIP Congress 77*, B. Gilchrist (Ed.), Amsterdam: Elsevier/North-Holland, pp. 939–944.

Clocksin, W.F. and Mellish, C.S. 1981. *Programming in Prolog*. New York: Springer-Verlag.

Codish, M. 1985. 'Compiling OR-parallelism into AND-parallelism'. MSc thesis, Department of Applied Mathematics, Weizmann Institute of Science, Rehovot, December.

Conery, J.S. 1983. 'The AND/OR process model for parallel interpretation of logic programs'. PhD thesis, Technical report 204, Department of Information and Computer Science, University of California, Irvine, June.

Conery, J.S. and Kibler, D.F. 1981. 'Parallel interpretation of logic programs'. In *Proceedings of the ACM Conference on Functional Programming Languages and Computer Architecture* (Portsmouth, New Hampshire, October), Arvind and J. Dennis (Eds.), New York: ACM, pp. 163–170.

Conway, M.E. 1963. 'Design of a separable transition-diagram compiler'. *Communications of the ACM*, **6(7)**, 396–408.

Crammond, J.A. 1986. 'An execution model for committed-choice non-deterministic languages'. In *Proceedings of the 1986 Symposium on Logic Programming* (Salt Lake City, Utah, September), Silver Spring, MD: IEEE Computer Society Press, pp. 148–158.

Crammond, J.A. and Miller, C.D.F. 1984. 'An architecture for parallel logic languages'. In *Proceedings of the 2nd International Logic Programming Conference* (Uppsala, July), S.A. Tarnlund (Ed.), Uppsala: Uppsala University Press, pp. 183–194.

Darlington, J. and Reeve, M.J. 1981. 'ALICE: a multi-processor reduction machine'. In *Proceedings of the ACM Conference on Functional Programming Languages and Computer Architecture* (Portsmouth, New Hampshire, October), Arvind and J. Dennis (Eds.), New York: ACM, pp. 65–75.

Darlington, J., Field, A.J. and Pull, H. 1985. 'The unification of functional and logic languages'. In *Logic Programming: Relations, Functions, and Equations*, D. DeGroot and G. Lindstrom (Eds.), Englewood Cliffs, N.J.: Prentice-Hall, pp. 37–70.

Dausmann, M., Persch, G. and Winterstein, G. 1980. 'A method for describing concurrent problems based on logic'. Research report, Institut für Informatik, Universität Karlsruhe.

DeGroot, D. 1984. 'Restricted AND parallelism'. In *Proceedings of the International Conference on Fifth Generation Computer Systems* (Tokyo, November), H. Aiso (Ed.), Amsterdam: Elsevier/North-Holland, pp. 471–478.

Denelcor. 1982. *HEP hardware reference manual*. Denelcor, Inc., Denver, Colorado.

Dennis, J.B. 1974. 'First version of a dataflow procedure language'. In *LNCS 19*, New York: Springer-Verlag, pp. 362–376.

Dijkstra, E.W. 1976. *A Discipline of Programming*. Englewood Cliffs, N.J.: Prentice-Hall.

Dwork, C., Kanellakis, P.C. and Mitchell, J.C. 1984. 'On the sequential nature of unification'. *Journal of Logic Programming*, **1(1)**, 35–50.

Finn, S. 1985. 'The Simplex programming language'. Technical report, Department of Computing Science, University of Stirling, March.

Foster, I.T., Gregory, S., Ringwood, G.A. and Satoh, K. 1986. 'A sequential implementation of PARLOG'. In *Proceedings of the 3rd International Logic Programming Conference* (London, July), New York: Springer-Verlag, pp. 149–156.

Foster, I.T. and Kusalik, A.J. 1986. 'A logical treatment of secondary storage'. In *Proceedings of the 1986 Symposium on Logic Programming* (Salt Lake City, Utah, September), Silver Spring, MD: IEEE Computer Society Press, pp. 58–67.

Foster, I.T. 1986a. 'Logic operating systems: design issues'. Research report, Department of Computing, Imperial College, London.

Foster, I.T. 1986b. 'PARLOG Programming System: user guide'. Unpublished report, Department of Computing, Imperial College, London.

Friedman, D.P. and Wise, D.S. 1976. 'CONS should not evaluate its arguments'. In *Automata, Languages and Programming*, S. Michaelson and R. Milner (Eds.), Edinburgh: Edinburgh University Press, pp. 257–284.

Friedman, D.P. and Wise, D.S. 1980. 'An indeterminate constructor for applicative programming'. In *Proceedings of the 7th ACM Symposium on Principles of Programming Languages* (Las Vegas, Nevada, January), New York: ACM, pp. 245–250.

Furukawa, K., Kunifuji, S., Takeuchi, A. and Ueda, K. 1984. 'The conceptual specification of the Kernel Language version 1'. Technical report TR-054, ICOT, Tokyo.

Gelernter, D. 1984. 'A note on systems programming in Concurrent Prolog'. In *Proceedings of the IEEE International Symposium on Logic Programming* (Atlantic City, N.J., February), Silver Spring, MD: IEEE Computer Society Press, pp. 76–82.

Glauert, J.R.W., Holt, N.P., Kennaway, J.R., Reeve, M.J. and Sleep, M.R. 1985. 'An active term rewrite model for parallel computation'. Research report, School of Information Systems, University of East Anglia.

Goguen, J.A and Meseguer, J. 1984. 'Equality, types, modules and generics for logic programming'. In *Proceedings of the 2nd International Logic Programming Conference* (Uppsala, July), S.A. Tarnlund (Ed.), Uppsala: Uppsala University Press, pp. 115–125.

Gregory, S. 1980. 'Towards the compilation of annotated logic programs'. Research report DOC 80/16, Department of Computing, Imperial College, London, June.

Gregory, S. 1984a. 'How to use PARLOG'. Unpublished report, Department of Computing, Imperial College, London, August.

Gregory, S. 1984b. 'Implementing PARLOG on the Abstract PROLOG Machine'. Research report DOC 84/23, Department of Computing, Imperial College, London, August.

Gregory, S. 1985. 'Design, application and implementation of a parallel logic programming language'. PhD thesis, Department of Computing, Imperial College, London, September.

Gregory, S. 1986. 'The Sequential PARLOG Machine'. Research report (in preparation), Department of Computing, Imperial College, London.

Gregory, S., Neely, R. and Ringwood, G.A. 1985. 'PARLOG for specification, verification and simulation'. In *Proceedings of the 7th International Symposium on Computer Hardware Description Languages and their Applications* (Tokyo, August), C.J. Koomen and T. Moto-oka (Eds.), Amsterdam: Elsevier/North-Holland, pp. 139–148.

Gurd, J.R., Watson, I. and Glauert, J. 1980. 'A multilayered dataflow computer architecture'. Research report, Department of Computer Science, University of Manchester, March.

Gurd, J.R., Kirkham, C.C. and Watson, I. 1985. 'The Manchester prototype dataflow computer'. *Communications of the ACM,* **28(1),** 34–52.

Halim, M.Z. 1984. 'Data-driven and demand-driven evaluation of logic programs'. PhD thesis, Department of Computer Science, University of Manchester.

Hansson, A., Haridi, S. and Tarnlund, S.A. 1982. 'Properties of a logic programming language'. In *Logic Programming,* K.L. Clark and S.A. Tarnlund (Eds.), London: Academic Press, pp. 267–280.

Henderson, P. 1980. *Functional Programming*, Englewood Cliffs, N.J.: Prentice-Hall.

Henderson, P. 1982. 'Purely functional operating systems'. In *Functional Programming and its Applications*, J. Darlington, P. Henderson and D. Turner (Eds.), Cambridge: Cambridge University Press, pp. 177–192.

Henderson, P. and Morris, J.H. 1976. 'A lazy evaluator'. In *Proceedings of the 3rd ACM Symposium on Principles of Programming Languages* (Atlanta, Georgia, January), New York: ACM, pp. 95–103.

Henderson, P., Jones, G.A. and Jones, S.B. 1983. 'The LispKit manual'. Technical monograph PRG-32, Programming Research Group, Oxford University.

Hoare, C.A.R. 1974. 'Monitors: an operating system structuring concept'. *Communications of the ACM*, **17(10)**, 549–557.

Hoare, C.A.R. 1978. 'Communicating sequential processes'. *Communications of the ACM*, **21(8)**, 666–677.

Hoare, C.A.R. 1983. 'Notes on Communicating Sequential Processes'. Technical monograph PRG-33, Programming Research Group, Oxford University, August.

Hogger, C.J. 1978. 'Derivation of logic programs'. PhD thesis, Department of Computing, Imperial College, London.

Hogger, C.J. 1984. *Introduction to Logic Programming*. London: Academic Press.

Ito, N., Shimizu, H., Kishi, M., Kuno, E. and Rokusawa, K. 1985. 'Dataflow-based execution mechanisms of parallel and Concurrent Prolog'. *New Generation Computing*, **3(1)**, 15–41.

Jones, S.B. 1984. 'A range of operating systems written in a purely functional style'. Technical report TR.16, Department of Computing Science, University of Stirling, September.

Kahn, K.M. 1984. 'A primitive for the control of logic programs'. In *Proceedings of the IEEE International Symposium on Logic Programming* (Atlantic City, New Jersey, February), Silver Spring, MD: IEEE Computer Society Press, pp. 242–251.

Kahn, G. and MacQueen, D.B. 1977. 'Coroutines and networks of parallel processes'. In *Information Processing 77; Proceedings of the IFIP Congress 77*, B. Gilchrist (Ed.), Amsterdam: Elsevier/North-Holland, pp. 993–998.

Kasif, S., Kohli, M. and Minker, J. 1983. 'PRISM: a parallel inference system for problem solving'. In *Proceedings of the Logic Programming Workshop 83* (Albufeira, Portugal, June), Lisbon: Universidade Nova de Lisboa, pp. 123–152.

Kasif, S. and Minker, J. 1984. 'The intelligent channel: a scheme for and/or parallelism in logic programs'. Technical report CS-TR-1412, Department of Computer Science, University of Maryland, June.

Kawanobe, K. 1984. 'Current status and future plans of the Fifth Generation Computer Systems project'. In *Proceedings of the International Conference on Fifth Generation Computer Systems* (Tokyo, November), H. Aiso (Ed.), Amsterdam: Elsevier/North-Holland, pp. 3–36.

Keller, R.M. and Lindstrom, G. 1981. 'Applications of feedback in functional programming'. In *Proceedings of the ACM Conference on Functional Programming Languages and Computer Architecture* (Portsmouth, New Hampshire, October), Arvind and J. Dennis (Eds.), New York: ACM, pp. 123–130.

Keller, R.M., Lindstrom, G. and Patil, S. 1979. 'A loosely-coupled applicative multi-processing system'. In *Proceedings of the National Computer Conference* (June), AFIPS, pp. 613–622.

Kowalski, R.A. 1974. 'Predicate logic as programming language'. In *Information Processing 74*; *Proceedings of the IFIP Congress 74*, Amsterdam: Elsevier/North-Holland, pp. 569–574.

Kowalski, R.A. 1979a. *Logic for Problem Solving*. New York: Elsevier/North-Holland.

Kowalski, R.A. 1979b. 'Algorithm = logic + control'. *Communications of the ACM*, **22(7)**, 424–436.

Kowalski, R.A. 1983. 'Logic programming'. In *Information Processing 83*; *Proceedings of the IFIP Congress 83*, R.E.A. Mason (Ed.), Amsterdam: Elsevier/North-Holland, pp. 133–145.

Kusalik, A.J. 1984a. 'Bounded-wait merge in Shapiro's Concurrent Prolog'. *New Generation Computing, 2*, 157–169.

Kusalik, A.J. 1984b. 'Serialization of process reduction in Concurrent Prolog'. *New Generation Computing, 2*, 289–298.

Kusalik, A.J. 1985. 'Semantic issues with Concurrent Prolog'. Presentation at Imperial College, London, May.

Lam, M.Y.C. and Gregory, S. 1986. 'PARLOG and ALICE: a marriage of convenience'. Research report, Department of Computing, Imperial College, London, November.

Landin, P.J. 1965. 'The correspondence between Algol 60 and Church's lambda notation'. *Communications of the ACM, 8(2)*, 89–101.

Levy, J. 1984. 'A unification algorithm for Concurrent Prolog'. In *Proceedings of the 2nd International Logic Programming Conference* (Uppsala, July), S.A. Tarnlund (Ed.), Uppsala: Uppsala University Press, pp. 333–341.

Lindstrom, G. and Panangaden, P. 1984. 'Stream-based execution of logic programs'. In *Proceedings of the IEEE International Symposium on Logic Programming* (Atlantic City, N.J., February), Silver Spring, MD: IEEE Computer Society Press, pp. 168–176.

Lusk, E. and Overbeek, R.A. 1984. 'Implementing multiprocessing algorithms now'. Technical memorandum 32, Mathematics and Computer Science Division, Argonne National Laboratory, Argonne, Illinois, August.

MacLennan, B.J. 1981. 'Introduction to relational programming'. In *Proceedings of the ACM Conference on Functional Programming Languages and Computer Architecture* (Portsmouth, New Hampshire, October), Arvind and J. Dennis (Eds.), New York: ACM, pp. 213–220.

MacQueen, D.B. 1979. 'Models for distributed computing'. Rapport de recherche 351, INRIA, Paris.

Manna, Z. 1974. *Mathematical Theory of Computation*. New York: McGraw-Hill.

Matsumoto, Y. 1986. 'A parallel parsing system for natural language analysis'. In *Proceedings of the 3rd International Logic Programming Conference* (London, July), New York: Springer-Verlag, pp. 396–409.

McCabe, F.G. 1984a. 'Abstract PROLOG machine – a specification'. Research report DOC 83/12, Department of Computing, Imperial College, London, revised June.

McCabe, F.G. 1984b. 'The Sigma machine'. Research report, Department of Computing, Imperial College, London.

McCarthy, J., Abrahams, P.W., Edwards, D.J., Hart, T.P. and Levin, M.I. 1965. *LISP 1.5 Programmer's Manual*, Cambridge, Mass: MIT Press.

Mierowsky, C., Taylor, S., Shapiro, E., Levy, J. and Safra, M. 1985. 'The design and implementation of Flat Concurrent Prolog'. Technical report CS85-09, Department of Applied Mathematics, Weizmann Institute of Science, Rehovot, July.

Miyazaki, T., Takeuchi, A. and Chikayama, T. 1985. 'A sequential implementation of Concurrent Prolog based on the shallow binding scheme'. In *Proceedings of the IEEE Symposium on Logic Programming* (Boston, Mass., July), Silver Spring, MD: IEEE Computer Society Press, pp. 110–118.

Moens, E. and Yu, B. 1985. 'Implementation of PARLOG on the Warren Machine'. Technical report, Department of Computer Science, University of British Columbia, Vancouver.

Monteiro, L. 1984. 'A proposal for distributed programming in logic'. In *Implementation of Prolog*, J.A. Campbell (Ed.), Chichester: Ellis Horwood, pp. 329–340.

Moss, C.D.S. 1980. 'Logic and dataflow'. Unpublished report, Department of Computing, Imperial College, London.

Moss, C.D.S. 1983. 'Computing with sequences'. In *Proceedings of the Logic Programming Workshop 83* (Albufeira, Portugal, June), Lisbon: Universidade Nova de Lisboa, pp. 623–630.

Moto-Oka, T., Tanaka, H., Aida, H., Hirata, K. and Maruyama, T. 1984. 'The architecture of a parallel inference engine – PIE'. In *Proceedings of the International Conference on Fifth Generation Computer Systems* (Tokyo, November), H. Aiso (Ed.), Amsterdam: Elsevier/North-Holland, pp. 479–488.

Naish, L. 1982. 'An introduction to MU-PROLOG'. Technical report 82/2, Department of Computer Science, University of Melbourne.

Naish, L. 1983. 'Automatic generation of control for logic programs'. Technical report 83/6, Department of Computer Science, University of Melbourne.

Pereira, L.M., Monteiro, L., Cunha, J. and Aparicio, J.N. 1986. 'Delta-Prolog: a distributed backtracking extension with events'. In *Proceedings of the 3rd International Logic Programming Conference* (London, July), New York: Springer-Verlag, pp. 69–83.

Pereira, L.M. and Nasr, R. 1984. 'Delta-Prolog: a distributed logic programming language'. In *Proceedings of the International Conference on Fifth Generation Computer Systems* (Tokyo, November), H. Aiso (Ed.), Amsterdam: Elsevier/North-Holland, pp. 283–291.

Pollard, G.H. 1981. 'Parallel execution of Horn clause programs'. PhD thesis, Department of Computing, Imperial College, London.

Reddy, U.S. 1985a. 'Narrowing as the operational semantics of functional languages'. In *Proceedings of the IEEE Symposium on Logic Programming* (Boston, Mass, July), Silver Spring, MD: IEEE Computer Society Press, pp. 138–151.

Reddy, U.S. 1985b. 'On the relationship between logic and functional languages'. In *Logic Programming*: *Relations*, *Functions*, *and Equations*, D. DeGroot and G. Lindstrom (Eds.), Englewood Cliffs, N.J.: Prentice-Hall.

Reeve, M.J. 1981. 'A BNF description of the ALICE Compiler Target Language'. Unpublished report, Department of Computing, Imperial College, London, July.

Reeve, M.J. 1985. 'A BNF description of the ALICE Compiler Target Language'. Unpublished report, Department of Computing, Imperial College, London, March.

Robinson, J.A. 1965. 'A machine-oriented logic based on the resolution principle'. *Journal of the ACM*, **12(1)**, 23–41.

Robinson, J.A. 1979. *Logic: Form and Function*. Edinburgh: Edinburgh University Press.

Roussel, P. 1975. 'PROLOG: manuel de référence et d'utilisation'. Groupe d'Intelligence Artificielle, Université d'Aix-Marseille, Luminy, September.

Saraswat, V.A. 1985. 'Problems with Concurrent Prolog'. Technical report, Department of Computer Science, Carnegie-Mellon University, June.

Sato, M. and Sakurai, T. 1983. 'Qute: a Prolog/Lisp type language for logic programming'. In *Proceedings of the 8th International Joint Conference on Artificial Intelligence* (Karlsruhe, August), Los Altos, CA: William Kaufmann, Inc., pp. 507–513.

Sato, M. and Sakurai, T. 1984. 'Qute: a functional language based on unification'. In *Proceedings of the International Conference on Fifth Generation Computer Systems* (Tokyo, November), H. Aiso (Ed.), Amsterdam: Elsevier/North-Holland, pp. 157–165.

Schwarz, J. 1977. 'Using annotations to make recursion equations behave'. Research report 43, Department of Artificial Intelligence, University of Edinburgh.

Seitz, C.L. 1985. 'The cosmic cube'. *Communications of the ACM*, **28(1)**, 22–33.

Sequent. 1985. 'Balance 8000 system technical summary'. Sequent Computer Systems, Inc., Beaverton, Oregon, December.

Shapiro, E.Y. 1983. 'A subset of Concurrent Prolog and its interpreter'. Technical report TR-003, ICOT, Tokyo, February.

Shapiro, E.Y. 1984. 'Systems programming in Concurrent Prolog'. In *Proceedings of the 11th ACM Symposium on Principles of Programming Languages* (Salt Lake City, Utah, January), New York: ACM, pp. 93–105.

Shapiro, E.Y. and Mierowsky, C. 1984. 'Fair, biased, and self-balancing merge operators'. In *Proceedings of the IEEE International Symposium on Logic Programming* (Atlantic City, N.J., February), Silver Spring, MD: IEEE Computer Society Press, pp. 83–90.

Shapiro, E.Y. and Takeuchi, A. 1983. 'Object oriented programming in Concurrent Prolog'. *New Generation Computing, 1*, 25–48.

Sleep, M.R. 1980. 'Applicative languages, dataflow, and pure combinatory code'. In *Proceedings of the 20th IEEE Computer Society International Conference* (San Francisco, February), Silver Spring, MD: IEEE Computer Society Press, pp. 112–115.

Sleep, M.R. and Burton, F.W. 1981. 'Towards a zero assignment parallel processor'. In *Proceedings of the 2nd IEEE International Conference on Distributed Computing Systems* (Paris, April), Silver Spring, MD: IEEE Computer Society Press, pp. 80–85.

Takeuchi, A. 1983. 'How to solve it in Concurrent Prolog'. Unpublished report, ICOT, Tokyo.

Takeuchi, A. and Furukawa, K. 1983. 'Interprocess communication in Concurrent Prolog'. In *Proceedings of the Logic Programming Workshop 83* (Albufeira, Portugal, June), Lisbon: Universidade Nova de Lisboa, pp. 171–185.

Takeuchi, A. and Furukawa, K. 1985. 'Bounded buffer communication in Concurrent Prolog'. *New Generation Computing*, **3(2)**, 145–155.

Takeuchi, A. and Furukawa, K. 1986. 'Parallel logic programming languages'. In *Proceedings of the 3rd International Logic Programming Conference* (London, July), New York: Springer-Verlag, pp. 242–254.

Tamura, N. and Kaneda, Y. 1984. 'Implementing parallel Prolog on a multi-processor machine'. In *Proceedings of the IEEE International Symposium on Logic Programming* (Atlantic City, N.J., February), Silver Spring, MD: IEEE Computer Society Press, pp. 42–48.

Tick, E. and Warren, D.H.D. 1984. 'Towards a pipelined Prolog processor'. In *Proceedings of the IEEE International Symposium on Logic Programming* (Atlantic City, N.J., February), Silver Spring, MD: IEEE Computer Society Press, pp. 29–40.

Treleaven, P.C. 1982. 'Data-driven and demand-driven computer architecture'. In *ACM Computing Surveys,* **14(1)**, 93–143.

Turner, D.A. 1981. 'The semantic elegance of applicative languages'. In *Proceedings of the ACM Conference on Functional Programming Languages and Computer Architecture* (Portsmouth, N.H., October), Arvind and J. Dennis (Eds.), New York: ACM, pp. 85–92.

Ueda, K. 1985a. 'Guarded Horn Clauses'. Technical report TR-103, ICOT, Tokyo, September.

Ueda, K. 1985b. 'Concurrent Prolog re-examined'. Technical report TR-102, ICOT, Tokyo, November.

Ueda, K. 1986a. 'Guarded Horn Clauses'. Doctoral thesis, Information Engineering Course, Faculty of Engineering, University of Tokyo, March. To be published by MIT Press.

Ueda, K. 1986b. 'Guarded Horn Clauses: a parallel logic programming language with the concept of a guard'. Technical report TR-208, ICOT, Tokyo, October.

van Emden, M.H. and Kowalski, R.A. 1976. 'The semantics of predicate logic as a programming language'. *Journal of the ACM,* **23(4)**, 733–742.

van Emden, M.H. and de Lucena, G.J. 1982. 'Predicate logic as a language for parallel programming'. In *Logic Programming*, K.L. Clark and S.A. Tarnlund (Eds.), London: Academic Press, pp. 189–198.

Vuillemin, J.E. 1973. 'Proof techniques for recursive programs'. PhD thesis, Stanford University.

Wadsworth, C.P. 1971. 'Semantics and pragmatics of the lambda-calculus'. PhD thesis, Oxford University.

Warren, D.H.D. 1977. 'Applied logic – its use and implementation as a programming tool'. PhD thesis, Department of Artificial Intelligence, University of Edinburgh.

Warren, D.H.D. 1979. 'Coroutining facilities for Prolog, implemented in Prolog'. Working paper, Department of Artificial Intelligence, University of Edinburgh, August.

Warren, D.H.D. 1980. 'Logic programming and compiler writing'. *Software – Practice and Experience,* **10**, 97–125.

Warren, D.H.D. 1981. 'Efficient processing of interactive relational database queries expressed in logic'. In *Proceedings of the 7th International Conference on Very Large Data Bases* (Cannes, France, September), pp. 272–281.

Warren, D.H.D. 1982. 'Perpetual processes – an unexploited Prolog technique'. In *Logic Programming Newsletter*, Universidade Nova de Lisboa, Summer.

Warren, D.H.D. 1983. 'An abstract Prolog instruction set'. Technical note 309, SRI International, Menlo Park, California, October.

Wise, M.J. 1982. 'A parallel Prolog: the construction of a data driven model'. In *Proceedings of the ACM Symposium on LISP and functional programming* (Pittsburgh, PA, August), New York: ACM, pp. 56–66.

Wise, M.J. 1984. 'Concurrent Prolog on a multiprocessor: a critique of Concurrent Prolog and comparison with EPILOG'. Technical report, Department of Computer Science, University of New South Wales, Sydney, January.

Yang, R. 1986. 'A parallel logic programming language and its implementation'. PhD thesis, Department of Electrical Engineering, Keio University.

Yang, R. and Aiso, H. 1986. 'P-Prolog: a parallel logic language based on exclusive relation'. In *Proceedings of the 3rd International Logic Programming Conference* (London, July), New York: Springer-Verlag, pp. 255–269.

Yasuura, H. 1984. 'On parallel computational complexity of unification'. In *Proceedings of the International Conference on Fifth Generation Computer Systems* (Tokyo, November), H. Aiso (Ed.), Amsterdam: Elsevier/North-Holland, pp. 235–243.

Index